DAVID R. BAILLY

AMERICA
...Still Going

Published by Seacoast Press, an imprint of MindStir Media, LLC
1931 Woodbury Ave. #182 | Portsmouth, New Hampshire 03801 | USA
1.800.767.0531 | www.seacoastpress.com

Printed in the United States of America
ISBN: 978-1-7356983-3-5

*Dedicated to my
beloved partner & best friend, Jan.*

CONTENTS

PREFACE

This is the second book in a series about how the "Greatest Generation" in America is becoming the "Forgotten Generation". If you have not read "*AMERICA Going, Going…*", I suggest that you take on that read first in order for this addition to make sense. The mentors and teachers we experienced and learned from taught those of us who are baby boomers about how to live a good life with love and respect for others, taking responsibility for and learning from our mistakes, and being solid law-abiding citizens. It is appearing more and more every day that those lessons which molded us into the older Americans we are today are being thrown to the curb in favor of a self-centered society. That model could lose its' way on the road of life in the current fast-paced global environment in which the stakes are not only high, but indeed could determine life and death and the very future of our country and the rest of the earthly world which surrounds us.

An apology (of sorts) is probably in order to those of you who read *AGG*. I learned a lot during the publishing of that book, especially that when you are writing in part about current events and there is a separation of six months between the completion of writing and the book availability, those episodes of news can become very "dated". I realized early in the process of getting that book to the presses that I needed to find a publisher that would permit changes to the text much further along in the process than was permitted by my initial partner. "Live and learn", and I did. I will endeavor with this writing to keep the "current" in current events.

I have been journaling on and off for over 40 years. I realized during my early years of education that writing things down helped me to remember those thoughts, sometimes for years. As I age, those periods of memory are reduced significantly. Do any of you rely on "lists"? Those tools have been integral for me to keep my life on track, especially when there can be hundreds of things to recall.

It was frustrating during the over six-month publishing project for *AGG* to hear and read about many (if not most) of the ideas which I had written about in my book. Then it occurred to me that many people were interested in the topics about which I had written, but there would not be a single place other than my book where they were accumulated together.

As I document my thoughts about social media, it occurred to me on many occasions that a large number of the players I would read and hear about (mainly because of the amount of "followers") are in reality "forgettable" people whose ideas would never see the "light of day" if it were not for that electronic platform (which could basically preserve their concepts forever)! The downside is obviously for those whose rantings are basically incoherent yet could remain in public view for eons. Much of which I write is based on what I have considered to be common sense, with the warning of Voltaire in his *Dictionnaire Philosophique* (1764) that "Common sense is not so common." How true that is in the chaotic times in which we find ourselves today.

One thing I learned about following the publication of *AGG* was the importance of "reviews" by those who would read the book. I was attracted initially and especially to those on the

Amazon site, but not for a very positive reason. The reviews there call for a rating of "1"(poor), "2", "3" (average), "4", or "5" (must read). When my Liberal sister (a wonderful educator for her career) first learned I had written a book, she was not interested in reading it (whew!)(even though it was dedicated to our parents) but simply asked me to keep her informed about how the reviews were doing. This should have tipped me off but didn't. My first review was from one of my best friends in grade school through high school who had become a successful media/marketing agency owner for his career (despite being an "artist" and "musician"). My father always taught me that it was difficult for artists to become successful in business, because of the structures encountered. The old "free style" clashing with barriers and rules. And year after year this friend had become increasingly Liberal, as well as separated from "the church"—now an atheist I presume. His single complaint cited in an Amazon review would come from a business concept (of course) based on what I had been taught. The rating was a "1", purported to quote me from the book (with four glaring mistakes), and involved the historic method for determining a person's wage from employment—their "value to/in the marketplace". That principle has also been used to calculate how the government provides benefits through various programs. I can understand how this matter of "judgment" could be offensive on the Left, even though it is the marketplace rather than the employer which sets the "value" through a budgeting process. A long story (already) shortened, it took several weeks and considerable consternation by me until I received a "4" and three "5s" to raise the composite rating to an acceptable "4" which was retained for the duration. Lesson learned: watch out for Liberals, some of whom are inclined to be sloppy in retirement—because they just don't get it nor care to.

I will use the same chapter titles in this book in order to attempt to maintain some continuity in the existence of the challenges which I believe do and will face us in this twenty-first century...

at least until there is so much change in our society and its' participants that results in those concerns which we cannot currently
envision nor the catalysts which will produce them.

I also intend to be visible in the months and years to come, God
willing, to take part in other aspects of mass media to address
existing and new problems as they morph and arise, and to
interact with those of you who agree with my writings or think
I am crazy. It is only through interaction, renewed civil dialogue
and the exchange of information and positions that we can ever
hope to bring back America from the verge of destruction. I am
committed to doing anything and everything I can to make this
a better country, and I assume that many of you will share in this
endeavor. I may only have a few valid plans to improve who we
are and where we are going, relying on you and many others to
frame a consensus about what needs to be done as well as the
methods necessary to accomplish the plan — "Bringing Back a
New and Better America".

The original *AGG* was dedicated in part to my father, Charles
Bailly, a great mentor to me and hundreds of other people over
the years. There is an annual event in Fargo at which the "Charles
Bailly Leadership Award" is presented to a deserving contributor
toward excellence in our region. This year the YMCA of Cass
and Clay Counties described him in this way: "The most memorable contribution of Charles Bailly was his courage — courage
to risk views and efforts amongst colleagues, courage to explore
potentials of a better way of doing things, courage to place the
greater needs of a community above individual fears. The Charles
Bailly Leadership Award goes to those who are willing to take
courageous steps on behalf of the greater good. The impact of
their courage transcends generations, economic conditions and
time itself." Thank you to my many friends at the "Y" for those
complimentary words in describing this amazing man who
served mankind for his entire life. My life today continues to

be guided by my father and my awesome mother, Helen. They taught me the most important things about life.

October 7, 2019 became an important day for the writing of this second book. That is the day that I began to actively use the Twitter account for "*America Going, Going…*" (@america_going) that I had set up in March and which had been unused until October. This provided an active source of information and writing for "*America…Still Going*". I apologize up front to those of you who follow me on Twitter, as you will experience some duplication of what you have already learned about me from the first book and from my "Tweets".

What has transpired in American politics and living since I was forced to finish the writing of "*AGG*" in December of 2018, including the arrival of the COVID-19 pandemic and the street violence with destruction following the tragic death of George Floyd, has been shocking, life-altering, and without any semblance of a reasonable explanation. At least that is my view from 30,000 feet above. This is the story of how it all looked from one pair of eyes.

It is time to get back at it.

CHAPTER 1

THE SELFISH "SELFIE" SOCIETY: INCIVILITY, MEANNESS, AND VANISHING "HIGH ROAD"

"Inside of me there are two dogs. One is mean and evil, and the other is good. They fight each other all the time. When asked which one wins, I answer the one I feed the most." Sitting Bull. Over the past seventeen months since completing my writing of *"America Going, Going…"*, I have been working on this follow-up book. During this time, I have listened to the Left and Right and am convinced overwhelmingly that the Liberals have been over-feeding the mean and evil dog while the Conservatives have left that dog to starve. Many on the Left are foaming at the mouth while those on the Right are mostly carefree and happy. I thought near the end of 2018 that the lack of civility in America had reached a pinnacle, but I turned out to be so wrong. There seemed to be great energy in the Republican Party as the impeachment inquisition was starting to fade away, while I sensed that the Democrats were showing signs of fatigue and desperation. Let's look back to see what transpired before us during 2019 while the decade came to an explosive close.

As the 2020 Democratic Presidential candidates hit the streets, they were espousing the Obama mantra of "hope" as what was the desire of their constituents. Is this because those on the Left have lost all of theirs as a result of the Donald Trump victory over Hillary Clinton in 2016? Probably. These candidates have apparently forgotten that there is hope on the Right—the hope that Trump is victorious in 2020 as well and that four years is turned into eight.

The response of the Left to the release of the redacted Mueller Report was predictable and uniform, as they often times practice the same phrases and terms to appear unified. The Liberal media called the Report "frenetic", "deplorable", and "disturbing". Was it? Many of us found it to be fair, revealing, and as expected. I used to have some respect for NBC commentator Brian Williams, but when the Report was released he referred to Attorney General William Barr as "Baghdad Bill Barr". And that was just the beginning of his incoherent tirade. Williams revealed his true self as a fraudulent journalist, a charlatan, and quack, ultimately costing him his job and vocation. Shame on you, news wannabe!

Oh, where to position this little ditty? It also could have been placed in the "War" Chapter, but I decided that it lends itself more to the lack of civility today in the US than the sexist rant it was towards men. Our former FLOTUS once again crawls out of the woodwork with some of her pearls of wisdom. With all of her gaffs, it is shocking to me how well respected she remains among women in the US. During an appearance in front of a group of people, she stated that being in America today was "like living with a divorced dad". How insanely stupid and thoughtless are those words and whatever the meaning they were meant to portray. This almost reaches the levels of the "deplorables" and the "back to where you came from" assertions by Clinton and Trump. "If only I had delayed my communication by a minute to ponder its' potential impact on the listeners present and the world via social media." But alas none of those comments were caught in time and had considerable legs to carry them a great distance. Reminder of past lessons, we must always "look before we leap" so that we don't jump off a cliff into the perils below.

Animal bigots are among America's most dangerous people. As a former cat owner (the two of them died of natural causes) and various small animals of our daughters while they were growing up, I am now an animal "lover"—mostly the behaved animals of our family and friends. I and my siblings did not have furry animals growing up as too many of us had allergies to pet dander. I also agree with Fox News commentator Greg Gutfeld that "Animals are Great!" Do the "ends justify the means" relating to the impact of animal testing in order to save lives from disease? I tend to lean in favor of such justification as long as it is shown to be necessary. One of the latest entries of People for the Ethical Treatment of Animals ("PETA") is their mission to take animal and insect names out of common phrases and sayings—and there are many. I agree with some of the ideas, but not all. It is probably time to replace "more than one way to skin a cat" by substituting "peach" for "cat". But I am not sure that "you're acting like you have ants in your pants" should become "have an itchy butt", or that "counsel is badgering the witness" would be "pestering the witness". And the same goes for "you dog" or "you rat" changing to "you bad person". I do not believe that change is always needed when a statement includes the name of an animal. "You snake in the grass" can never be "you slime ball in the grass", just as "I would love to be a fly on the wall" would not be the same as "a concealed microphone in the room".

Many of us in America agree with Arthur Brooks, social scientist and President of the American Enterprise Institute: "We don't need to disagree less; we need to disagree better!" This obviously applies to both sides of the debate and is similar to recent remarks made by Louisiana GOP Sen. John Kennedy. In assessing the degree of success (or not) in the negotiations between Republican and Democrat members of the House

Judiciary Committee regarding the amount of unredacted portions of the Mueller Report that needed to be turned over with background information to the Committee, Kennedy stated that "both sides are doubling down on stupid". At least he is decent enough to tell things as he sees them.

Democratic 2020 Presidential candidate, Mayor Pete Buttigieg of South Bend, IN, has joined the "rank and file" of his fellow wannabes in declaring that "America was never that great that we would want to return to it." That is a perspective of our country to which I and millions of others have never subscribed. The US has not been perfect, but it has been the best country in the world. Many of us want to get back to that, with appropriate changes to make us better. I was taught to say that: "I've been around the block once or twice". When you experience something that is very good, one naturally wants to make a return trip. Maybe Mayor Pete has not traveled around those same blocks. Later in the campaign, Buttigieg drops the race card (as he and his fellow politicians on the Left are "want to do") when he says that Trump supporters are facilitating the POTUS "racism" in standing behind him. Suggestion to Pete - You had better settle any issues about "racism" with your constituents in South Bend before you point the finger at others whom you do not even know—that "casting the first stone" concept to which we continue to return in the case of politicians and others on both sides.

Baby boomers were raised under the banner of "live by the sword and die by the sword." In other words, society does not allow us to change the weapon based on a change in our circumstances. If we choose a potentially lethal instrument to fight a battle, we are not permitted to cast aside the armament when it appears we are or our position is in trouble. This ties in with the related phrases of "choose your battles [weapons] wisely". We don't need to chase flies in the fall with high-powered rifles when a fly swatter would do just fine. Leaders on both sides of the political spectrum are guilty of using too much "fire power" in simple skirmishes with our opponents. This is most likely based on a personal desire to be armed with more artillery than you need, just in case. The greatest generation taught us to save hate for wars with our enemies, and to not use it against our friends and neighbors—as that was not prudent based on our personal and religious beliefs. Pray for your enemies and those who persecute you, turning the cheek which has been struck to offer the other as well. Are such teachings no longer relevant in our scrambled world? I take the position that they are still worth pursuing. And if we are to believe that Rep. Nancy Pelosi prays for President Trump, as she says she does, then maybe even the unlikely is possible in our sharply divided world. Follow up: shortly after the prayer claim by the House Speaker, she once again reverts and descends to the "dark side" in stating that she is hoping for a Trump "intervention". I have an idea: maybe it is Pelosi who is "crying out" for such treatment. The Democrat "talking point" drafters get to work and come up with the thought that she is "getting under his [Trump's] skin." Or is this one of those vice versa deals?

One of the most prominent examples of our self-centered American society today is the movement to oppose the vaccination of our children—for any reason or irrationality. Segments of our population are being duped by online quacks who claim (without evidence) that necessary inoculations cause almost everything from autism, sudden infant death syndrome, to other chronic conditions. In our litigious world, parents who refuse to give these preventive shots to their infants and adolescents are now being sued in greater numbers when that decision is believed to have resulted in serious illness to others such a measles, mumps, whooping cough, tuberculosis, meningitis, polio, influenza, and others. If any of you "never-vaccinators" are out there and reading this, just get it done if you care at all about your family and your neighbors. The recent outbreak of measles (which was declared eliminated in the 1970s(?)) is further evidence of today's selfishness which I have labeled as the "Selfie Society". Thousands of US parents in their infinite wisdom and based on those same online falsehoods and conspiracy theories have decided to not have their children vaccinated for some of the most common ailments which disappeared with those inoculations. At one point in time during the recent past, there were seventy new cases of measles diagnosed within a single week—many of them in a community of Hassidic Jews. Do we need to tighten our laws which require that all young people are vaccinated for these now routine but potentially dangerous health conditions? If we do not go down that road, then maybe we have no alternative but to punish those parents whose children infect others with an otherwise preventable disease. We cannot expose innocent citizens with the poor choices of their neighbors.

Is there any humility today? You sure don't see it in DC. That is not surprising as "ego" is the primary enemy of being humble and also one of the regular residents of our nation's capital.

A prime example of how the Democrat-controlled US House is waging war on the Trump administration is evidenced by House Judiciary Committee Chair Nadler. He has led the issuance of more subpoenas against administration employees than have been used in the past 60 years. That is such an absurd abuse of power.

The mocking, childish, and bullying actions and rhetoric on all sides of the political spectrum must come to an end. This is not how we were raised to behave in the 50s and 60s. Many used to justify this conduct of President Trump by thinking: "how would you respond to constant taunting, lies about you, unmitigated and senseless criticism, and hatred against you and your family on an hourly, daily and weekly basis—incessantly?" But the President has now had almost four years (at the time of my writing) to get over this and on with his real life. It is time for the high road that was the way we were raised to respond to such vile conduct aimed our way. On the other side, I would not expect that those on the Left will ever tone down their destructive behavior toward the President, as it simply would not be consistent with the content of their hearts. They are beyond repair, having plunged into the mire of evil and brain death. It is all more of that waste-filled swamp land that surrounds us.

The boomers were raised with the phrases "what a difference a day can make" and "hope springs eternal". These were meant to emphasize that strange things can happen when least expected. Such revelations occurred recently with House speaker Nancy Pelosi. On June 5, 2019, she said "I don't want to see him [Trump] impeached, I want to see him in jail!" Then on day four of the Democratic action to impeach him (September 27, 2019), Pelosi related that she was "praying for the President"! We did not see that coming. Or was she just being facetious? You decide for yourself. I cannot believe that Pelosi would joke about praying to God! Then I remember that the insane persons on the Left will say and do anything because of their overwhelming hatred of anything and everything Trump or Conservative.

AOC, the "de facto" leader of the US House Democrats, states that: "The US has concentration camps for immigrants on the border with Mexico", or at least to that effect. The response on the Right is that our country has only such detention centers on the US/MX border as are required based on federal laws and Congressional inaction to make any changes. Do something bipartisan about it. Just who do you think you are Ms. Ocasio-Cortez? Your inflammatory words are an affront to every Jewish person in the world, except those who would buy in to your senseless anti-Semitic blubbering. And what is the response of and discipline by Speaker Pelosi, her Democratic partners in the House, and the rest of the Left to these vulgar anti-Semitic ravings—nothing, bring back the crickets!

Meanwhile, AOC's colleague from "The Squad" (which I have nicknamed "the four horsewomen of the apocalypse"), Minnesota Democratic US House member Ilhan Omar, blames Trump for all of the tensions with Iran—of course she does. She loves any country that hates and wants to destroy Israel. What Trump has done has been to appropriately withdraw the US from the lopsided and enabling Joint Comprehensive Plan of Action ("JCPA"/Iranian Nuclear Deal), implemented debilitating financial sanctions on Iran, and moved our military into the Straits of Hormuz to protect the free flow of oil tankers from Iranian aggression. Trump is seriously against the US taking a role as the "world police" under virtually all circumstances, but there are certain actions that only we will undertake to stand up for our allies against the tyrannical bullying of belligerent terrorist regimes. Omar also manufactured a story alleging that an Hispanic-American woman was arrested and fined $80 for stealing a loaf of bread to feed her children. Later upon a return to Minnesota, she pledged "to continue to be Trump's nightmare" by yelling it with a bullhorn to a handful of her "peeps"—more evidence of her self-righteous bigotry and hypocrisy. One can only assume that Omar will be dumped by her District constituents in 2020.

MN State Parks are adding "selfie stations". Great idea from some government employee with a lot of idle time (by no means one of the vast majority who work hard for the citizens of the State).

Trump is like Lutefisk, grilled liver & onions, Scotch, or cilantro—you either love it or hate it. During his trip to Minneapolis yesterday (10-10-19), I was anxious to see the response of the opposition protestors. I was horrified to see the same hatred we see in other less-refined areas of the country—fires started, vulgar insults, police officers and their horses assaulted, and people saying they did not care if police died. Shame on you urban Minnesota. It is a whole different world when you experience the "Children of God" in the rural parts of the state.

The great State of #NorthDakota recently joined the *AGG* selfie society with the change of its tourism motto from a beautiful "North Dakota — *Legendary*" to a bland "North Dakota — Be Legendary". One small word, big difference, big mistake.

Teamwork is incompatible with selfish individualism (there is "no I" in Team). The boomers were taught from our very early years about the importance of working as a team ("Teamwork makes the dream work!"). As such, we could make the optimal use of our own talents by joining them with those of others on the team. There was the family team, our home room group at school, the fellow students in our physical education class, early sporting activities, musical ensembles or debate teams, Sunday school classmates, scout troops, indeed any and all opportunities to be joined with our peers in a common mission. I could write volumes about the power and importance of teamwork training. But let's just leave it here by saying that without education and experience in developing each of us as a part of a team, we are missing out on one of the most important life lessons that prepares us to be active participants in building toward necessary uniform goals and destinations.

During the summer of 2019, a magazine supplement to our local newspaper dedicated to regional home building and furnishings features a contributing writer and local arts advocate traveling on a "tea train" in England, as well as a story about an area wine sommelier vacationing in Greece, and gardens in Belgium. And these writings have what to do exactly with our homes in the Northern Plains and lake country? That would be "nothing". They simply further the selfie society in which we find ourselves.

The lives of these people in no way impact our world but rather separate us away from our real values. Can we please return to local.

Some political cartoons are not immune from claims of "fake news" as well as a lack of civility and personal sensitivity. No one nor anything should be excluded from those considerations. Most of us know this when we see it.

It would be wonderful if there was a "vanity meter" available today to measure the unparalleled level of that vice which we see everywhere around us. The boomers were taught that vanity was not something to be proud of creating for oneself. A favorite song of our generation was *"You're So Vain"*, released in 1972 by Carly Simon. It was a moderate criticism about one or more of the men in her earlier life who loved her and left her. Vanity can certainly develop into an obsession with the way one looks. We see this condition suffered by men and women of all ages. One of my least favorite manifestations of vanity is when a peer of mine who is 65 or older gets "braces" on their teeth. Creepy! Is this just a problem that I experience? Most of the time I thought my friend had excellent teeth to begin with and is just looking for a way to spend excess cash. I should not judge but many times think: "doesn't [George we will call him] have better things on which to spend his money? Like a charity?" Get a life, Bailly.

Liberals seem to derive pleasure from effectively ousting great people and Americans from positions of power in the Trump administration. A perfect example of this was the recent and successful effort to expel Secretary of Labor Alexander Acosta from that position. He was a "shining star" in an unprecedentedly talented cabinet which the President had assembled. The wheels came off for the Secretary when the press learned that he had been involved in an earlier arrest and jailing of American financier Jeffrey Epstein who had been exposed again through new complaints and photos relating to sexual misconduct. Acosta had been a federal prosecutor in Florida when state charges were brought against Epstein and was a party to a settlement agreement reached with the financier. The media seemed to ignore reports that Acosta was apparently an integral and positive part of the negotiations through his insistence that the perpetrator would be imprisoned and required to register as a sex offender for the remainder of his life. Acosta became a victim of the "hindsight is 20-20" notion—he "shoulda/coulda/woulda" done more to push for a greater penalty against the predator Epstein. So another virtually flawless career by an amazing public servant is destroyed by the elitist Liberal media mob in for them just another routine day at work.

Trump-hater Mitt Romney and the bogus Twitter handle "Pierre Delecto" comes to light in late-October, 2019. This is further proof that there are some Republicans who do not use social media for "transparency". I used to like #MittRomney when he was a Republican. Update: Now (in early January of 2020) the "never-Trumper" appears to be the only Senator on the Right who is demanding impeachment witnesses, including John Bolton. Trump's past criticism of Romney has come home to roost. And I do blame that on the POTUS.

"Will & Grace" stars, Debra Messing and Eric McCormack, had to backtrack on their suggestion that Hollywood "out and boycott" Trump supporters there while claiming that the comments were "misinterpreted"? That is a common excuse by Liberal elitists who actually believe that most people (excluding themselves) are just plain stupid. They had said that they wanted a list of people from Tinseltown who were attending a Trump fundraiser there so they could be aided in determining the celebrities with whom they would (or would not) want to work in the future. Critics rightly accused them of "McCarthyism". Nice try by two idiot actors whom I do not watch at the present time nor would ever intend to do so in the future. And that is not the same McCarthyism they showed, but merely personal choice about what is entertaining and what is not.

It is a quiet day in DC on October 25, 2019, but there are partisan fireworks at (of all places) the Elijah Cummings funeral in Baltimore. I stop watching following Hillary and Pelosi "bashing" POTUS. How shameful and sickening. That was not the proper time nor place for such vitriol. #DisappearHillary #PelosiMelting

In a late-October (2019) tweet, has-been Bette Midler criticizes a Rand Paul tweet about the Kurds, saying that the beating of Paul by his neighbor was therefore somehow justifiable. Midler was allegedly later seen climbing out of a gutter. #GoBackToTinseltown

Do we believe those people who are claiming to be ignoring/not listening to the "negative talk" all around us? That is only possible for someone who is using earplugs, "noise-reduction" headphones, or listening to music with ear buds on a 24/7 basis.

"Hot off the press": Democratic NYC Mayor de Blasio and his administration in the city have fostered and facilitated disrespect of the police (one of the best and most admired forces in the US). According to the leader of the police union, the situation is "out of control". This is another one of those cases of "sickening but not surprising". Throughout the big cities of the US, the Liberals have driven a wedge between the residents and law enforcement while labeling the civil servants with all of the negative terminology—racist, bigots, homophobes, xenophobes. You know the "schtick".

Memo to future POTUSs: When you take over the office, "clean house" virtually everywhere to eliminate as much of the "deep state" in your administration as possible. #DeepState members seem to be everywhere!

"Shifty" Schiff yesterday (November 16, 2019—weekend between weeks one and two of the Inquisition) in CA: "We will send that charlatan in the White House back to his golden throne." So much for the #PelosiMeltdown "bipartisan" Impeachment Inquisition.

Never a question in my mind that #Democrat and "resist" activist "Reverend" Al Sharpton has always been a "slimeball". President Trump refers to him correctly as one of the foremost "racists" in our country. Now we hear he received over a million dollars from the charity he runs. Figures. #SlimySharpton

Most of the environmentally-active "envirocrats" (or now "envirocrites" because some of them are "hypocrites") who recently attended the $20 million Google "Camp" (July of 2019) traveled to the event in Sicily by airplane, including an estimated 114 private jets. Attendees included Prince Harry, Leonardo DiCaprio, Barack Obama, and Katy Perry. So much for protecting the earth to join the group of world elitists.

More "selfie" deaths in California at Yosemite National Park. NBC once again takes the snowflake road and refuses to identify the victims. Pardon me. The citizens of the US are entitled to know what stupidity looks like. This reminds me about a portion of the driver education the boomers received in the early-60s. The gory movies had names like "*Signal 30*" and "*Mechanized Death*", actual photos of the victims of auto crashes covered in blood. Needless to say not very pretty, but probably somewhat effective as a deterrent to thoughts about erratic or impaired driving. Is it time to show our young people exactly what can happen with that selfie in a precarious location? How else will this insanity end? Or has the generation been so protected in their bubbles that the result would be permanent emotional damage? And there are not enough of the selfie survivors to travel around to school auditoriums to provide the "don't do what I did" presentations. Back in the day this was called the "swift kick in the pants" lessons in life. Now we could just take away the kick. Update on May 13, 2020: an unidentified (of course) female recently entered a closed Yellowstone Park and was severely burned when she backed up for a shot near the Old Faithful geyser, right into a scalding "thermal feature". We will eventually learn if this was simply a stupid and uncoordinated albeit legitimate photographer or a selfie-seeking millennial, or both.

When is the last time you remember an immediate-past President criticizing his successor—like never? Well, when Trump beat out Hillary and followed Obama into the Oval Office, you might have figured that this tradition would change abruptly, and it has. On July 26, 2019, the former President shared an op-ed in the Liberal Washington Post in which Trump was criticized for the "poisoning of our democracy". No, Barack. That has been the result of the Left-winged media and others who have hated Trump since long before the 2016 election. It does not seem fair to blame someone else for the insane actions of his detractors that followed a lawful election and an outcome they considered impossible. Update on May 13, 2020: and how about the actions of the second Obama-Biden administration now dubbed "#ObaMAGAte"—their surveillance of the Trump presidential campaign prior to the election and up to the date of the inauguration. This will all further diminish the already dismal reputation of the treasonous cronies of Barack Hussein Obama and his henchman Biden.

Who is responsible for the craziness in America as we prepare to enter 2020. That would be those who voted in 2018 to empower the Leftist insanity and hatred by voting for the #Democrats and giving them the majority in the US House. Think about it.

If the Republicans had maintained control of the House in those mid-term elections, we would not be staring impeachment in the face as the Christmas/Hanukkah/Kwanzaa holidays season is upon us. And there would have been much more time for all of Congress to be debating and acting upon the substantive issues facing America today, especially immigration reform and reigning in federal spending which is out of control and adding to our deficit.

I am waiting to hear and/or see the exact language used by POTUS in his comment in Battle Creek, MI on "impeachment night" about their late-Rep. John Dingell "looking up" at them that night. Could he have meant "from his grave" rather than "from Hell"? Is this just more #FakeNews? I will admit if I am wrong. Then we see that the words used were to the effect that the late-Representative was looking down at them "or maybe up". I will try to give the President "the benefit of the doubt", but that was not a direction most of us would have chosen to go in talking about the respected and deceased former Democratic Representative.

We will remember that 2019 became the year that Anthony "The Mooch" Scaramucci turned on President Trump following a nearly two-year stint as one of his strongest supporters. He started as a ten-day White House Communications Director before getting fired upon the recommendation of incoming administration Chief of Staff John Kelly allegedly because the Mooch could not get along with anyone on the inside nor the outside. He continued to be a fan of the POTUS as a Fox Business Network contributor and elsewhere before a 180-degree turn. It was stunning to many that anyone who was a first team cheerleader for Trump could make such an abrupt and total change of direction seemingly overnight. Someday we will learn more about how this was possible and came to be reality. Until that day, we will continue to be amazed at how quickly and decisively a "worm can turn". As a result of the about face, Scaramucci went from being a "persona non gratis" with the media to being a poster child for the resistance, including the #FakeNews Liberal media, Trump haters throughout America, and those people with TAD ("Trump Affective Disorder").

Liz Warren was a Democrat 2020 Presidential hopeful and their "Selfie Queen"—a perpetrator of that egotistical, dangerous and degrading practice. She claims to have done more than ten thousand of the photos. It is all about her though, isn't it? Shame, Shame. #LyingLiz Would anyone I know want to be in a cellphone photo with the candidate? I cannot imagine that to be the case. Well, on second thought, I probably do know a few who would.

Anti-Semites Tlaib and Omar refer to President Trump as the "occupant of the White House" in remarks following a closed briefing today (1-8-20) re Iran/Soleimani. I am done listening to any more of the putrid garbage and hatred that they spew from their mouth. #Anti-Semitism

Antifa is being considered for classification as a "domestic terrorist group". Excellent thinking. How about organizations such as "Proud Boys" (alt-Right neo-fascist skinheads) and/or the "Three Percenters Militia Group" (far-Right paramilitary organization advocating individual gun rights and resistance to federal government involvement in local affairs)? Should they be included on that list as well? From past activities, it would appear that the "Boys" are a definite "yes" with the "3%ers" subject at this point to a "wait and see" position to monitor how violent and disruptive they become. Right or Left should not be an issue here. Dangerous groups at both extremes should not be tolerated, no matter what potentially reasonable and lawful positions they claim to advocate.

Now for something completely different, but still on the theme of selfishness. Television and movie celebrity as well as Weight Watchers "pusher" Oprah Winfrey has a $90 million home. I cannot help but wonder if she is one of those rich folks referred to in *The Bible* under the category of the "eye-of-a-needle" people. That amount of money tied up in a residence does seem to many of us as a bit extravagant, but we will still leave the judging to others.

Joe Biden referring to the POTUS during an interview: "we're going to make him feel the pain"? Really, Joe? Ouch. I am not so sure Biden could fight his way out of a paper bag let alone hurt our President with his actions. If you are trying to sound tough, Joe, it ain't working. Instead, I tend to feel sorry for him.

When Kirsten Gillebrand dropped out of the Democratic 2020 Presidential race, some of us were a little disappointed as she was a regular source of strange actions and statements. And her ego was as large as any candidate in the field. One of her best efforts was when she criticized several of her uncles who had voted for Donald Trump, even though they knew how much she loved Hillary. Now how could that not make anyone a little saddened? Shame on those uncles!

I could include this story in the "journalism" Chapter, but that would be inappropriate as Bill Maher has never been nor will ever be considered one. So, we will chalk this one up to incivility. Only hours after it was announced that David Koch (one of the Conservative "Koch Brothers") had died, Maher states on the air: "I am glad he is dead!" Really? How shallow and callous can a person be? Extremely in the case of Maher. Trying to give the Liberal host the benefit of the doubt, he is probably only trying to build up a cushion for when he passes on, as I can only assume that there will be many thousands of people who will cheer that event (though I will not be one of them if I am still here). Follow up regarding the Koch Brothers: a local (Fargo) office for "American's for Prosperity" (founded by the family) is vandalized by anarchists (such as the fascist group Antifa). Bizarre, as incidents like this have virtually never happened here because of our inclusiveness and tolerance.

Over the past ten years or so, the "glam" (for "glamour") photography business has exploded. It seems to be a combination of too much makeup and soft tones that sometimes totally change the appearance of the subject. It appears to be more prevalent in female Facebook photos and in pictures of young Native-American women. At least that is where I have experienced them the most. I should probably do more study of this phenomenon before I say too much more as I am clearly out of my element with this topic. There is one thing that I learned probably twenty years ago about the idea of personal photos that caught my attention and was memorable. I have forgotten the person who said this but remember and agree with the basic content—in real time look worse than you appear to be in a photo so the people who see you after viewing the picture are surprised at how great you look in person. Needless to say, I will not be looking for a marketing or executive position in that photo industry.

Conservative radio commentator, Rush Limbaugh, speaks regularly about his vision that there are many millions of Americans who are quietly seething and enraged at how President Trump has been treated by the Left since well before the 2016 election. We will probably find out if this is true as we approach the 2020 Presidential election.

Tweets have made the Trump administration by far the most transparent in history. My advice to the POTUS: keep on tweeting but try to adjust with less of the bullying and name-calling. You are leading with your actions and now you could consider adding more "high road" to the rhetoric. #highroad

A Minnesota Union of snowplow operators examines the forecasts during the winter in order to schedule strikes. Back in the day, they used to call such efforts "extortion". Now it is simply "strategic planning".

A Federal District Court Judge (DC District) ruled on March 25, 2020 in favor of the Standing Rock Sioux Tribe and against the Army Corps of Engineers regarding the Dakota Access Pipeline. The COE was ordered to do more extensive study about the environmental impact of the pipeline which passes under the Missouri River to the north of the Reservation in the exact location as several other pipelines. This pipeline has been carrying oil safely for the past three years. The Tribe erupts in dance! Suggestion: don't dance too much until the appeals are handled by the Court of Appeals and SCOTUS, keeping those shoes ready to go. The Tribe needs something to celebrate with COVID-19 unemployment rates on the Reservation probably 70% or more (as a guesstimate).

A Facebook post from me on May 2, 2020 (Happy Birthday, Charlie): "Okay, enough. I have been inundated over the past several days with posts about how selfish people are during the COVID-19 pandemic. This is why the first chapter in my recent book (*AGG*) is entitled "The Selfish 'Selfie' Society...". This "new America" has been building for the past 30 years, and apparently has become more evident to some during our fight against the virus. My generation was taught to not worry about something if you cannot control it — so I do not. Good luck if you continue to be shocked and amazed by the 40%+ of our population who are either insane, or on the doorstep. I will no longer read any of these posts."

The big question of the day (on May 11, 2020): should the former POTUS BHO be sent to prison once his felony conspiracy is proven, and which resulted in "#Obamagate"? I say sure, why not? Michelle can visit him on weekends.

During the July 4, 2020 weekend, a female hiker taking photos with her family off of the regular trails slips and falls to her death. Selfie or not, be careful if you are trying to preserve special moments in a dangerous place.

To put a wrap on this chapter for "*ASG*", the subject matter to me was obvious. About the time that you feel the level of political incivility could not reach any higher level, it then explodes in your face. I admit being naïve about and guilty of believing that the seriousness of the Coronavirus pandemic would bring the warring parties in America closer together at a time of national crisis. It is now obvious that I missed that one by a mile—make that a thousand miles! On one hand we have the Trump-loving Conservatives praising the POTUS for the amazing response of the administration, the federal government, and the President's Task Force for a nearly miraculous effort in identifying issues and challenges created by the virus and in then finding the solutions during what for all of us has been unchartered waters. Then on the other side we have the Trump-hating Liberals who would not give the President credit for a single grain of sand being properly positioned on any beach around the globe—the POTUS is a conniving, lying and egotistical imbecile who is personally responsible for every COVID-19 death on the planet as well as those which we will be facing for decades to come. Then multiply that times ten! The detractors on the Left have been so demented by Trump Affective Disorder (TAD) and Trump Derangement Syndrome (TDS) that they have evolved into blithering idiots, unable to cope with the possibility that the coalition of patriots on the Right has carried out a series of COVID attacks that have saved hundreds of thousands of lives and begun the preparations to fight the next thousand-year pandemic. Accurate history will sing the praises of many battles in the trenches of the virus that resulted in positive outcomes amidst a mostly invisible foe that threatened to take down the world. With all of this caused negligently or intentionally by the People's Republic of China, one might think that such a factual realization would bind all sides of our country together—another example of wishful but seriously flawed thinking. Instead, the finger-wagging on the Left in the direction of our President alone will leave tens of millions of Americans with chronic joint damage and no cure in sight. The United States of America is so polarized right now that whoever wins the White House on November 3, 2020 will face certain and fierce opposition but will still be "my President".

CHAPTER 2

THE PROBLEMS WITH SOME MILLENNIALS

It continues to seem that there is at least one new statistic released every day regarding our millennials in America. Recently a new factoid was released. Seventy percent of all members of that generation (aged 18-34) are at least partially dependent on their parents for financial support. And a further study indicates that those in the generation are not dating, because it is "too expensive". Both of those are worthy of a "wow".

In a recent expose, a story came out that some young people are faking their vacations—"fake it until you make it!" This is obviously also an appropriate entry for my chapter on the "truth". How sad is it that we have created a society in which some of us believe it is better to deceive others (including our friends) than to acknowledge that it is not a good time in our life to be able to travel or even have a "stay-cation". It might be an acceptable time for these individuals to seek counseling to improve their self-esteem. That could probably be more helpful and less expensive than any old vacation.

Is it possible that the millennial generation will be better parents than they had (if they become parents at all)? I would rate the chances to be unlikely or nearly impossible, which would be a disaster for America in the partial loss of two generations in a row. With a number of other countries breathing down our necks in the technology race, we cannot afford to squander any and all chances we have to excel. It will take a super-human effort to improve our education system to even come close in this life and death competition.

Many of us watched with amazement and disappointment as "Game of Thrones" concluded its' eight-season run. It was one of the favorites of all time for my spouse and me. While we thought the final episodes were shocking at times, a little slow moving, and merely surprising in other instances, we know that not everyone shared our views in such matters. That was apparently the case with over 1.7 million fans who signed a petition demanding a remake of the season with new writers. WHA? Who were those idiots joining in such a futile effort? Do they not understand that what has been written, produced, and presented in Hollywood or virtually any place else in the world does not get a second chance to "get it right"? I can only assume that most of these disgruntled "Throners" were of the millennial variety, many of whom had probably been spending too much time on the "porcelain throne" from whence their position fomented. Everything in the universe is not necessarily all about you. Endings in life could have at least thousands of different outcomes. One of the beauties of art and theater is that others make those decisions—mostly without the input from watchers/arm-chair quarterbacks. As my wife points out to me regularly, those "should have beens" are simply our personal slant or opinion, rather than binding determinations from the initial arbiters. To those who were deeply offended and even injured by the final twists and turns of a classic drama: get over it. Life goes on and may even get better for you despite this momentous set-back. If things continue to spiral down that worm hole of life, it is probably once again a good time to consider professional help. (And I still hope and even pray that I am wrong with my original demographic assumption regarding this amusing effort.)

Some advertising these days is quite amusing, even when it is probably not meant to be. JG Wentworth will exchange a lump-sum monetary payment for a stream of income to which you are presently entitled. They have an ad on the airwaves that is classic millennial "bashing". It depicts a male from that generation who is on the phone with the company expressing his interest in getting <u>his</u> money "right away"! Yah. And how do you think that will go? I do not see such an exchange as ending well. Instead, the money could be squandered/wasted, leaving the young person with nothing but regret. That is unless the young man (in this case) was to risk the monies in a brilliant startup business that makes him a gazillionaire ("The Expected Millennial Dream")! And what is the likelihood of that happening—approximately? Probably slightly greater than zero, with "slightly" being the operative word.

Are millennials notorious for wanting something for nothing? Here is a recent story that follows that theme. Paul Stenson opens a new hotel and restaurant in Dublin, Ireland. He is contacted by a 22-year old YouTuber and social media "influencer" Elle Darby who apparently felt she was entitled to a "free room and board(food)" in exchange for positive social media exposure. This was until Stenson met Darby head on. He set forth her 186K Facebook followers, 32K on Instagram, and 12K on Twitter, and proclaimed that those numbers "did not make her better than anyone else or afford her the right to not pay for something." The answer was "no". He went further to declare all bloggers banned from the hotel and restaurant. The social media response was swift and mostly negative for Darby, some calling influencers "self-entitled Kardashian wannabes" and "no more than useless professional beggars". Some but not many defended the influencer, while Stenson and others suggested that she "go out and get a real job to be able to pay for goods and services like everybody else." I would call this the "best laid plans of mice and [influencers]." Sorry, Robert Burns. Or, if the shoe fits, wear it—in a manner of speaking.

Many of the baby boomers were taught by their parents to know and use some basic "fix-it" activities. It certainly is nice to be able to do some simple tasks when it does not make sense to call someone to make repairs. We are learning that this tendency by the greatest generation is no longer being followed by some subsequent generations. It is said that millennials are not "do-it-yourself" (DIY) people. Their parents left out many of these lessons for some reason(s). This is one of the factors why the personal hand tool industry is in trouble today. Young people are not buying basic tools like they used to. And the "handyman" market as a vocation is exploding. My spouse was raised on a farm, and I in a city. She has never considered me to be very skilled in repairing anything. From time to time, she is shocked to witness that I am actually pretty good with some common tasks. I thank both of my parents for training me to handle many of those routine activities.

There are local groups around the US called "One Million Cups" who gather regularly for networking opportunities with fellow "entrepreneurs". That is a term which has gone through considerable change over the years. As the boomers were being taught by the greatest generation, entrepreneurs were typically brash young innovators who were willing to make a calculated "roll of the dice" to change traditional ways of creating the "widget" (that generic term for any product). These daring "recreators" were using whatever resources they and their friends had and were risking it all for a desired outcome. In training me, my father would often say that success was achieved by those with enough courage to risk failure with their "skin in the game", their fortune on the line: "no risk means no reward". There was a need "to pay to play". The "entrepreneur" of today has been diluted to be one who is out of work looking for that next big deal, while probably having very little idea of what it would look like. A good friend for mine, Bruce Gjovig, was responsible for developing and leading the University of North Dakota Center for Innovation and resulting in one of the top schools in the country for entrepreneurship. Now that is the reality of entrepreneurism that my generation was taught to seek out and achieve. All of this is much different than the new meaning of "entrepreneur" that we are expected to embrace—a synonym for "unemployed millennials" rather than the risk-taking business innovators who steered America from the 1970s and through the 1990s.

For most (if not all) of the baby boomer formative years, the greatest "fears" of Americans were as predictable as the days on a calendar. The greatest fear was "public speaking", followed closely by the "fear of death". For any of you who ever took a course in Speech which included making presentations in front of your classmates, that primary fear was very evident from the physiology of your presenting friends, i.e. shaking, sweating, stuttering, a flushed face. The memories come back to me as if the experiences were yesterday in Mrs. Hanson's junior high class. Fast forward to today with the millennials according to writer Pranjal Mehar, citing in part a study from Face a Fear at the British Heart Foundation. Some of the modern fears for this generation are spiders (37%) (twice the rate of 55-year olds), phone running out of battery (31%), sending a text to the wrong person (26%), having no wi-fi (24%), social circumstances (20%), and having your photo taken from a bad angle (19%). Okay, I did leave a few of the unimportant ones out. Just under a quarter of millennials (24%) admit to having lost friends due to fears, and 20% say fear has destroyed a relationship. The Chapman University Survey on American Fears has recently cited another major fear for young people—that a server in a restaurant will forget about them (which is easily rectified by flagging down another server or talking to the manager). The great news is that 84% of these young adults believe that they need to overcome their fears—a very good start. Alas, in the Chapman Survey, "dying" as a fear in now relegated to 54th place, and "public speaking" in 59th, just slightly ahead of "stalking" (63rd), "Hell" (64th), and "the Devil/Satan" in 66th place (or is that really "666th"?). Cue the spooky music.

In the past few months, over two million people signed an online petition on Facebook to storm Area 51 on September 20, 2019 in Nevada (the US Air Force Test and Training Range) which has been rumored over the years to house the remains of alien beings and spaceships from visits to earth in the 50s and 60s. Why do I place this in the "millennials" Chapter you might ask? It is because of an educated hunch that most of those who committed at least informally to attend were members of this generation. The promoters pulled the plug on the event about 10 days prior to the intended gathering, supposedly upon the realization that it was probably not a very good idea. Sound thinking. When over a thousand people came anyway, there were two humans arrested and no alien beings found nor incarcerated.

The times sure are a changin'. Take, for instance, how we meet our "soul mate". In 1980, 80% of couples met their spouse through friends and family. Fast forward to today: 66% of couples meet through online action or services. No problem. Whatever works is the important thing, as long as it is working. It appears that there is not that much difference in the longevity of marriages beginning in the 70s—it still runs about 50% of those who make it and those who do not. That changes significantly with "second" marriages which only last about 35% of the time, and "thirds" which are at the 25% level. "Rule of Life"—make sure the first time that you are with the right mate.

A local TV station interviews a millennial who says that Daylight Saving (or "Savings") Time "fall back" messes up his schedule and life?! Study: the number of workers "sleepy at work" has increased from 30.9% in 2010 to 35.6% in 2018. Related? That is a call for you to make. #SleepyMillennials

Rpt: Most millennials "paid" for their entire 2019-20 holiday season on credit/with plastic. Probably a lot of "used clothing" with which they are obsessed. And that was followed up with the stat that 86% of you spent an average of $500 over your budget during the previous year. That is a lot of extra spending on the gifts of experiences and memories that you are allegedly buying. It may take some time, but you will learn to follow a thoughtful and deliberate budget for such things. #BlameTheParents

New study: millennials around the country are drinking less alcohol—than they used to, and than their predecessors do and did. Two comments about this study: it is obviously not true in ND where the millennial drinking numbers are staggering (sorry (not really) for the pun), and one of the reasons elsewhere is probably that they are unemployed and cannot afford to drink so much.

A new college admissions scam has emerged involving millennials. Some of their wealthy parents relinquish parental rights so that their son or daughter can be eligible for a scholarship/grant/financial aid. When we boomers were growing up, it was common for many of our parents to put money in savings accounts or purchase education bonds for our college costs, enabling us to be able to afford higher education without securing loans. Today it is not uncommon for some college students to graduate in four or five years with six-figure debt. The planning in the old days was obviously superior to the current trend of deferring the ultimate costs of higher education until after graduation, and potentially for decades after that.

We have reached a point where school-age children who can legally work are choosing to not do so—the old all school and no work plan. This is a sad commentary about the laziness we are building into our society. These used to be great learning opportunities for kids and a chance to understand at a young age the power of turning employment into the cash resources which could help support their efforts to attain success in life. We should learn from the words of Sophocles in about 425 BC: "without labor nothing prospers." Sounds like the truth to me (but I come from the state that WalletHub named the #1 hardest working state is the US for 2019!).

Tess Brigham, a millennial therapist (I should have but did not realize there was such a person) reporting on CNBC.com, says that "the generation has everything they need", but should have "planners" to help choose from so many options in life. This is part of the generational challenge of being indecisive and the inability to prioritize what is "important" in life and what is "necessary". And it also comes out as the "Holidays" approach that they do not like "Secret Santa" programs at work, as the "Grinches" think it is too much of a "hassle". Bah, humbug!

It is not difficult to become attracted to the writings of journalism student Sonal Gupta, as she wrote in "*The Indian Express*" about the philosophical battles being waged these days within millennial minds. She says that we may be reaching a point in which the generation is solving its' existential crisis and determining a purpose in life (what some of us boomers have called a "raison d'etre" since being taught that in our teen years by the likes of Albert Camus and/or our junior or senior high French teachers). Gupta quotes a dejected Morty of the Netflix animated series, "*Rick and Morty*", who is speaking with his sister: "Nobody exists on purpose. Nobody belongs anywhere. We're all going to die. Come watch TV." The series which attracts this "lost" generation shows unquestioning support of science at the expense of, among other things, a belief in God. This is what Arundhati Roy refers to as "public despair". This loss of self-esteem, direction, and faith in the future appears to this writer to be a result from these young adults not having been taught and trained about how to think on their own two feet but rather how to find out about what others from different generations think. There is little if any ownership of independent thought as opposed to determining what the leader of the lemmings was saying and how best to be additional followers on that course of destruction. The retort "ok boomer" made famous by a 25-year old political activist from New Zealand, Chloe Swarbrick, seems to be just more of the laziness of the generation with the development of a simple response to be used universally in all instances to denounce the wit and wisdom of those elders who were trained over many years to use their brain for creativity, unique thinking based on analysis, and to thrive on the challenges in life placed in front of us as hurdles over which to bound rather than barriers to block us. In *AGG* I wrote about the passion of millennials to search for and locate that instant gratification and success rather than having their skills exploited by others for the satisfaction and benefit of others. Why share the fruits of my labors rather than enjoying all of the abundant harvest for myself? We can call this the "Name-In-Lights Syndrome" (NILS) from many but not nearly all of these struggling souls. You know and can name most of the causes of this condition.

At a Democratic Socialist gathering in Iowa with hundreds of millennials in attendance, there were complaints about "sensory overload", so they agreed among other things to ban colognes in an effort to protect their sense of smell and for the auditory problems they would use "jazz hands" instead of clapping. Such delicate flowers.

As we have just started 2020, Finland's 34-year old female Prime Minister, Sanna Marin, becomes the poster child for millennials worldwide with her proposed 4-day/6 hours per day work-week—just what our "lazy" and "unmotivated" planet needs to plunge it into the abyss. Imagine the position in the economic world we would attain with our young crop of workers ascribing to this type of schedule? This is a "no" for me, but I am not so opposed to the old 4-10s schedule (as well as the shotgun).

We are learning about a new camping and learning opportunity for interested young people. What a positive and engaging world we live in! It is called an "Emoji Camp". Doesn't this make you want to just kick yourself for not thinking of this amazing educational gathering? The goal is to help children learn better how to recognize and communicate their emotions, albeit with cartoon-ish figures and objects rather than spoken or written words. How helpful will these sessions be in bringing our youth from the brink of failure and isolationism into the arenas of high finance, global competitiveness, and world influence? Okay, probably not so much. But as the boomers were taught to think: "it is the thought that counts". Or is it? Just don't sign me up for one of these camps.

Not to worry millennials and Gen-Zers, Alexandria Ocasio-Cortez is a "fan" and has your backs. She claims that your generations are the most "aware", "literate", and "informed" generations in the world today. This is notwithstanding the fact that 20% of your generations in the teens and above are not aware of what the "Holocaust" was. As a group you are "willing to go to the streets" and "to puncture more taboos". It is reassuring that there are national leaders who are working for and with you to make a major positive impact in the world.

Some millennials are putting their future lives where their mouth is. They are partnering up with the UK, AOC, and the Birthstrike movement relating to global climate change, planning to not have children based on the premise that there is no reason to have them now because the beginning of the end of the world is only a little over a decade away. They see the results of climate change as a worldwide famine which will make food sources too scarce to cover the feeding of their children. That is clearly the minimalist/scarcity position versus the proactive solution of raising several children, teaching them about the perils of climate change, and working with like-minded people to solve the dilemma on a global basis. Thank the Lord that the boomers did not buy into the world destruction arguments decades ago, as the millennial and Gen-Z generations would not even exist today.

Pop singer Taylor Swift claims that she is "obsessed with politics". In this infirmity, she is joined by millions of other Trump-haters from the millennial generation. The obsession appears from the outside to be nothing more than a lingering hangover from Election Night 2016, the shock that Hillary Clinton would not be known as "45". Hopefully this sickness will pass them by at some point in the future, before it is too late.

YouGov poll in February of 2020: Nearly half of the millennials surveyed would rather live with socialism than capitalism, and 71% of those surveyed could correctly identify at least one of the economic systems. More than a third of those who responded said they approve of communism. Vox found that 30% are lonely (loneliest generation) and desire companionship, while 22% have "no friends". Forty percent (40%) consider themselves to be "religious" (that is good)! Black millennial women are the most entrepreneurial group within the generation and advocate the importance of self-employment.

Many millennials believe that the disappearance of the dinosaurs was as a result of climate change. That is partially correct, but the dramatic changes are thought to have been caused by volcanic activity and the aftermath of a huge asteroid hitting the earth in what is now Mexico.

According to a 2019 CreditCards.com poll, women and baby boomers are the best tippers, with millennials in last place. A lot of this appears to be consistency, as when millennials do tip, they will go as high as 22%. What is the sense in that? They don't tip as often, but when they do they sometimes go overboard.

UCLA is joining the list of our colleges and universities that are adding programs to assist in the coddling of the millennial and Gen-Z generations. Their latest effort is called the "Kindness Institute".

The financing company named SoFi has been advertising recently with young people who have refinanced their student loans, credit cards, and other debt through the company and then declare: "It is an incredible feeling to be debt free!" Time out. Don't you still owe this consolidated debt, only with a single company and monthly payment to that company? I do not read that SoFi is simply writing off those debts. In fact, these loans are generally repayable in three to seven years with interest rates of 5.74% to 16.74% according to bankrate.com. They used to call this false and misleading advertising.

The millennial lifestyle movement known as "FIRE" ("Financial Independence Retire Early") from around 2010 continues to gain traction via online vehicles—save 75% and retire at 30?? Really?

Not surprisingly many of our millennials and Gen-Zers are ignoring the social separation requirements of the national COVID-19 response. These people are partying around the country with their peers during the cancelled Spring Break. At the same time there is an initial confirmed case of the virus in Arizona, causing some of their peers to careen off the rails. Chill. Will they ever "get it"? May God help us. #SpringBreak

I read with much curiosity about the types of products which are disappearing from America (and the world) today because the millennials are not "buying in". This came from Paige Steinman in cooperation with Vaneer Studio. Much of this will not surprise you, but certainly some of it will. Here is a smattering: cars & gasoline (driver's licenses for their generation are down by 25%); fabric softener; traditional gyms; cereal (inconvenient); business suits; homes; regular milk; weddings & diamonds; movie theaters; bulk groceries (Costco/Sam's); traditional domestic beers (Budweiser, Coors, Miller); cruises; beef; napkins; mayonnaise; irons; land lines; lottery tickets; postcards; high-heeled shoes; life insurance & investments (stocks & bonds); doorbells; cable; McDonalds; hotels; golf; bar soap; casual dining; department stores; fast food; savings (62% are living paycheck-to-paycheck); designer clothing; wine with corks; motorcycles. That is a lot of stuff to which we are saying "goodbye".

According to a study by "Business Insider", fifty percent/half of millennials admit to having left a job for "mental health" reasons. I suppose they felt they would "go crazy" if they stayed in the position. The 2019 Deloitte Global Millennial Survey categorizes millennials and Gen-Zs as a "generation disrupted", unsettled and frightened about their future. The biggest concerns of millennials internationally are climate change, pollution, and terrorism, while those in the US are focusing on corruption/lack of trust, pollution, economic instability [before the COVID-19 "crash"], income inequality, and climate change. And around the world, these young adults are showing considerable interest in political and social activism. We will see how that turns out.

It is wonderful to learn new names and phrases. One of these for me is "neck beards". These are apparently nerdy millennial guys who thrive on board games and live in their parents' basement. Sounds like fun.

News out of our neighbor Minnesota which is confusing, at least to me. Drug use by a population in the state is leading to a critical need for foster care. It must be about millennial parents. I apologize if I am wrong.

A study by the Annenberg Public Policy Center found that the most likely persons to believe the falsehoods about the safety and content of vaccines are millennials and Gen-Zers who are active in their use of social media. Pardon the supposition, but that does not seem to be a glowing endorsement about the positive power of social media—possibly more of a condemnation.

According to the Wrike, Inc. 2019 stress statistics, 94% of Americans are stressed at work, with almost 30% feeling those levels to be high or unreasonably high. The Liberal *New York Times* tabloid declared the US to be the most stressed country in the world (of course due mostly to fear about President Trump). Millennials were considerably more stressed out at the office than baby boomers, partly because the latter generation is generally content with what they have while the millennials want it all and want it now.

An article in the local newspaper that I almost skipped (not being interested in reading about a 23-year old former area college student who had recovered from COVID-19) somehow lured me in for a glance, and I was glad I took it on. It was worth it for this tidbit of her philosophy: "I feel like I need to apologize for my generation just for not protecting other generations and other people as much as they could." She was not alone in those sentiments.

As we are in the middle (hopefully) of the COVID-19 pandemic, there is much serious concern that the results of the virus will be tougher on the millennials than any other generation. Think about all they have had to endure so far during their relatively short lives. They had to experience the tragedy of 911 while they were receiving their primary education. They were required to suffer through the financial pain of the "Great Recession" as they were graduating from college or had started building a career and family. Now as they are trying again to grab the golden ring of life, they are colliding head-on with a careening train that is out of control and will take too many of them at a quite tender age. Then add the George Floyd tragedy and unrest to that. This chapter has not been very kind to that group of our family, friends, co-workers, and neighbors, and I am pushed to imagine how the boomers would have fared under similar circumstances. One of the mantras during the COVID crisis has been that "we are all in this together and will survive it together", just as a team of any other individuals would be assembled to experience and succeed. I am fully committed to doing whatever I can in the little time I have left to help this group of Americans experience full and productive lives. They have suffered enough—much more than most of the rest of us can even imagine.

CHAPTER 3

A GOVERNMENT OF MEN AND WOMEN, NOT OF LAWS; THE GROWING LIBERAL "DEEP STATE" AND THE OVERBUILDING OF GOVERNMENT

Someone you may remember, Hillary Clinton, has spoken out about the Mueller Report and President Trump. Maybe you don't care about anything she would say, but here goes. She said that anyone else facing all those facts would have been indicted. But Hillary, as a lawyer you must know that a sitting President cannot be indicted. This all reminds me of a recent situation which involved an illegal computer server installed and used by a US Secretary of State. Some of the communications were assuredly hacked by foreign governments. When this equipment was subpoenaed, it was cleansed and/or destroyed, and thus not available to be investigated. And that person was not indicted because of protection by the deep state, contravening federal laws and placing her "above the law". How convenient for an accuser of others and compulsive liar.

"Ignorance of the law is not a defense." This was one of the principles of law that was taught to my classmates and me in our Criminal Law classes at the UND School of Law in the mid-70s. This should have been a lesson in school for Hillary Clinton, James Comey, and many other politicians on both sides of the aisle.

Trump refused to claim Presidential privilege for the contents of the Mueller Report. Would that hurt any of his subsequent efforts to fight with former White House counsel Don McGahn against the Congressional subpoena for the attorney's testimony? We will keep this updated. Shortly after I wrote my notes regarding this matter, the President said "no" to any more compliance by members of his administration with the plethora of Congressional subpoenas served on his current and former staff. So far as of August 7, 2019 there has been no House Committee appearance by McGahn. (The courts later support this privilege claim by him.) House Judiciary Committee Chair Jerry Nadler threatens that those persons who ignore his Committee subpoenas could face jail time and $20,000 per day fines. This seems like harassment to me. And those efforts by Nadler and his Congressional thugs on the Left continued with the sickening and juvenile hearing when Attorney General Barr refused to voluntarily appear before House Judiciary Committee—more political "theater" which I would categorize under the genre of "farce".

A classic lesson in how the federal government should be operated rather than what it has become. Ford Motors announces in mid-2019 that it will eliminate 7,000 white-collar management positions. These programs need to be extended to the bureaucracy in DC, but on a much larger scale. There are too many tiers of employment in most of our government departments and agencies. We need to remove many of those levels and some entire departments to revolutionize our federal offices. Some entire departments could also be merged to reduce the total number considerably.

Our "government of laws" took a major "hit" during the summer of 2016, four months or so before the presidential election. The FBI was conducting a covert counterintelligence investigation which they named "Operation Crossfire-Hurricane" (OCH) into a rumored link (from the fictitious "Trump Dossier" funded in part by the Hillary Clinton campaign) between the Trump campaign and the Russians. OCH went far enough to question as to whether Trump was a "Russian spy/operative" or susceptible to blackmail for his previous activities in Russia. This raises a critical question about the lack of transparency of the Obama administration and its' Department of Justice: "why was the Trump campaign not alerted by the FBI or DOJ that there may be collusion between members of his campaign staff and the Russians?" It now appears likely that this was because there were high-ranking agents in the FBI who wanted to prevent Trump from being elected President, or they wanted an "insurance policy" to remove him from office under the unlikely chance he was elected. In essence, this constituted possibly treasonous conduct by powerful agents in the government—an unprecedented "bloodless coup d'état" in America for the first and hopefully last time in our history. And we elders in this country thought that the egregious conduct of the Nixon administration with the unexplainable "Watergate break in" was serious stuff. Little did we know how dangerous such matters could ever become. It may be decades until we know the expanse of these efforts by certain Americans to circumvent the election process.

Historically, some Native American activists have been among the most radical and violent leaders of a "resistance" movement in the US—probably with some justification as the "white man" killed thousands of them and stole their land over a period of decades and continues to "occupy" Tribal lands. Two of the leaders of this fight as the "American Indian Movement" (AIM) were Russell Means (who died in October of 2012) and Dennis Banks (who passed away in October of 2017). Means and Banks were among the leaders of the February-April, 1973 (71-day) armed takeover of Wounded Knee in the Pine Ridge Reservation of South Dakota, for which they were later charged (and then dismissed for governmental improprieties). In 1975 (also at Pine

Ridge), AIM members fired on FBI agents in a massive shoot out, leading to the controversial conviction of Leonard Peltier for first-degree murder and sentencing for two consecutive life sentences (which he continues to serve). These were tough times for Native-American relations in the Dakotas and other adjoining states. Since those times it seems that the white man and Natives have peacefully coexisted to a certain extent with living conditions on the Reservations improving for some and deteriorating for others. Infusions of cash from minerals, gaming and reparations have been mostly squandered by those who have continued to suffer from alcoholism and drug addiction. And acts of violence on the Reservations continue to plaque the Natives, including those which have led recently to the movement to investigate and publicize the problem with Missing and Murdered Indigenous Women (MMIW). What has happened to the law enforcement on these Native lands through the Bureau of Indian Affairs (BIA) Police departments? Apparently not enough to protect the residents from seemingly uncontrolled assaults, murders, suicide, illegal drug sales, poor healthcare, and general mayhem. Then there are the controversial oil pipelines, some of which carry their oil. Certain segments of the protests against Keystone and Dakota Access are based on valid concerns such as the environment and sacred Tribal lands, while others have been a sham to bring in outsiders to fight the Native "war" for "control". Decades ago my father wrote his opinions about the problems on our Reservations and his belief that the entire system needed to be scrapped in favor of protecting our indigenous peoples and their cultures and heritage. That will never happen, but it is obvious that something needs to be done to improve the lives and legacy of our Native-American population. My Episcopal Church in the US has attempted to contribute by bringing Jesus Christ into the lives of this population, in combination with the beautiful spiritual world of the Natives through which they lived long before we outsiders arrived on the scene. Whatever the solutions, they must be reached "under the governing laws" through dialogue which has improved lately in my State of North Dakota, mostly from education, listening, compassion, and recognition. Whomever solves these dilemmas of Natives and their roadblocks toward positive futures will make a name for themself(ves) in the history of our republic.

When George Orwell's "*1984*" hit the bookstands in mid-1949 and migrated to every junior high and high school in the US during the 1960s, little did we realize how many of the predictions in that book would become reality, and certainly not the timing of those changes. Some of the warnings about the issues raised predated the writing and release, such as suggestions about our potential loss of privacy. One of the favorites was from 1890 when American lawyer Louis Brandeis (who later served on the US Supreme Court (1916-39)) expressed concerns that the emerging use of photography was a threat to the right of Americans to their personal privacy. Today in September of 2019, the American Civil Liberties Union (ACLU) complains that the use of facial-recognition software by the Transportation Security Administration (TSA) as people are boarding airplanes in the country is a potential invasion of their privacy if the TSA maintains the photos in a database for any extended period of time. And yet in China, the government has created and stores facial images as well as dossiers on virtually all of the citizens of that country. We were warned about that in "*1984*" as the actions of "Big Brother" in controlling the lives of everyone. We are slowly but certainly seeing the images of a strictly managed society creeping into our world.

Speaking of the ACLU (which was founded in 1920), baby boomers are old enough to remember when that organization was a defender of the personal human rights of all Americans rather than only those on the Left as we find today. On a rare occasion over a decade we are shocked that they come out in support of the rights unique to those of a Conservative bent—truly infrequent "gotcha" moments. This is why it should become the ACLFLU. I trust that you can figure that one out. Or if it must remain as the ACLU, it could be the "American Causes Liberal Union". "Same difference" as we were taught to think and say. Many of us yearn for a non-governmental entity which would become a beacon of rights protection for all Americans. I suppose that is why we need to have and retain our amazing local, State, and federal courts, the premier system for justice and law enforcement in the world—much copied but never duplicated. And I will give a self-serving "shout-out" to most of the attorneys out there who ably assist in our legal system, but only those who diligently and effectively serve the interests of their clients.

Florida Democratic Congresswoman Frederica Wilson says: "those who criticize members of Congress, online or offline, are criminals and should be prosecuted." Pardon me, but I thought this was America with a First Amendment rather than Communist China?! I would say that the Congresswoman has gone a little elitist on us with her position "going to her head".

Never in the history of America has there been a more insidious exposure of the deep state than we have now witnessed with the multiple "whistleblower" complaints lodged by partisan federal employees bent on bringing down President Trump and resulting in the impeachment inquiry waste of time and energy which will take us well into election year 2020! Adam "Shifty" Schiff, Chief Justice of the Star Chamber in the US House Intel Committee Impeachment Inquisition, is a conflicted leaker, liar and louse. He needs to recuse himself from the Committee leadership for as long as the Inquisition continues. I could write more here but will wait for other chapters to discuss this incredible new "witch hunt" at the hands of traitors who protest actions and words by our President which are expected of and protected for him.

It is humorous to watch the Liberals quacking about transparency as we have transitioned over the past nearly three years from the least transparent administration in history to the most transparent. They rue the day that Twitter was unleashed upon the world. It seems like every day that President Trump gets into trouble for saying exactly what he is thinking while not speaking with the "swamp" dialect.

The "crazies" in California are at it again. They pass a law directed at President Trump which will attempt to prevent his name from being a candidate for President on their 2020 primary election ballot unless he releases his tax returns for a period of years. Are they unaware that the laws, rules and regulations relating to candidates for national office are regulated by the federal government and cannot be infringed upon by the states? Of course they knew that. They are simply interested in sticking a knife in the President and giving it one more twist to create pain for a political opponent they hate. Don't blame lawyers for all the increased litigation in the country. The Liberals are responsible for more than their share. If you did not believe before that there is a shortage of adequate mental health services in California, this and similar real-life developments will probably help you realize the truth of that absence of available and effective treatment.

During 2019, we have witnessed one of the biggest scandals in the history of college admissions unravelling before our very eyes. Many parents in the corporate and Hollywood elite attempted to buy the way of their children into colleges which otherwise probably would not have admitted them. Some of these caring mothers and fathers bought fake admissions test scores or fabricated sports abilities with tens of thousands of dollars donated to fake "charities" of the perpetrators. What an intriguing "double dip"—buying the way of your child(ren) into a prestigious college and then attempting to deduct the fraudulent payments as a charitable deduction. Actress Felicity Huffman was sentenced on September 13, 2019 to fourteen days of jail in exchange for her guilty plea in one of the least expensive of the schemes while some of these brilliant-minded celebrities are refusing to settle and taking the process to the full courtroom conclusion. There is no expectation Huffman will serve all of her time, assuming she will be let out early for "good behavior". Lori Loughlin now faces additional bribery charges as her time for a plea deal expires. Proverbs 16:18—pride goes before destruction, and a haughty spirit before a fall. Time to get off your high horse or prepare for the plunge. #HaughtyInHollywood There have been and will be many more dispositions in this scholarship scandal. Most people who are interested seem to be waiting patiently for the Laughlin trial with her husband (Mossimo Giannulli), and that outcome which could potentially involve at least months in jail if there is a conviction. Update: they finally settle and will be sentenced about when this book is published—probably a slap on the wrist with a wet noodle.

In September of 2019, a "whistleblower" from the deep state madness comes forward with concerns about what the POTUS said in a phone communication with the leader of The Ukraine. It appears that there were requests for the investigation of claims about leaders in that country who supported Hillary in 2016 and possible efforts to cover up Biden and Clinton taking millions of dollars from a Russian oligarch. There certainly will be much more coming forward about these claims. Follow up: How unprecedented is the (forced) release of the transcript of a phone call between the POTUS and the head of state of a foreign country. What a chilling impact this will have on the US Presidency and vital communications with other countries—forever! And don't people realize that there are usually ten or more listeners on every Presidential phone call from the White House?

In *AGG* there was a proposal to increase the auditing of federal government departments and agencies. The purposes would be to have better control of purchases and expenses, and to be able to identify where the largest costs (payroll) can be reduced through restructuring and fewer employees/less bureaucracy. A similar state program conducted by the North Dakota State Auditor has created considerable controversy as it appears that no matter what level or type of government is involved, there are huge numbers of deep state staff members who are fearful that their jobs are vulnerable to elimination. I have always believed that most governmental agencies could run as efficiently with at least one-third fewer administrative personnel.

Lt. Col. Alexander Vindman(?) is deposed by the Impeachment Investigation today (October 29, 2019) for his "opinion" about the Ukraine call. No one seems to know who he is, even POTUS. Does he have any new and "earthshattering" information about the transparent call, or, was he one of the whistleblower's "sources"? Hmm. We will eventually find out. The whistleblower complaint has 17 references to information learned from the Leftist US news media, which casts grave concern about whether it is worth the paper it is written on. There should not be many more questions about this infamous intercontinental telephone communication since the transcript of it was released weeks ago in yet another attempt by the Trump administration to show 1000% more transparency than we saw from his predecessor. #DeepState Just one day earlier, #ShiftySchiff opined when an Impeachment Inquisition witness was a "no-show": that nonap-pearance makes it presumable the witness would have adversely implicated the POTUS. At what law school was legal scholar Shifty taught this? We can only presume based on the substance of the pronouncement that the renowned institution of very high learning was in California. Did Schiff and his staff help create the whistleblower? Who was the attorney that drafted the whistleblower's complaint? Any questions why Shifty (as of a day following the testimony of Vindman) has not deposed the whistleblower who started the Inquisition? Hmm. UPDATE:

"Whoever he is Vindman" is without employment on November 12, 2019. "Thank you for your service" and "you're fired". Advice to the Presidents who will follow Trump: during the transition be sure to fire from your administration as many members of the "deep state" as possible, lest they later come out to haunt you!

Nikki Haley as she comes out with her new book (*"With All Due Respect"*): Tillerson and Gen. Kelly sought her help in undermining President Trump. Treacherous conduct at best. Whatever happened to communicating about differences, and then resigning if they cannot be settled satisfactorily?

SCOTUS arguments today as I write (November 12, 2019): can the DACA protections illegally set up by Obama with an Executive Order be reversed by a Trump EO? DUH? Even Judge and Fox News contributor (and "never-Trumper") Andrew Neapolitan Ice Cream knows the correct answer here. #SCOTUSRules

"Joke of the Day" (No…how about the "year" so far): Dems — The "deep state" is made up of "patriotic career professionals". That is almost correct if you first replace "patriotic" with "partisan" and then remove "professionals" with "Trump-haters". #DeepState

Rep Greg Stuebe (R-FL) on the US House Judiciary Committee correctly sites that terrorists on trial by the US around the world have more rights than the POTUS has during the Inquisition process. Only in America can facts like this exist. We are a "government of laws", and yet we treat our President like the citizen of a country on the terror watch list. This is a sure example of what hatred can do. #ImpeachmentInsanity

The Cherokee Nation claims that Native Americans have the right to a seat in Congress from the 1785 Treaty of Hopewell. Why has it taken so long for the Tribe to strongly raise such a premise? It would seem that any such grant would need to be contained in the US Constitution or clearly elsewhere in federal laws.

It was alarming that so many Judges and DOJ alumni were protesting the DOJ recommended sentence reduction for Roger Stone, until we learned "the rest of the story". They (like the DOJ prosecutors) are mostly political operatives on the Left. Should have seen this coming. Followup: The sentencing of Roger Stone takes place today (October 20, 2020) for lying to Congress and obstructing their investigation of 2016 Russian meddling—process crimes. Judge Amy Berman Jackson gave him 40 months (3 years & 4 months), slightly less than the 7-9 years deep state DOJ prosecutors were recommending. Disgraceful performance by the DOJ. There is a story out on the street that POTUS has directed AG Barr to "clean house" at the DOJ (hopefully to include the Stone prosecutors) to remove as many partisans from those ranks to assure that incidents such as this are minimalized in the future. #DeepState

John Bolton is entering the realm of those leeches who "kiss & tell". I do not care what he is lawfully saying. It is just that he must have had a lot of writing done even before he was fired. At least the "Democrites" (Democrats + hypocrites) will read his book.

The Democrats have an extremely selective memory when it comes to the firing of Department Inspectors General. Joe Biden goes off the rails on May 20, 2020 when he learns that President Trump fired the IG of the State Department who was investigating Secretary of State Pompeo for allegedly using some Department staffers for personal errands? So what. Biden claimed to be unaware that Obama fired most of the IGs who were holdovers from President Bush. This is more of the reason why I have named them "Democrites". An incoming POTUS should probably fire all of these #DeepStaters, except those from their own previous administration.

This says it all: while #Liberals believe that the Federal Government can do everything, the #Conservatives know from experience that the private sector invariably outperforms the bloated Federal bureaucracy. Truth. #DeepState

125 leaks in the first 126 days of the Trump administration, compared to 8 for Obama and 9 for JW Bush. This is your "#DeepStateExposed" at work. I write suggesting future Presidents clean house during the transition.

An historic week for the SCOTUS starting on 6-15-20 with two seemingly Liberal decisions authored by Conservative Justices Neil Gorsuch and John Roberts. In a 6-3 decision, the Court extended the Title VII provisions of the 1964 Civil Rights Act to protect the LGBTQ+ community against certain types of discrimination, and in a 5-4 decision rejected the effort of the Trump administration to use an Executive Order to reverse that Order of President Obama relating to the DACA program benefits for the children of illegal immigrants who came to the US two decades ago. The Democrats (in tears) seem to have been hit with shock and awe, while the Republicans accuse the Court of "legislating from the bench" (something the rules do not permit it to do). This was actually a terrific civics lesson for the Liberals that the judges on the Court are selected to follow the law in a consistent manner using the principle of *stare decisis* wherever it may lead. No person nor issue is "above the law". If you are interested, be sure to read more about these decisions as my analysis here is extremely basic for very complex issues. Update a couple of weeks later: Chief Justice Roberts "flip flops" and joins the Liberals on the Court (by 5-4) in striking down a Louisiana law requiring abortion doctors to have admission rights in an area hospital (the opposite of his position with a virtually verbatim

Texas law), and then writes the opinion in an historic decision simplifying the ability of religious schools in securing federal funds, closing the gap between "church and state". There does not seem to be a dull moment with the SCOTUS. And the Trump tax returns decision should be out any day now as we move on to July of 2020.

I just don't get it on June 30, 2020. A leaker illegally provides possibly classified info to the failing *#NYTimes* about an unverified claim of Russian bounties for killing US soldiers in Afghanistan. Why are the leaker or the writer not in jail?

The following day, AOC (Anarchist Ocasio-Chaos) (D-NY) complains that a $1 billion cut to the NYC Police budget is not "de-funding"? She wants real cuts! Watch for crime in the Big Apple to explode from current huge growth levels. Unfortunately, this has become another city added to the US "do not travel" list (with Minneapolis-St. Paul, Chicago, San Francisco, Seattle, Portland, Los Angeles, DC, Baltimore, Detroit, St. Louis, and Philadelphia). This will presumably improve when Americans take back the streets from the control of the Leftist "mob rule" advocates.

Here is another chapter that has an obvious track for concluding thoughts as the writing hits mid-June of 2020. "45" (or President Donald J. Trump) has now been in office for forty-one months, most of which were fought out near the gates of Hell. I cannot possibly imagine in the slightest what it has been like for this person to face people who "hate your guts" (more boomer stuff) on a daily basis at such an extreme level and during that considerable expanse of time. Virtually all of us would have succumbed from such torture long before now. We have learned so many things during this period, among them: the "deep state" is real and dangerous, consisting of those holdover civil servants many of whom are as politically divisive as can be (we need to be able to identify and remove these cancers from a new administration as soon as possible before they do their otherwise inevitable damage); the Democrats as a party are on the verge of splitting into two or more parties (at least the Democrats for one and the Socialists for another); the "mainstream" media is basically a public relations arm of the Democratic National Committee; neither the Trump campaign nor the administration has colluded with Russia although the Russians did collude with some of the Democrats and did attempt unsuccessfully to interfere with the 2016 US elections; Big Tech is totally focused on spying into the lives of its users and in eliminating through censorship Conservative and Christian thought from the Internet, resulting in the need to break up the likes of Facebook, YouTube, Twitter and Google (for starters); Trump has not been found to have committed "high crimes and misdemeanors"; and lastly but certainly not the least, the Obama administration DID spy on the Trump Presidential Campaign and Transition Team from early-2016 into 2017 and followed by the actions of its' deep state minions after the inauguration until well into 2018. This final indiscretion has now been dubbed as "#ObaMAGAte" but could easily be "#ObamaBidenGate". The Democrats are trying to justify the spying as legitimate surveillance of Trump based on team contacts with the Russians, which the Republicans are not buying as the communications with Russia were either in the normal course of preparing a new government or were trying to learn more about the fake "Trump Dossier" created by Hillary and the Democrats. I will not extend my neck out too far on this one as there is not enough information at the present time to predict whether this is the most serious incident of treason and breach of federal election laws in our history, or simply serious errors in judgment by political zealots in attempting to sabotage a duly elected President of the United States of America. Or something in between. Whatever the outcome, it does make for some interesting investigations and debate.

CHAPTER 4

IMMIGRATION WITHOUT ASSIMILATION AND A BROKEN IMMIGRATION SYSTEM

The Democrats have finally acknowledged that there is at least a "humanitarian" crisis at the southern border. This surfaced in mid-June of 2019. They had refused to admit there were any challenges in those areas since before President Trump declared a "National Emergency" along the boundary with Mexico. The Immigration Court backlog for asylum claims now equals more than 869,000 cases, yet our federal Representatives are doing nothing to legislate for a solution to the mess. The Dems claim to be able to walk and chew gum at the same time, but we are not seeing it. There is some partisan legislation passed in the US House, but those efforts are going nowhere with the Republican-controlled Senate. And the glut of refugees is not aided by the radio ads in Central America that are encouraging residents down there to "go to the US".

At one point in July of 2019 (since my original writing of *AGG*), arrests of illegal immigrants at the US/MX border totaled 504,000 for a 7-month period compared to 396,000 apprehensions during all of 2018. That amounts to an increase of 118%. The US Border Patrol estimated that these numbers could end up at over one million arrests for 2019. Then Mexico agreed to get serious about reducing the flow of immigrants at its' Southern border and increasing patrols at the US border. That military deployment coupled with holding more of the asylum seekers in Mexico pending their US Immigration Court hearings appears to have significantly reduced the immigrant numbers as we enter September of 2019. Then the US Supreme Court rules in favor of the recent POTUS Executive Order requiring US asylum seekers to apply for such in the first country they enter while fleeing (or in the US Embassy or Consulate of their home country). Seems pretty reasonable.

In early June of 2019, US House speaker Nancy Pelosi opined regarding the efforts of the Trump administration to impose trade penalties against Mexico for their failure to stop the Central American flow of foreigners to the Southern US border stating that "tariffs are not a way to treat friends." Those on the Right responded that friends do not let foreigners travel through their country to invade an allied neighbor. And if she does not like the tariff solutions to trade imbalances, maybe she should do her job and legislate changes necessary to close down the flow of illegal immigration into America. Failure to act with a solution to these problems jeopardizes the best and fairest legal immigration system in the world—by far!

The Liberals are known to come off the hinges when they learn that ICE is embarking on an effort to remove from the country illegals who are the subject of deportation orders. Such is a lawful means of enforcing our current immigration laws. On the other side of their mouths, they accuse President Trump and the Conservatives of acting "above the law"? Indeed, it appears that it is the sanctuary jurisdictions and anti-ICE factions on the Left who are claiming that they and their causes are not subject to the same laws that our law enforcement community is sworn to uphold and protect. The antithesis of following the law is anarchy, not far from where the Liberals are currently placing their support. Another sickening result of sanctuaries took place in Montgomery County (MD) where there had been an epidemic of sexual abuse and rape allegations against male illegal immigrants there being protected from deportation and released back into the general population as a sanctuary county. Question: how has this policy protected the US citizens of the County (mostly female) who have been the victims of these outrageous criminal attacks?

Is there anyone who claims that the differences of opinion about the US/MX border security are not based on politics? A recent poll showed that Republicans concerned about border security was at 85% and 15% for Democrats. How is that even possible?

Bleeding heart Liberal and two-faced House Speaker Nancy Pelosi speaking about aid for the border emergency: "we need to treat [those unaccompanied immigrant minors] with dignity and respect." Question for you Ms. Pelosi: how about the minor children of citizens who are homeless in your California back yards, do they deserve even half of that same dignity and respect? It is a disgrace how you and your constituents are treating them. Many on the Left support treating illegal immigrants much better than American citizens who are down on their luck. Many illegals are receiving free medical care, housing and meals, transportation to be with family, and employment opportunities. Whatever happened to the philosophy with which we were raised—"Charity begins at home". That has been all but forgotten.

As I am writing, there has been a remarkable recent reduction in the amount of screen time for "Squad" member AOC. It is probably due to the fact that people with a brain have decided that what comes from hers and is transported to her mouth is not worthy of repeating or noting. Just an educated guess. In early-July 2019, she did however come up with a doozy. She claimed that immigrants in US/MX border detention centers were being told to drink water from toilets, and they were doing so. An investigation followed showing there was bottled water and water fountains everywhere in that particular facility. The whole fiasco was probably started with an ill-advised joke that someone interpreted as factual—much ado about nothing. And then we have a reemergence of AOC as she declares that illegal immigrants are merely "pursuing basic human rights" by coming to the US and showing up at our doorstep expecting to be admitted with red-carpet treatment. I must have missed this. Where does it say and who said that living wherever you want in the world is a "basic human right"? I guess this is your belief if you support open borders throughout the world. My suggestion to this "cub" Congresswoman is that she move from NYC and DC to the US/MX border for a few months and see what she thinks of the situation after that stay. "Me thinks she doth protest too much." And it is not then too far in the future when six members of MS-13 from Mexico and El Salvador in the country illegally are arrested for the murder of a rival gang member in Towson, MD. These are not good people.

The Trump administration is inconceivably blocked from adding the "citizenship question" back into the forms for the 2020 US Census. The question has been a part of all Censuses since the 1800's, only eliminated by the Obama administration (as was their right) for 2010.

Those of us who are Conservatives do not agree with much we hear from the Left when it comes to immigration, but some of us concur that ICE needs to shift some of its' focus on "Visa overstays" as we expel illegal immigrants from our country. This situation has gotten out of control over the past 30 years. If we are going to control our borders, we need to monitor those who enter the US legally and then "overstay their welcome".

Some of the incredibly stupid things that happen when there are "sanctuary cities/states": citizens who are injured by an illegal immigrant in a sanctuary city are unable to sue the city, but an immigrant who is "traumatized" at the border when entering the US illegally can sue the US government. When we boomers were growing up, we called things like this "bass ackwards"!

Following the massacre of nine breakaway Mormon Americans (women and children) by a "terrorist" drug gang in Northern Mexico near La Mora, our southern neighbor rejects a Trump offer to partner in a "war" against the drug cartels. Why? Answer: Mexico has no intention of destroying one of its' largest and most successful industries (killing Americans with illegal drugs). #SayNoToDrugs And as those victims were being laid to rest, "Scrooge" Sanders reveals his proposal for comprehensive immigration policy related to our southern border neighbor: stop deportations; eliminate ICE, CBP, and all immigration enforcement; open the borders wide and let everyone into the US; in order for the gangs and cartels to kill us all "to reduce the excess population." He has not sold me although his plans are at least seasonally timely with Christmas of 2019 approaching. #Democrites #CrazyBernie

The costs for immigration are being questioned today at every level of government. How much can US citizens afford to spend to bring people from around the world to America. One of the concerning study findings was that a total of 63% of non-citizens in the US are using the welfare system, and that the numbers grow to 70% for those who are still here after 10 years. That is very expensive for the country. We need to do a better job making sure that our newest neighbors from places around the world are not a financial burden to our citizens.

One of the most serious cases of hypocrisy we have seen over the past 13 years has been as a result of the <u>Reno v. Flores</u> case relating to US government treatment of unaccompanied minors who have illegally entered the country. The 1993 suit decided by the SCOTUS has been a thorn in the side of the Obama and

Trump administrations. The Obama administration protested about the case and the impact it had on our borders (especially the southern border with Mexico), and then the Left has railed against the Trump administration for being proactive and actively fighting against the ruling and doing something about it. And the video clips we see of minor children in cages are from the Obama years, not from recent years during the Trump border crisis. These circumstances must become a part of the comprehensive immigration policies overhaul which the 2021-25 administration will need to address.

The numbers are in: illegal immigrants arrested at the US/MX border during the fiscal year ending on September 30, 2019 totaled 977,509, an increase of 88% from fiscal year 2017-18. We would call that difference "whopping".

In an October 7, 2019 Special Communication from the Journal of the American Medical Association (JAMA), the authors assessed the level of healthcare spending in the United States as well as the estimated amount of waste in the system. They estimated that such costs approach 18% of gross domestic product (GDP) and that the amount of waste in those expenditures reaches 20-25% ($748 billion to $935 billion). Think of what could be done with those wasted monies if we were able to cut them by as little as 10%, and how about 50%! It is okay to dream, isn't it? Applying a 25% rate of waste savings using the lower amount, we could cover annual medical costs (estimated at $10,739 per person in the US in 2017) for over 17.4 million people! As Americans we need to make medical cost and waste reduction a much higher priority. The figures do not lie.

CHAPTER 5

THE DISAPPEARING NUCLEAR FAMILY
AND ENGAGING ALL CHILDREN

One of the most recent activities added to the list of options for newly-divorced women in the US is the "destination divorce party", recommended for Las Vegas. This has not caught on yet for men, and it probably won't any time soon. Personally, I wasn't raised to believe that ending a marriage ("until death do us part") created an opportunity for celebration—just old fashioned, I guess.

Many of us would enjoy seeing a study about how many of our children growing up today in America are required to perform daily chores or work for the family during their formative years. In the 50s through 70s, these personal responsibilities for the household were an important method of developing the meaning and purpose of our life and in building character and discipline. These were often simple and menial tasks which someone in the family was required to do, making it fair to spread the work out among the entire group of parents and kids so that no one person was required to bear a disproportionate burden. By the time the boomers raised our children in the 80s and 90s, this practice like many from the bygone era had mostly disappeared. Even so, we called upon our sons and daughters to help with activities that could build teamwork in the home, such as cooking, cleaning, and watching younger siblings. Chores around the farms for those kids continue today in many settings, resulting in those children being some of the most responsible as any in the country at an early age. This ties in with the training of work ethic we discuss in Chapter 12. If only we could revisit such habits today, we would be a much better place to live.

This "Father's Day" in mid-June of 2019, I pray for all of those fathers and father figures out there who are positively working with their kids and other children in need, as well as those children who do not have such a person who will teach, nurture and protect them. Being familial teachers and mentors for our children and those in need is a huge task nationwide that we must continue to encourage and expand.

As a part of a proposal for readily available mentoring throughout the US, it will be important to utilize many resources which educate, motivate, and inspire. Some of us learned early in life about the Biblical seven deadly sins and contrary seven virtues of life. Others credit Prudentius with the virtues in a poem or Pope Gregory with their creation. These writings were many centuries before James Spears penned his *7 Virtues for Success and Happiness* which was published in October of 2018. I was refreshed with "The Seven Virtues of Success" by a mentor, business partner, and friend, Stewart Hughes, in the 90s, and they went like this:

1. Integrity–Recognize the right thing to do and then do it.

2. Clarity–Work in specifics, measure the specifics, and report them to your mentor. If you don't measure it, you can't manage it.

3. Courage–The function of taking risk. Boldness is inspiring. If you aren't growing, you are dying. Leadership is conquest.

4. Diligence – All rewards come in the second mile. They don't show up when you need them but come through when you least expect them – and in work clothes.

5. Decorum – Dress appropriately, speak properly, and practice good health habits.

6. Patience – Life is uneven — get used to it.

7. Gratitude – Gratitude is incompatible with depression. Depression begins as a function of selfishness and later becomes a disease. We give thanks daily for our virtues and look forward to continuing success.

It has been proposed for America that we start a program to identify the fathers of African-American children in families in which there is no father at home. These determined fathers would then be responsible for their share of all the expenses required to raise their children. This would assist in some of the ridiculous situations out there in which fathers are not accountable for the children they are responsible for bringing into the world.

There have been times in the history of our country when children were actively taught "life sports", mostly by our parents, with our friends, and sometimes in school. These tended to be low-impact activities enjoyed by both (at that time) sexes that could be played with minimal equipment, virtually anywhere in the US (depending on season), and without the need for outside organization. It seems that there is less of this today for some reason. My guess is that the social media addictions have a major role in the inactions at the present time. And there seems to be a societal aversion against trying to single out or otherwise isolate people around us with different physical and mental capabilities. For whatever reason, the movement away from teaching life sports hurts us all, especially those who tend to be excluded because of their lack of knowledge and training. In my case, these sports were golf, ice skating, roller skating, bowling, cycling, tennis, horseshoes, hiking, surfing, sailing, running, paddleball then racquetball, handball, snowshoeing, ping-pong, pool/billiards, swimming, archery, cross-country skiing, and downhill skiing. (I have definitely left some out.) Then closely behind were those activities which required the right circumstances, interest, and equipment, such as water skiing (my personal favorite with golf), hunting and fishing. Purposely excluded are commonly team sports like baseball, softball, field or ice hockey, basketball, flag football, and volleyball. You who are the OK Boomers get the picture. While in our youth, we often spent the final hours of daylight each day throughout the year engaged in these life sports and continue to participate in many of them. That is why they are called life sports, as they can be played for most of a lifetime. For those of you who are parents of young children, I urge you to participate with your kids and their friends in as many of these sports as possible. The same goes for you grandparents with your grand-kids. And then there are those who have chosen to be leaders in youth organizations or as mentors of young people, you are probably in the thick of it with your charges. They say that with changes in our work schedules and responsibilities there will probably be more discretionary time in the future. It is difficult if not impossible to think of sources of good times with family that can be as much fun as these sporting experiences.

CHAPTER 6

A RETURN TO EDUCATION FOR ALL
WITH THE FACTS AND PROPER ENGLISH

There are many lessons for life which are long gone from any curriculum we see in our present-day schools. Some of these courses were left for parents to teach, which became difficult when the parents in charge disappeared or when they chose simply to skip these lessons for their children. An excellent example of this is with the "four t's" we boomers were taught by a combination of teachers, parents/family, and in Sunday school at church. Think for a moment about how different America would be today if our young people were diligent with "loyalty, honesty, modesty, and integrity." These were the building blocks used for discipline and the foundation of our life. Millennials and the Z generation would bully us and tell us to get out of their way before they ran us over. Point taken, but too bad that we do not and cannot expect many or any of these traits from the majority of our adolescents to young adults.

It continues to be astounding how our levels of government can keep throwing away good tax dollars for a declining college system. We read recently in amazement in our corner of the universe about how the Minnesota State Legislature is increasing the financial support for State colleges which are bleeding from losses in enrollment numbers. And how much longer can we acquiesce to the notion of "college for all" as Internet education (even local University of Jamestown (ND) is getting into it) is exploding in use and popularity while the costs of brick, mortar, instructor salaries, and administrator wages continue to surge higher? A recent study determined that higher education costs had increased by 150% over the past twenty years. We have reached the point where it is no longer fiscally responsible to consider traditional colleges for an education that does not succeed in preparing the students for a productive future. Still another example of this is a State University in Western North Dakota which when required to prepare a budget reduction comes back to the Governor with a proposal to eliminate fourteen positions and six programs. That sounds like a solution to considerably reduce the size of your student body at the same time.

On an increasing level, colleges and universities around the US are deciding to cancel Conservative speakers on campus based on "security" concerns. Isn't this a bit discriminatory? Why aren't the Liberal guests being turned away? Oh, wait, that's right. Virtually every institution of higher learning in America is controlled by administrators and instructors on the Left. For whatever reason, we must not endanger the cogs of the machines which produce our Liberal robots. And we certainly do not want good people on the Right to be physically exposed to the fascist violence of groups like Antifa (who are often the designated "greeting party" for those visitors).

Our generation was raised with daily homework in school. In my case it was an hour or more in grade school, up to two hours in junior high, high school was two or more hours, undergraduate college three or more hours per day, and law school at 5 or more hours. That work keeps a person sharp and maximizes learning. I suspect that some of those numbers have declined over the years. This all ties in with developing discipline over the formative years and continues in one's vocation. Social media usage and video game play are not valid excuses for reducing the educational environment which should surround our young people. For anyone who wants to excel in life, add time each day for additional learning out of the classroom or office. The results can be totally life changing.

Teachers around the country are complaining about the level of violence in their classrooms, leading to the "physical and mental injuries" they are suffering. I believe that the problem is as much about the inability of our younger educators to handle the pressures of instruction as it is from the precipitous rise of mental illness among the young people in America and the hopelessness they are being taught by their parents and peers. Schools have always been dangerous places, but our loss of instructors from the greatest generation and their toughness is helping to lead us to a crisis as we currently attempt to treat our children as "snowflakes". The solutions will center around separation, compassion, appropriate treatment, and reintegration. In America we need to step up our efforts to return the mental and physical toughness for which we have always been known and respected.

Another cliché of the day which is losing all appeal is "no symptoms is the main symptom". No. "Nothing" cannot become "something" in an effort to identify a challenge.

NBC announces that the millennial generation is the most educated of them all. That is probably true, albeit with a worthless and unusable education. This unfortunate situation is perpetuated with programs like "TEDx", the epitome of the "selfie" society. Millennials demand that everything possible in life is centered around them. Our local TEDx announces a "P.L.U.S." theme for 2020 (Play, Love, Unlock, Sustain). "These words help build ideas, foster effective communication, and encourage the free sharing of ideas." Perhaps. At least for snowflakes.

As the original edition of *AGG* indicated, it gives me the "willies" (creeps) when news commentators or interviewees use the same phrase over and over and over. One of those entries to the list of repetitive references: "at the end of the day"! You can hear this being stated a half dozen times or more during a single 90-second conversation (even guilty is one of my favorites (Ed Rollins) from the Bush era). How about mixing it up on occasion with the likes of "when it is all said and done" or "everything considered" or "in the end" or "when the dust settles" or "the bottom line" or "at the end of the road" or "when the chapter ends" or "all in all". This could have been raised in the "laziness" Chapter as well. Come on people, can't we use imagination and creativity in what we say in our communications? And I need to repeat one of my least favorite words that continues to be overused in ad nauseum. The word "even" is regularly utilized when describing something that is a logical extension of the original phenomenon. Our generation was taught that "even" was to be used to describe the extraordinary result rather than that which is generally expected. The biggest offenders here appear to be meteorologists and other weathercasters. Such as: "The thunderstorm will produce significant rainfall, and even thunder and lightning." Or: "The storms have [your community] in their sights and could even hit [a town in the path of the weather just beyond your community]." DUH? Please present your story with the assumption that the listeners have basic knowledge about the subject matter and geography. Update: this became a gagger during the COVID-19 reporting, which I will address later in the book.

Another one of those words that is used for a much different purpose than in the past. The word "dope" is now substituted for "cool" or "great". As I was growing up, it meant either a person with limited intelligence, or "illegal drugs". That is how it came about for people to ask, "why do you think they call it dope?". It would be interesting to hear how this usage to make something desirable came about. Some of us become disappointed when the meaning of a particular word or phrase is changed without a very good explanation. In a current Chevrolet commercial, an African-American man refers to a vehicle as "dope". So, they want to change "dumb" or "illegal contraband" to "awesome"? I do not think that I am alone in questioning this variation of "dope".

The concept of quality education for all is not always met with universal support. Lately we have seen commercials on the television sponsored by the Ad Council (which I had always thought was a legitimate entity). They want us to believe that receiving a high school diploma is "social". No. It must become the necessity for all our citizens.

Aristotle once opined that "educating the mind without educating the heart is no education at all." There was a lot more heart in education overall as the baby boomers were growing up in the 40s, 50s and 60s than there is today. There are pockets around the country in which heart will always be a part of the successful curriculum, as well as specific teachers who are noted for their compassionate style and results. Many of us still remember these important people and schools by name for the special treatment and attention we received from their hands. We will always recognize and reward excellence in teaching, just as we must continue to safeguard our children from those educators whose productive days in the classroom are coming to a close.

A local State college in our area has partnered with Planned Parenthood to train our K-12 teachers on how to educate their students for sex education. Is there any better evidence of the sources of some of the Liberal garbage our young people are being force fed in the public schools?

Our local newspaper reached a new low recently as it supported addressing "academic freedom" by blocking any attempts to question our Liberal system of education at all levels. This is not the way the baby boomers were taught to believe as we were raised sixty years ago. It appears difficult to defend K-College education today based on its curve to the Left, what we used to call "not your parent's classroom education".

A new program was announced recently at the University of Minnesota. The elderly are permitted to take college courses at a reduced cost of $10 per credit. Fine. Now how about a similar program for the appropriate low income high school graduates. We cannot afford to leave any people behind in the effort to make sure our entire population is educated.

"That's the tea" means "spreading news"? That must be a new English idiom. We can only hope that this will apply in the future to the Liberal media contaminating the tea rather than disseminating it.

Another "pet peeve" of mine comes generally from game shows on TV and sporting events. It occurs when onlookers yell out "you got this!" It seems to turn out about 90% of the time (approximately) that the participating contestant or athlete "does not got it". I know that the fan on the sideline is simply trying to support and motivate the person to whom their remarks are directed, although that does not appear to be working with the dismal success rate achieved.

The study of "real" history as the baby boomers were growing up taught us to be careful in avoiding the same pitfalls which were experienced by our various teachers and those persons featured in their lessons. One of the phrases used was: "look before you leap". This is still great advice today which breaks down to look, evaluate, decide based on experience and knowledge, and carry through or end the considered action(s). And all of this can happen in a split second. There is a clear tendency today to attempt to selectively erase such history that is deemed to be possibly disturbing to the recipients. That unfortunate practice does not prepare our children for what could be reasonably expected to occur in their lives. This item could have been easily made a part of any of Chapters 13, 14, or 18, but it probably fits better here as we discuss the quality and applicability of history being taught in the schools to our children and grandchildren. A public-school principal in Boca Raton, FL, has stated that it is "too political" for him to say to his students that the Holocaust happened or did not happen?! Since when does the "truth" of history become "political"? Such ignorance as this position displays is unacceptable in America. Have we reached a point in our country in which our young people are not able to handle fact-based history, the real truth? How sad and sickening would this be for us?

What is considered a "proper" education these days. In reading a description of a new leadership position the other day, I noticed that a South Dakota native is the Ozbun Executive Director of Entrepreneurship at North Dakota State University in Fargo. First of all, I have complained for years that North Dakota is so small that colleges and universities in the state should not duplicate courses of study—have one program and make it the very best. The University of North Dakota has a very highly-rated Center for Innovation and course of study in entrepreneurship. I would normally think that is enough. And then there is private Lutheran Concordia College across the river in Moorhead, MN with a College of Business and entrepreneurship program. That is surely enough. But no, NDSU needs to pile on with a duplicative course of study. Okay. So I look at the degrees of this new Executive Director. They include a master's degree from Norway (Arctic University) in Peace and Conflict Transformation? Who'da thunk it? I'll bet that this common course of study is not widely duplicated in that country!

In a frontpage lead article in our local newspaper on July 5, 2019, the headline read: "Spreading the Word". It described how the Lakota Dakota language is being taught at Sitting Bull College on the Standing Rock Reservation in North Dakota. I was fearful that such programs would decline in availability and funding following the removal by the NCAA of "Fighting Sioux" as the nickname of the University of North Dakota. And while I am pleased that the nickname loss has not resulted in a total disappearance of educational courses to maintain some of the important Sioux traditions, I am still disappointed that we lost a significant source of funding for such classes by not negotiating a settlement agreement to retain the nickname between the University/state and the Tribes. Too few "thinking caps" were being warn at the time, as the nickname use had been bestowed on the University in formal tribal ceremonies (yes, two) in perpetuity—which means "forever".

As we reach the 50-year anniversary of the US moon landing and first walk on that orb (Neil Armstrong on July 20, 1969), America needs to put its' space and US Space Force programs into warp drive. "One small step for man...one giant leap for mankind" needs to be translated into an effort to once again place our nation into the world lead position for outer space exploration and innovation—back to the moon, on to Mars, and beyond.

Another example of "use words wisely"—"lynching"—not a word to use because of the horrific connection with slavery and what followed. But I do see the application to the Impeachment Inquisition ("II") from the American "Wild West" of "vigilante justice" (ranchers versus cattle rustlers or horse thieves caught in the act) without a sheriff, Judge, jury, and due process. There is no place for "lynching" in our country, no matter what the perceived context is. So, the Left (including their media thugs) goes ballistic when Trump uses the word in a tweet to describe his opinion about the bogus II process. A new name today for the Democrats (at least I could not find it with a Google search)—the Democrites (remember: Democrats + hypocrites)! What a change a couple of letters can make. In short order, the Democrites are cleaning the egg from their faces and the glass from rocks through their windows after scolding POTUS for his use of the word. There must have been 20 videos which emerged of them using "the word". Oops, did they do that? Indeed, they did.

As the doors open locally for the fall semester at North Dakota State University, it appears that some of my predictions about the future of higher education are becoming reality. NDSU experiences its' most significant enrollment decline in five years, and the lowest student population it has seen since 2008. Meanwhile, other local colleges either show a decline (Concordia College) or are holding steady (Minnesota State University—Moorhead). We may be on the verge of a collapse of the college structure, at least in some parts of the country.

Many historians, educators, and civil rights activists say that they want to expand K-12 history class teachings about slavery in the US (which existed here for 246 of the past 400 years). There doesn't appear to be a clear and reasoned answer to the question: for what purpose? I will not get into the conspiracy theories for why such a shift in the American History curriculum for our children is advisable. This proposal does make me curious about whether the added information would include the fact that the slavery in America resulted in our Civil War between the anti-slavery Union Republicans and the pro-slavery Confederate Democrats. That would be beneficial.

Chicago teachers striking today (October 23, 2019) for Day 5. Those on the Left claim the dispute is not about money, but that of course is a lie. New Mayor Lori Lightfoot claims not enough money to pay the demanded higher wages for the teachers with the city looking at a $900 million budgetary shortfall. Solution: make that shortage $1 billion. #BrokeInChicago Is anyone with a brain surprised that the inner-city schools in the US are in shambles? The answer to the mess in New York City at the hands of Mayor de Blasio is to destroy the "charter" schools in the City—the only bright and shining light in the darkness of their public schools. The motto of the Left: "if you can't beat them, tear them down." #PatheticPoliticians

Are there some "shortcut" words that you do not appreciate in "journalism"? There are a few that "rub me the wrong way". How about "cop" instead of "police". I consider the former in place of the latter as a bit of a "cop out", which is what I wish they would do with it. And then there is "busted" replacing "broken", and alongside is "busted" rather than "caught" or "arrested". In North Dakota, we wish they would outlaw the use of the word "snow". It is so white and cold.

There are major concerns today in our country with the exploding numbers of children diagnosed with ADD (ADHD) as they enter our K-12 education structure. It is suspected that the increase in numbers is amplified by parents who are not enrolling these youngsters in preschool but are instead holding them out of the system until the public-school option is available. These challenged young kids probably need the earliest possible educational immersion more than almost any other group.

As the open Impeachment Inquisition ("II") hearings end, it becomes clearer to me about the power of words and people acting upon them. Think about the damages which followed these words in a joke from then-candidate Donald Trump in late-July of 2016: "Russia, if you're listening, I hope you're able to find the 30,000 [Hillary Clinton] emails that are missing." That statement was a factor in the whole "Russian Collusion" fraud perpetrated on the American people as well as the II which followed. Trump was merely stating what many on the Right were thinking—the emails which Hillary illegality destroyed are probably out there somewhere in the electronic universe, so why not see if anyone can produce them. At the same time, the Left was totally committed to the Trump impeachment process since the day of the 2016 election, so they would have found the means to achieve their ends with whatever rationale it took.

Is it just in the Northern Plains that teachers' unions and school administrators without a contract for the following year take the summer off and end up in August in the same position? These are supposed to be intelligent people with whom we entrust the education of our children, and yet another example of the "Snoozing and Losing Syndrome" (SALS). Time to get off your butts and do the job of negotiating and settling to avoid disruption. Locally, the teachers' union and school administrators took this past summer (of 2019) off rather than spending those months to negotiate a new contract for the coming/current school year. The reason given for the inaction was that the educators who would be involved in the talks were "unavailable". Now in the late summer we find that the sides are at an impasse. Duh? My advice to both camps in the discussions: find people who are available to meet and make decisions during the summer months. This is not a "rocket science" deal. Follow-up: the teachers' union and the school board DECLARE AN IMPASSE in the fall (of course they do), leading to major distractions when the focus should be on a quality education for our future leaders. "Haste makes waste" seems to apply here together with the SALS.

A recent local study comes to the conclusion that girls are not as interested as boys in STEM study and careers because they are "better readers"? When you figure out what that means, please let us know. And as we expand STEM opportunities to all, let's bring back "home economics/econ" with a new name like "Living

Basics" so that all of our young adults are better prepared for life away from home. Think about how many current issues for millennials and Gen Z'ers could be improved with some commonsense lessons about how to live a better life.

Will we ever return to a time when children (and adults) are taught how to correctly pronounce words? I would hope so but am not so sure that it will happen anytime soon. Statistics show that we humans use so little of our computer-like brains, leaving a lot of room to remember how we are supposed to use phonetics. One of the challenges is that we have been trained to take short cuts all throughout life, including this aspect of our language. Let's use two names of people as examples. Since when did "Favre" become "Farve"? The former would be a common French or Cajun name and pronunciation. And Brett is from Louisiana, isn't he? Is it easier to say "Farve"? Probably. And a more recent example of this issue is with our recent "Squad" member "Tlaib". Why does everyone (except me) call her as if it was spelled "Talib"? That is a stumper. A September 28, 2016 article in the *Huffington Post* by Katherine Brooks and attributing some of her material to authors Ross and Kathryn Petras (*You're Probably Saying it Wrong*), cites the most commonly mispronounced words in the English language, such as acai (ah-sigh-EE), gif (jiff), flautist (FLOU-tist), wash ("wosh" and not "worsh" (a Boston thing))(I have a friend from there whose wife is "Donna"; in consecutive sentences he will call her "Donna" and "Donner"; I chuckle; sorry, Mike), mischievous (MIS-chuh-vus), niche (neesh or nitch), chutzpah (KHUT-spa), important ("tent" and not "dent"), turmeric (as "term" rather than "too mare"), Wednesday (wenz-dey), February (feb-roo-air-ee), asthma (just like it is spelled and not "az-ma"), nuclear (noo-clear), colonel ("ker-nul" as opposed to "koll-a-nel"), or endive (EN-dive or ahn-DEEV). But then again, how many times a day (a month, a year, or in a lifetime) are you called upon to say these words. And be careful pronouncing Polish names, except if you ARE Polish and accomplished in figuring the names out. Just don't get me going on SPELLING, such as (according to the *Oxford Dictionary*): accommodate, which, receive, grieve, until, hoard, occur/occurred/occurrence, occasion, separate, hygiene, marshmallow, quaere (question), piqued, government, definitely, pharaoh, tranche, or publicly. Or the misuse of words: there/their/they're, are/our, your/you're, lie/lay, would of (should be would've), here/hear, affect/effect, chalk/chock, or irregardless (should be regardless). Okay, English is a difficult language, even before you add "spell check" and idioms. For some of us when we see the mistakes, it is like chalk on a screechy chalkboard (or is it "skreechy chalk board"?). It is the former. All we can do is try to do our best, use "spell check", and verify that "spell check" doesn't change your word in a crazy way (which happens all the time).

New study data assessing the state of our current K-12 system in our country: 10% of NYC school children are homeless, two-thirds of 8th graders do not read up to that standard grade level, one-third of US citizens aged 18-29 think there are better countries in the world than the US, and 48% of that same group are "not patriotic". Welcome to the results of American education. Can we expect that these dismal numbers will be turned around in the future? Certainly not without a major nationwide overhaul of our system and curriculum. Meanwhile in NYC, Mayor de Blasio continues to destroy K-12 there. As his #Liberals plan fails, his new program is to tear down successful programs such as charter schools rather than building up positive alternatives.

Ahh. We arrive at picking up the tab for higher education/college tuition, room, board, books, and incidentals. This is not an inexpensive task. The boomers remember the days when we were raised as many of our parents saved throughout their lives to cover the costs of their children attending college. We have morphed from that planning to parents now ignoring those future costs in favor of instant gratification in their lives. Young high school graduates are being thrust into higher education where they may or may not belong and forced to incur often catastrophic debt to secure or attempt an undergraduate degree and possibly beyond that for one or more post-graduate degree(s). The current system of personal college financing is pure insanity. It was developed by President Obama who "owns" the problems created by shifting the student loan system away from banks to the federal government. Candidates on the Left are now touting "free" college and plans to forgive student loan debt which currently exceeds $1.5 trillion for 44 million Americans! And this would be paid (where else) by more taxes on the wealthy and middle class. And what is the proposal to reimburse those families and students who have already paid from their own pockets for this education? Will there be reparations? Guess again. In the P-14 proposal I set forth in *AGG*, much of this issue would become "moot" or nonexistent. Students would plan their future vocations in or prior to grades 10-12, so that a portion of the specific training needs could be determined and begun or completed as well as how those costs would be paid. A greater responsibility for the expenses of the training and caring for day-to-day needs could be borne by a combination of parents/guardians, and current and/or future employers of the students, including local, state and the federal governments. These young people and others in the programs for re-training would be compensated for their work and would receive the specific skills education required for their career. Colleges as we know them today will be reimagined, recreated and retooled as well as consolidated to meet the needs of the changing jobs marketplace. The liberal arts colleges will be the hardest hit, with many if not most of them fading into the sunset as once useful but now archaic dinosaurs of our educational structure. And we will do a much better job preparing our young adults for the basic aspects of life they will be experiencing in real time and otherwise right out of the stage-14 shoot. Much training will be provided by each of the critical industries which make up the employment grid as the costs of educating our future generations are covered internally rather than by the governmental entities and the taxes they collect. Truly the times they are a changin'.

IBM has come up with new terminology for some of their jobs which are high paying, in big demand, and do not require a college education. They call them "new collar jobs". We will see so much of this in the future, not a great omen for the traditional men's and women's business attire industries.

The Liberals are dumping their "adversity score" for standardized SAT scores which would have been used to penalize children from better schools in favor of minorities. The "Landscape Plan" is not a solution but rather a band aid to find a quick fix for serious issues surrounding the whole entrance exam industry. The answer is to significantly change these traditional standard tests and coordinate with the ACTs as well to remove the current focus on mathematics and verbal areas of knowledge. The exams should be a more accurate measure of basic intelligence and skills. On May 22, 2020, the decline of America continues with the California universities announcing the elimination of ACT and/or SAT scores for admission. "No", the tests are not biased. It is rather that the exam takers are not educated enough.

There are a couple of common teachings I learned while growing up and which were reinforced when I attended law school. They have always come in handy for their intended applications and occasionally for other settings in which their use was unexpected. "Never assume anything" was one of these jewels, and the other was "never ask a question for which you don't already know the answer." In the legal context, these pearls of wisdom were especially useful in the courtroom or otherwise in adversarial matters. As for the assumptions, the value of knowing the basis for a factual problem makes itself provable if necessary. And the matter of questions relates to not being put in a position of asking for something favorable for your client or cause and receiving an answer that does not match up with your needs and intentions. Both of these lessons have served me well over the years and will never be discarded nor forgotten.

It was typically in our family home that the boomers learned about manners and proper etiquette. This course of study is currently lacking with our youngest generations. It seems that parents are abdicating their responsibility today and are not making sure that the children they are helping to prepare for life are leaving the house with some basic skills about how to treat others and how one is to conduct themselves in a group. We may need to make a decisive change in this training in an effort to make sure it is getting done — and correctly.

Sanctioned middle school "walk-outs" to demand climate change action are a farce. Participation by teens is minimal, driven by Liberal school teachers, and the local gatherings are punctuated by signs with foul language. The US leads the world in carbon emission reductions and is committed to much more.

Disturbing news from Ohio University: they plan to eliminate all national social Fraternities on campus in order to get rid of hazing. That is absurd and like throwing out the baby with the bathwater as those same Fraternities already prohibit hazing in all their chapters around the country. We cannot take the lazy way of life and harm a vast number of innocent people in order to solve a problem which is not pervasive in an entire population of that college campus.

Harvard announces on 3-10-20 that it is going to online classes indefinitely based on the COVID-19 threat. This supports the projections made in my book (*"AGG"*), that college campuses are dying with the emergence of e-education. #colleges #highereducation

A Nutri-System ad exposes the weakness of math today: "Two months for the price of one—it's like getting a month free!" Duh? They said there would be no math, and they apparently mean it. This used to be referred to as a "dumbing down" of our society. We need as many STEM courses and proficiency in the US as is possible. You can bet that countries like China and Russia are not letting up, and we cannot afford to be left behind. A recent report from the National Center for Science and Engineering Statistics shows how the US has lost its world dominance in science based on reductions in "Research and Development" (R&D) here compared to other countries. We cannot afford to take a secondary role in STEM education, knowledge, and leadership. We have never been dependent on other countries in the scientific arena and must not continue to slide backwards now.

A Minnesota Department of Education report shows that American Indian students in the state still face a persistent achievement gap compared to their white peers. NSS? The tribal schools are spending so much time in their studies to preserve their language and heritage that they are not emphasizing the necessary core education courses which provide the basic topics for learning to these poor Native students. Some day they will get this right, hopefully before too many more lives are wasted.

Please explain to me the importance of having a "Doctorate in Indigenous Health" course of study and degree?

As local school students begin virtual online classes (4-1-20) (no fooling) amid the COVID-19 pandemic, I learn of a new (to me) "animal" in the K-12 education game—Connections Academy, a free online public school! It will be interesting to see how their curriculum compares to the rest of the Liberal contributors. Inquiring minds want to know/I want to know. Time is what we have, and wisdom is how we spend it.

Local State U President says (on 4-18-20) that more budget cuts "could" be on the way? Duh. Enrollment continues to decline and the '20-'21 year is in jeopardy. I predicted the demise of our present college system in "AGG" but did not expect a virus as one of the catalysts! #CollegesDying

As we close the door (at least for now) on the matter of a great education for all young people, that learning remains as probably the most important factor in building the future of America and the world. What is a singular element of today's learning that is missing from what the older generations in our country experienced? It may be a short supply of "curiosity". Back in the 60s, we may have been told that curiosity "killed the cat", but we also possessed a generational desire for learning that has been unmatched since that time. We were constantly being challenged by others and ourselves to reach higher and broader levels of knowledge to prepare to excel in the future. In the relatively small city of Fargo, North Dakota, we were taking classes beyond what were expected of children our age around the US. I was trained with competent instructors in French for six years (grades 7-12) in the language that enabled me to challenge and receive a "minor" level of proficiency in it at the collegiate level without taking a single class at the University. Math was not my favorite course of study in high school, but I was good enough at it to qualify for Advanced Placement (AP) classes such as Statistics, Chem Study (Calculus plus Chemistry) and Modern Math Theories. These experiences to learn were fascinating for me. They piqued my curiosity as to how high and far I could go. I was being constantly trained in methods to "learn how to learn". I never touched another math book after high school, instead accepting the challenges of accounting, political science, and law. I had always wanted to be a lawyer like "Perry Mason" who was often able to make others say what they did not want to say—in front of a judge and a jury. Enough about boring me. My suggestion to the current group of P-14 students: develop that "thirst for knowledge" that can take you wherever you want to go and to do whatever you want to do. Curiosity may have indeed killed a few cats over the years, but it also helped in the creation of amazing careers that can be with you and your peers for a lifetime. Carpe diem!

CHAPTER 7

ACCEPTING RESPONSIBILITY
FOR POOR RESULTS

This chapter follows what we were taught in the 60s by a very intelligent and visionary President and statesman, John F. Kennedy: "Let us not seek the Republican answer or the Democratic answer, but the right answer. Let us not seek to fix the blame for the past. Let us accept our own responsibility for the future." Sometimes we need to be reminded that responsibility does apply equally to the past, present and future.

It is not just young people who refuse to take responsibility for their actions. Joe Biden is also guilty of this behavior. He has stated that Americans would have never seen Russian election interference during the Obama-Biden administration. Wha? A question for Joe: what do you think was the primary focus of the 2-year Mueller Investigation? Uh. That would have been Russian election interference in 2016 (during the Obama-Biden administration)! Shame on you, Joe—how dumb do you think we are?

And then there are some sad stories as well. As freshman Congresswoman Katie Hill (D-CA) resigns from her position in Congress (for which she was hand-picked by fellow Californian Nancy Pelosi) following an "inappropriate" affair with a young staffer and being a revenge-porn target, she takes a page from the Hillary Clinton playbook—it was all the fault of a conspiracy by the Conservative media? Really? #NoResponsibility

In 2019 one of the largest and most successful companies in the world is facing extraordinary scrutiny for one of its' newest and most successful products. Was the Boeing 737 Max 8 jet problem which apparently resulted in the death of 346 passengers caused by manufacturer "laziness"? The victims were on Lion Air and Ethiopian Airlines planes which crashed in late-2018 and early-2019, respectively. Should the training simulator for the plane have been focused (at least in part) on the MCAS responses to false sensor alerts? There were stories disseminated that the simulators did not even address the possible challenges which allegedly resulted in the crashes. Someone will find the truth. In April of 2019, Boeing formally accepted responsibility for the crashes, and they have since that time settled approximately 50 lawsuits relating to the Lion Air crash and have set aside cash to cover the victims from the Ethiopian crash and the dozens of legal actions that followed. The airplanes in fleets worldwide will continue to be grounded well into if not through 2020. The biggest hurdle which the aviation giant faces now and in the future is probably to help passengers in its' planes (especially the 737 Max 8) feel perfectly safe again. #BoeingInTrouble Update: still no sign of the Max 8 coming back into regular use as we enter the summer of 2020.

As wildfires again rage in various parts of California in late-October, 2019, did Governor Gavin Newsom declare that utility PG&E is responsible for cleaning combustible brush in the State's forests. That is what it sounded like he said. The federal government has accused the State of improper and insufficient forest management, resulting in the wooded areas of the State being cluttered with tinder-dry underbrush that constitutes perfect fuel for the fires. This is quite curious to a forestry novice, as I read that the State has a California Department of Forestry and an additional Department of Forestry & Fire Protection. What is the responsibility of these two governmental Departments? This is obviously a huge problem for California, and it seems to me that it would be best for all related entities to work together to meet the challenges head-on. They cannot afford to continue to pass around the "hot potato", while expecting somehow that the situation is going to take care of itself and without even more serious conflagration. Welcome back to #LaLaLand.

A month later, fired Navy Secretary Richard Spencer "quacks" to CBS about being dedicated to "good order and discipline" in the military and his inability to follow an order by his boss (the Secretary of Defense). Instead, Spencer broke the "chain of command" and went directly to the POTUS. That is a "no-no"! In his retirement, Spencer should probably take a refresher course in Military Protocol 101. #UnableToTakeResponsibility In a later similar fiasco this time involving the subsequently acting Navy Secretary Thomas Modly, he flew to Guam at a cost of $243,000 to remove USS Teddy Roosevelt nuclear aircraft carrier commander Capt. Brett Crozier for ignoring the chain of command in a demand for the COVID-19 safety of his crew. Modly called Crozier's leadership "too naïve or too stupid". Shortly after that disaster, Modly resigned from his post. Hopefully the Navy can get its' act together — soon!

The OK Boomers were trained in life to understand that actions have consequences, and to be careful and think ahead about the potential outcomes of what we say and do. As we screwed up, there would eventually be a time to "fess up" by taking the lumps we deserved and moving on to our next activities.

The federal jail in New York City, the Metropolitan Correctional Center, where wealthy investor and pedophile Jeffrey Epstein died, is in the crosshairs of a "who's responsible" scandal. The facility has blamed the Epstein death on two guards who were allegedly sleeping at the time, failed to make timely cell checks on the decedent, and then apparently faked and forged records in an attempt to protect themselves. The guards have sued and claimed that the facility was grossly understaffed. Some pathologists have ruled the death a suicide, while others claim that their findings point toward murder with a self-inflicted death virtually impossible. In all scenarios, the death while in custody was a disaster and unconscionable result. Will this all end in a clear and convincing manner with a definite resolution? That is highly unlikely. One thing is sad but true. There can be a lot more certainty today with all of our fancy computers, cameras, motion detectors, other recording devices, and eyewitness testimony than what we experienced thirty years ago or more. Inquiring minds want to know what happened—but that will probably not happen in this case and in many more.

On April 29, 2020, #AndrewCuomo is a fool to think Americans do not know he is trying to shift blame to @realDonaldTrump and the US government for the NY #CoronavirusPandemic debacle. A major cause of the New York disaster was the decision to place elderly COVID patients back into nursing homes/long-term care facilities that were not equipped to isolate and protect those vulnerable people. Suggestion to Gov. Cuomo: buck up buttercup and accept rightful responsibility for your failures.

Eventually in the future we will once again have a generation that becomes noted for their ability to accept responsibility when that is dictated by the facts. That is a much-awaited milestone and will be a cause for celebration, as well as a source of respect for those young people.

CHAPTER 8

SOCIAL MEDIA KILLS
AND IS SKEWED TO THE LEFT, LITERALLY

Some of what is written here may seem to be duplicative, but there are no apologies being made at this end. A portion of those repeats are advisable because they address some of the most serious problems we face today as a society. Social media in its' present form is destroying individuality and increasing the stigmas of personal looks, fashion, size, and identity. This leads to an increase (sometimes dramatic) in suicides for those who lose hope of succeeding in the "competition". To the parents in our midst: be very careful about the amount and content of social media to which your young children and teens are exposed. Just like other "excesses" out there in the world, the volume of social media can often determine the detriment that is created, and you have the power to put reasonable controls on the who, what, where, and why for those you love and nurture. The stakes are high now and are rising dramatically with every passing day.

Social media giant Facebook is staring a $5 billion fine down the barrel for violating the privacy rights of its' users. It can be difficult to fault FB for this as there are incredible amounts of money available in exchange for the information turned over. And this is more and more a problem being faced by all of us. According to a recent (June 2019 release) Pew Research study, approximately 78% of all adult women use social media compared to 65% of adult men. So, the disastrous effects of social media have entered all of our age groups, moving everyone closer to the promises of Orwell's "*1984*". A new study has shown that the use of social media and resulting isolationism tends to breed violence in our streets, affecting us all. These are far from positive developments.

This issue could have been placed in a number of different chapters, but the results of these efforts on the Left tend to be placed on social media for their viewers to consume. One of the extremely sad outcomes from mass shootings in America is the flooding of Liberals to the electronic airwaves for fundraising purposes within literally hours following the senseless occurrence. This happened recently following the El Paso and Dayton attacks. It appears that the candidates wanted to "tug on the heartstrings" of those who blame the innocent deaths and injuries on the abundance of firearms in the country as the result of innocent people exercising their Second Amendment rights. There is seldom a mention in the advertising of the mental health or criminal elements of the horrific acts. Absent from the ads of Elizabeth Warren were any mention that the deranged Ohio shooter was one of her supporters. One can see how that might not have been a good idea to align with one of the perpetrators. These matters should not be regulated (as we have too many of those already), but could probably continue to be left up to the better and commonly compassionate judgment of the candidates—maybe a gap of a couple of days?

"Swatting" (often with the use of social media) is continuing to grow. This is a practice of intentionally reporting a fake dangerous situation to disrupt someone's life. The communication usually results in a SWAT team being deployed to the site of the supposed deadly situation. Some of the victims of these criminal activities end up dead or significantly injured at the hands of the first responders who are expecting armed and dangerous perpetrators on the premises identified. Swatters in the future will need to be fully prosecuted for the results of their criminal behavior, including injuries to persons involved, property damage, and the governmental costs for those who are required to respond to the hoaxes.

Social media has had the effect of putting our law enforcers and other first responders in harm's way as they are in the field addressing community concerns. Police officers state that they feel betrayed following the emergence and proliferation of cell phone cameras and social media on which those digital videos are displayed. How would you feel if you were sent out on a domestic violence call as a part of your job? For me, I would make sure that I had plenty of backup with me, as much as possible. There are a lot of armed and dangerous mentally ill people out there on the streets and in homes, and they seem desperate enough to attack our civil servants who are focused on keeping our residents safe.

Social media execs are well aware of how the overall result of increasing social media exposure will lead to an intellectual decline for our American children. This is why many of those industry leaders don't let their own kids get caught up in the online intoxication and madness.

Fake news disseminated through social media can be quite deadly for a company, creating the ultimate negative publicity that can and does result in the destruction of tens of thousands of innocent people. A false rumor was spread online in August of 2019 by zealots on the Left that the owners of the Olive Garden restaurant chain were helping to fund the Trump 2020 campaign.

This activity led to a proposed boycott of the restaurants for their heinous activities. The falsehoods were not only proven to be untrue, but it was shown, in fact, that employees of the owner Darden Restaurants had donated $8,407 to the Hillary Clinton campaign for 2016 while $886 had been given for the Trump campaign. Talk about "biting the hand that feeds you".

CHAPTER 9

NEW ADDICTIONS AND EPIDEMICS: OPIOIDS, CELL PHONES, VIDEO GAMES, AND MENTAL ILLNESS

Writer Samuel Johnson has been quoted as saying: "The chains of habit are too weak to be felt, until they are too strong to be broken." How true that can be for almost any addiction. By the time you realize you are "on the ropes" [of a boxing ring for instance], you are headed through them and on to the concrete floor below. And that plunge will leave a mark. As a society, we need to work on being better able to identify personal problems in ourselves and others while remedial intervention is an option to head off the challenges before the victim is tumbling out of control. We appear to be doing just that in the Northern Plains of the US with the addition of new facilities to treat destructive habits as well as actively expanding existing in-patient and out-patient services.

As I went to press with *AGG* in mid-December of 2018, I sounded the alarm near the end of this chapter about an issue I viewed as serious at that time but which was receiving little or no attention from those of us in the mainstream of America—a possible vaping epidemic on the horizon. Little did I realize then what exactly would materialize with this new craze within our young people, especially those in the K-12 category. As I write in early-November of 2019, dozens of people have died from vaping-related illnesses, over a thousand Americans are confirmed as being sick from vaping, and alcohol vaping has been added to THC vaping as a major health concern. According to one study, 85% of vaping lung patients are under age 35. No shock there. The obvious underlying factor in all of this is that we need to have considerable studying done to identify whether vaping in any form is safe for the consumers—from youngsters to adults who are trying to "kick" the tobacco smoking addiction. All of this is in the light of a serious increase today in nicotine consumption, much of which is a part of some vaping. A recent study claimed that one in three teens now uses tobacco. It is sad for those who have been dragged into the vaping habit by the "cool" way it looks and are becoming statistics evidencing the dangers behind the scenes. #JustDon'tVape

AGG also did not focus on traditional addictions, such as alcoholism. The abuse of alcohol continues to an incredible extent throughout all age groups from teens to octogenarians. And in our region, North Dakota and cities Fargo and Grand Forks lead many national surveys in the consumption of alcohol. The former notoriety here of "having a church on every corner" has now been replaced with "a bar on every block". It doesn't help that we have a number of small to medium-sized colleges in the area with millennials and Gen-Zers who feed the bars and restaurants. We also have rural areas and frigid winter weather that enhance the opportunity to be home-bound with nothing to do but watch television, play games, and drink. According to the National Institute of Alcohol Abuse and Alcoholism and the 2017 National Survey on Drug Use and Health, 56% of those responding said that they drank alcohol during the past month. Over 26% of those 18 or over have engaged in "binge" drinking (generally a regular pattern of consumption that brings the blood alcohol concentration (BAC) to .08 g/dl or above) in the past month. That is approximately 4 drinks for women and 5 for men over a period of 2 hours. 6.7% reported heavy alcohol use during the previous month. The number of admitted adult alcoholics totaled 14.1 million people (5.7% of the population), nine million men (7.5%) and 5.1 million women (4%). Youth numbers are approximately 1.5% of the population (1.4% of the males and 2.1% of the females). An estimated 88,000 people (62,000 men and 26,000 women) died in '17 of alcohol-related causes. That is the third leading cause of preventable death, behind tobacco use and poor diet/physical inactivity. Alcohol misuse cost the US $249 billion in 2010, with 75% of those costs attributable to binge drinking. Alcohol continues as a major health problem in America and worldwide, and there are no signs that it is going away any time soon. Ultimate "bummer": being arrested for DUI/DWI without drinking a drop, because a fungus in your gut is turning carbs into alcohol ("Auto-Brewery Syndrome"). This would be even worse if you are "recovering"! #UltimateBummers

An 18-year old girl from Mankato (MN) was charged with distracted driving for traveling at 96 miles per hour in a 65 miles per hour zone while video-chatting on FaceTime. She chuckled at the State Trooper who was explaining to her the dangers of such conduct. This behavior consists of a combination of addiction, failure to admit and take responsibility, and a lack of respect for constituted authority—all shocking but not really surprising.

And now an addition to the challenges of our youth/teens—sexting! It is rising dramatically with 15% of them having sent sexually explicit messages and/or photos, and 25% having received them. In our training by the greatest generation, the baby boomers were taught to be modest when it came to our body—the "temple" as it was described in *The Bible*. What are the lessons being taught today to our young people about morality and immorality? It appears that the teachers and lessons have changed significantly. This could be loosely connected to the shocking rise of pornography and a corresponding addiction to it. Such an addiction, apparently similar to an addiction to sex, appears to cross all lines of education, wealth, and physical location. Most offensive to this writer are those of these mental illnesses involving children, as with child pornography. Particularly shocking are those perversions conducted by well-educated professionals such a respected or at least respectable college professors or administrators, physicians, lawyers or accountants, K-12 educators, and pastors/clergy, for instance. There is considerable evidence in my mind that these aberrations are serious diseases, as how could it not be with the vast majority of the population totally offended at even the thought of being aroused by such materials. It must be a serious sickness for the abuser. Enough about this here as such matters are far outside of my education, knowledge, and comprehension.

Gambling addiction is much more understandable to me. It would seem to mirror the teachings we learned from the greatest generation about the scientific chances of an event occurring in one's life. The adage is that "insanity is defined as doing something over and over again and expecting different results". Chronic gamblers seem to believe that the "odds" of something happening, the winning of large sums of money, will be different for them, that they will defy the laws of probability. How often do we hear what some problem gamers are thinking: the next repetition (hand of cards, pull of the lever, roll of the dice, purchase of the ticket, spin of the wheel) will be the big winner, and if they fail to take that chance they cannot succeed against the odds. I have been a "calculated risk-taker" in life and do not find it too difficult to understand how a person's mind can be distorted into believing that they are at the doorstep of "the big one" and must take that chance—again and again and again. How often do we hear about the spouse who takes their paycheck and attempts to double or triple it in a night of harmless entertainment, resulting in the wages disappearing in a flurry of gaming? While driving through Las Vegas, I can still remember vividly how our father would say: "the people who own that fancy resort did not pay for it; it was paid for by the people inside who are gambling and almost always losing their money." A powerful and important lesson in life that will always stay with us. How many of us have had or have friends who have lost everything or came close because of their gambling sickness? It is several for this guy.

An update on the allegedly addictive video game "Fortnite". Many parents have said that the use of the game by a child has adversely affected their financial condition and has subjected their private family information to hackers. It does not help the addictions when a 16-year old boy wins $3 million in the international "Fortnite" competition—further facilitating the challenges.

Now as we reach November of 2019, there are new warnings about the Chinese-owned social media app, TikTok. Its' use is being fueled by US millennials and Gen-Zers, young people from around the world, and terror groups such as ISIS. It is being used by over a billion people. The video format is being widely used for activities from dangerous stunts to beheadings. There is considerable concern about what the Chinese are documenting from the app participants. The warning to parents—do not let your children use this app!

Not a candidate for the smartest business decision of the century so far: Starbucks will add needle disposal containers to bathrooms in their retail operations. Is this really necessary? Maybe it is in Washington and California, but certainly not in Fargo.

Studies are showing record levels of stress in the United States. This is most likely the result of what I have coined as "TAD" (or "Trump Affective Disorder"), and what others have named as "Trump Derangement Syndrome" or "Trump Traumatic Stress Disorder". Our needs in America for additional mental health services are increasing faster than any physical health condition in the history of the country. The shocking impact of Hillary Clinton being defeated by Donald Trump in the 2016 election will undoubtedly become the single-most catastrophic event in the history of our republic. More on this below.

The pregnant mother who says that "smoking pot was the only thing that gave me hope!" That sounds like Michelle Obama, except substitute the "smoking pot" reference with "my husband's primary victories". And for the pot head, why not substitute the safer pills, liquid, or food marijuana without the THC? This is not so much addiction as it is stupidity and a dangerous "crutch". Meanwhile as there is a feeding frenzy of lemmings who want to grow or sell pot for personal non-medicinal consumption, the US Surgeon General simultaneously issues more serious warnings about the adverse results of cannabis use. This will be one of the major social issues in America until it is one day resolved in a manner that protects our citizens rather than placing them in an additional set of crosshairs. Very much contrary to my opinion in the 1970s, I am now inclined to believe that recreational pot needs to be shut down totally in the US.

According to the *Chicago Tribune* in an article on November 29, 2018, iPhone use for persons who have had a device for three years or more now averages 277 minutes per day (about 4 hours and 35 minutes), with users checking their phones an average of 77 times per day. Is this evidence of addiction? It sure could be as this is simply an average and not indicative of how some people use their cellphone for longer than average or much more than average. Is it a surprise that many tech executives do not let their children use their devices anywhere near the average amount? Not shocking to this writer. UPDATE: Since *"AGG"* was written and included this chapter about new addictions (including cellphones), the usage problem for our young people in America has nearly doubled according to a report from Common Sense

Media, a nonprofit group which assists children and parents in all matters relating to social media and personal electronic devices! Their study shows that an average US teen spends more than seven hours per day on screen media, a majority of that time (53%) on YouTube. Twenty-nine percent (29%) of that age category spend over eight hours per day. All of this is beyond exposure to screens in the classroom and for homework. How insane is that? The dysfunction this creates in our 13 to 19-year old's is evident in virtually every negative statistic out there, such as depression, stress and anxiety, distracted driving, isolationism, drug use, aggression, bullying, and (of course) personal physical harming and suicides. Twenty percent (20%) of teens received their first mobile device at the age of 8 years old. Gaming is the predominant entertainment for boys (70%) with girls at just 23%. The usage is less for higher income children than those with lower incomes. Bottom line: we can expect that screen use by young people will continue to be a challenge to their mental health and overall physical and mental wellness. This is on you parents out there to monitor and guide your children with their social media practices. Good luck with that and be prepared for the possible need of medical professionals to assist you in assuring that your young ones are practicing healthy habits with their social media devices. Wise counsel for some (but not me as a proud OK Boomer) comes from PutAwaythePhone.com: "Your cellphone has already replaced your watch, camera, calendar, and alarm clock. Don't let it replace your family!" One can be more easily remedied than the other.

Prediction: for years in the future we will see PTSD claims made not only from those who served our country heroically with the military in armed combat (a major valid condition), but also from those who were supporting and voted for Hillary Clinton in 2016 and who are now irreconcilably "Trumpatized" from that loss and the subsequent stress and absence of all hope. Hence the name: "Post-Trumpatized Stress Disorder" for which there is no known cure and probably never will be. We knew this was inevitable when we witnessed the election-night tears from all of those "Hillaryites". Maybe most of us have led a sheltered life as this was a new phenomenon following the loss of any candidate in any election. Fox News medical consultant Dr. Marc Siegel summarized the "state" of our country very succinctly and correctly on October 30, 2019: "Worry and division are destroying America's psyche." I probably would have said simply that "there do appear to be a lot of 'crazies' out and about these days." Update as the COVID-19 pandemic continues (on 4-13-20): we will see tens of millions of American first-responders, healthcare professionals, and those citizens stricken with the virus or severely economically impacted by it added to the rolls of PTSD victims who will require treatment for the disorder. This is very serious stuff!

There is an update on "real" PTSD and its treatment in November of 2019. Will the Stellate Ganglion Block procedure (SGB) work in fighting PTSD? *Anxiety.org* is not so certain that it will. This methodology has been used on a fairly wide basis since 2008. We will be hearing a lot more about this in the coming months and years. Whatever can be done simply, safely, and effectively should be utilized as we continue to learn much about the vast extent of people affected by the disorder.

More of a hatred than any sort of addiction, a large number of our big city residents have had enough of "scooters" on the sidewalks and streets. This is not so much a physical sickness as it is a mental one. Maybe the detractors have been nearly taken out by one, or they are simply jealous that the users are arriving at their intended destination in less time and with incredibly reduced effort. Some cities are also complaining that these modes of transportation are destroying their sidewalks. Not to fret, as this method of moving people from one place to another will inevitably disappear when technology is perfected to "beam us" to our location of choice.

Before this entry about "obesity" into *ASG*, I "navigated it" to see how many times it was already mentioned. The number produced was "zero". I was shocked that neither the condition nor the word had been raised yet. This will be another instance of a very superficial overview of an incredibly serious problem today in America as well as in many other parts of the world. A statistic that drew me to writing this paragraph is that the incidence of obesity has increased in the US by over 300% since the 1970s. Currently about one-third of all Americans (or 115 million people) are obese, with Mississippi and West Virginia having the highest rate (almost 40%) and Colorado as the lowest at 23%. That is astounding to me as well as very saddening. As a clear novice in the healthcare and weight management fields, my expectations are that this dramatic explosion of significantly overweight Americans has been caused by a decline in physical activity, the pathetic increase in consumption of "fast food" at the expense of balanced homemade and healthy foods, rampant depression and resulting isolationism, and the epidemic of social media and video/electronic games, as well as a combination of two or more of those culprits. A recent regional study has shown that less than 10% of Minnesota teens are obese while the rate for their peers on the Indian Reservations in the state is 28%. It appears that protecting the body needs to be added to Native priorities such as conserving the earth, eliminating missing and murdered neighbors, and reversing climate change. Just as the intervention of diagnosis and treatment is an integral part of all the new obsessions and epidemics discussed in this chapter, the same is certainly true to turn obesity off and return the body to reasonable weight and conditioning. For your further reading and education, I recommend *The Obesity Epidemic* by Zoe Harcombe.

Drug overdoses in the US (commonly caused these days with fentanyl-laced heroin) are more than double the firearm deaths in the country. There are many, many books dedicated to these topics. I will leave it here with this short blurb. We need to dramatically increase our efforts in America to reduce both drug-related deaths and gun violence. Too many good people are taken from us each year, in both cases with a dangerous weapon in the wrong place and hands. Are we to believe the results of a recent study that claimed 97.8% of mass shootings from 1980-2018 occurred in "gun-free zones"? Meanwhile virtually 100% of overdose deaths left behind shocked and grieving family and friends. All very tragic.

The American Medical Association (AMA) calls the deaths of eighteen transgender persons in the United States during 2019 an "epidemic". These were mostly male-to-female individuals of color. Let us pray that this was simply an aberration for that year rather than a trend that will continue and possibly even grow in numbers. This sounds like statistics that would be true of intolerant places in Africa as opposed to the more accepting confines of America.

On a lighter note, current STD ("Sexually Transmitted Disease") levels in our country are at record highs. It appears that our laziness in the US extends to protecting ourselves from being exposed to and spreading venereal conditions. That is a very sad and easily solved situation.

The American Psychological Association defines "anxiety" in January of 2020 as: "an emotion characterized by feelings of tension, worried thoughts and physical changes, such as sweating, trembling, dizziness or a rapid heartbeat." Our local "rag" embarks on a six-day feature about the current Gen-Z anxiety epidemic which is following on the heels of the millennial epidemic. There was nothing like this as the Boomers were growing up in the Heartland. Our greatest worries were the choices about how and with whom we were going to have fun in life.

Caution: Well-meaning people (including the media) share positive stories during times of crisis. Seems fine for those who can handle it but may be the opposite for those millions suffering from mental illness—adding to their feelings of isolation and loneliness. Be careful that your efforts to lessen a problem are not adding to it with pain and anxiety. #MentalIllness

For an excellent read about addressing the medical, addiction, and mental problems of today, I highly recommend *Make America Healthy Again* by Dr. Nicole Saphier.

CHAPTER 10

AMERICA DISTRACTED

Where do I place this update? It could have been in any of the chapters relating to selfies, millennials/Gen-Zers, addictions, or right here. So here we go. Over the past few months, there have been numerous stories of young people falling from dangerous places (many times in prohibited areas) while taking a selfie photo. Some of these incidents resulted in death and/or serious injuries. I am suspecting that in hindsight many of these immature amateur photographers would have made a different plan for the "shot"—or maybe not. As we were taught at a young age, it is best to use one's brain through reasoning rather than a quick impulse that could be irrational. "Look before you leap."

Likewise, this addition could have been made in any of several chapters—millennials/Gen-Zers, addictions, or here. Liberty Mutual Insurance announces on August 17, 2019, that the biggest challenges today leading to auto accidents are from millennials auto habits and distracted driving. Over 80% of the generation admit to using their cellphone while driving and 57% say they send texts while driving (that is no doubt a lower number than the actual figure). When will these people learn how dangerous their behavior is? Some states are trying the implementation of "hand's-free" rules, but it may be necessary to ban use by drivers totally in order to keep our streets and highways safe—at least until we are all riding in self-driving vehicles.

Changes coming to our baseball parks throughout the US, because of a rash of injurious incidents involving fans being hit by line drives while sitting along unprotected portions of the foul-line seating. One of the reasons why such protection becomes necessary today is that the active bats and balls create a more dangerous situation with higher speeds than in previous times. And then there is also the fact that many game attendees are not as attentive in watching the game as they were in those years prior to the cellphone and social media addictions. This is a required action in extending the protective netting along the seating to the foul poles, but unfortunate as it will diminish the vision of fans in those areas.

On November 5, 2019, we see graphic video of a man being pulled at the last second by a transit worker from the path of a BART train in Oakland, CA. Initially, I was so intent on seeing the extraction that I did not look for an answer to the ultimate question—how in the heck did he end up on the tracks? So I watched the video online a few more times. I hope this is "fake news" as I write it, but it appeared to me that the man simply appears out of nowhere with a phone pressed against his ear and then steps off the platform for the fall to the track…total distraction, not even remotely aware that he was approaching any tracks. The platform was pretty full of Oakland Raiders fans returning home after their game nearby, so we should find out more from witnesses in the future. From what I saw, it seemed to have been one of those videos we see of a distracted cellphone user falling into a mall fountain, only the results here could have been far more disastrous.

Sometimes we Americans are too busy with life to notice what is happening around us—we are "unable to see the forest from the trees". Where were you in 2019 when Google's "Project Nightingale" accumulated healthcare data on 50 million Americans in just months. Whatever happened to HIPAA? *1984* is here. #HealthcarePrivacy

CHAPTER 11

WHATEVER HAPPENED TO BUYING LOCAL AND SUPPORTING THOSE BUSINESSES?

Our country is rapidly losing sight of how important it is to patronize locally owned small businesses rather than the Big Box stores, local businesses owned outside of the area, and online retailers. This revolution is obviously being fueled by the millennials, Gen-Zers, and Gen-Xers. That is not surprising as these younger generations have never been taught about the benefits of buying local. This is one of the final chapters I am working on in *ASG*, as I found that when I completed the basic writing of the book this was the only topic from *AGG* which had virtually no activity while the remainder of the book was being written (at least until the COVID-19 pandemic was thrust upon us). Hopefully enough of those young persons will read this or learn elsewhere just how important local businesses are to our everyday life and well-being.

Normally over the past couple of decades, we hear annually as we prepare for Christmas/Hanukkah and the "holidays" the debate about whether we should be buying gifts locally or through online resources. My wife and I continue to do our spending through-out the metropolitan area and use sources such as Amazon only on an "as needed" basis. We have no intention of changing these habits at any time in the future.

Recently, we have all witnessed some of the local purchasing focus since the Coronavirus outbreak, starting with the buying we need to accomplish to get our food, adult beverages (for some of us), necessities, medications, and fuel. There has also been an area push to help support our favorite restaurants by ordering their food for take-out or delivery and investing in gift cards to assist with their current cash flow needs. It has been reassuring to hear about some of those success stories. It is not positive to hear the speculation about how many of our local small businesses are not expected to survive the pandemic. Lives and livelihoods are being destroyed or at least dramatically changed in real time right in front of our eyes. It is saddening to think that many of our youngest residents will not even understand what is transpiring all around them at least until it happens to a relative or someone else they know, or until it is over and they see that many of the active shops they once passed are now shuttered for the duration. The pandemic we continue to face will not end well for ourselves, our neighbors, and our communities. I cannot even come close to imagining the pain that many people are facing today as I write on April 1, 2020 (no fooling) with ten percent (10%) of them having lost their livelihoods while rent and other monthly bills are coming due and with no income to pay them, a savings account which is woefully inadequate, and excruciating fear about what the future has in store for them. The levels of stress and anxiety are through the roof.

Suggestion: each time you think about or proceed into an online retailer, consider your friends and neighbors who sell similar products and depend on those sales to pay their rent and put food on their table. This is serious stuff when we take the time to consider it. "Think globally, act locally" can and does make a big difference right where you live.

I do not see a clear place for these thoughts, so I will put them here. Americans at one time were raised to believe that "they [manufacturers] don't make things like they used to!" It was true then and it continues to be true today. When you purchased a product "Made in the USA", it was usually of a better quality than you would receive with the same item from a foreign producer. Those countries which were most often the victims of such criticism were Japan, India, and China. For example, my wife and I still have old products that we inherited from the family, or purchased when we were young, or received as wedding gifts (1979) that work as well today as they did when we started using them. The quality of craftsmanship and materials was superior to that which we see today in similar widgets. Sometime in the 1980s or 90s, producers learned about something called "planned obsolescence"—why make your product so well that it will last forever and limit your ability to replace it in the next 5-10 years or so? Some previously quality and durable products became virtually "disposable" almost overnight. And we have been paying for this ever since. You can still pay for quality, but at a hefty premium in cost. And sometimes there are local artisans who can make better items that "do not cost an arm and a leg". The lesson here can still be buying local with the added suggestion to buy quality that can pay off with the longevity of use.

On April 14, 2020, #WallStreet celebrates the record high stock value for #Amazon as online sales explode amid the #CoronavirusPandemic. This is great news for Jeff Bezos and the new 100k+ Amazon employees but is a disaster for #smallbusiness in America!

There has never been nor hopefully will ever again be a more cataclysmic attack on small local businesses than what we have experienced so far with the Corona Virus pandemic. How many small businesses and farms will be lost and financial lives destroyed before it is all over? And where will the victims be employed once the carnage has been meted out? There are estimates of 25% to 90% of various once-going enterprises being sucked up into the large black hole which is being created by COVID-19. Who has any idea of what the landscape of self-employment and entrepreneurism will look like when we are viewing the virus in the rearview mirror? There will undoubtedly be tens of millions of casualties in the US alone. Make way for the mega graveyards housing the best-laid plans which will be plowed under in our cities and towns which make up the American landscape. I pray that I am all wrong about my visions of future doom and gloom. Only time will tell.

May 21, 2020: IT IS TIME TO #BOYCOTT ONLINE PURCHASES EXCEPT LOCAL! We need to save our local small businesses!

CHAPTER 12

SOMETHING FOR NOTHING, LAZINESS, AND ENTITLEMENTS — THE VANISHING WORK ETHIC

Everything is being delivered these days, and by everyone. Walmart announces that they are now delivering groceries right into your kitchen. Great idea, or a "how lazy are we" moment? Those who bought into this trend with the DoorDash restaurant food delivery system may now be paying the price after that company was hacked and their customer records stolen.

We talk often about the fact that it is difficult to make things up when we are surrounded with so much "craziness". Then we read about Amazon's new "shock bracelets". The wearer gets a small electric shock when they vary from "healthy habits" (in whose judgment?). How lazy and dumb are we becoming in 2019 (the new "*1984*")?

The boomers were taught to "never ever quit". "Winners never quit, and quitters never win". That is a pretty solid rule of life. Can there be exceptions? I sure hope so, as I recently resigned from a volunteer leadership position based on irreconcilable management methods. Mine developed from fifty plus years of experience did not match with those of my "boss". Another firm rule: "one needs to do what one needs to do." And still more: "a fight is not over until someone is on the mat." That is good to know: stay off the mat while you wrestle your opponent.

It was intriguing to me to learn that groups of millennials and feminists have agreed on a common thread—their desires for a four-day work week. This piqued my curiosity as I have spent much of thirty out of forty-three years as an attorney working four ten-hour day schedules, beginning in 1984 when my first daughter was born. This decision was in response to those of my legal colleagues who advised me not to make the same mistake they had made in not spending enough time with their children as they were growing up. I would love to know how many of these advocates have ever worked for ten hours in a day. It is by no means an easy thing to do. The idea sounds wonderful to be able to enjoy a three-day weekend. My boomers were taught that "the proof [of something] is in the pudding", meaning that the validity of an idea or concept is determined by testing it out in real life. This saying was derived from an English phrase: "the proof of the pudding [commonly homemade sausages] is in the eating." The reality of "4-10s" (the days instead of the shotguns) seems quite illogical in this day of laziness commonly occupying the space which used to be filled with solid work ethic. Pardon my skepticism/cynicism. I would be wary of such a plan today, at least in most parts of the country.

Breaking News in the laziness category: a young (millennial perhaps?) software engineer has implanted a starter for her Tesla automobile into her body. Now that is being rated very high on the scale for the lazy index. But can we today really expect a person to have that remote starter on their keychain? Sure.

A "rare" Sunday ("Day of Rest") tweet on 4-19-20 amid the Corona Virus pandemic: Time to #GetBackToWorkAmerica!

One of the major #CoronavirusPandemic recovery challenges today as businesses start to reopen on May 1, 2020, is the unavailability of employees (with 30 million recently unemployed) as they are receiving State unemployment benefits plus $600 per week from America to not work! Ouch! Those unemployed must lose their federal benefits if they refuse to go back to work in their previous position. #ReopenAmericaNOW

There was not a shortage of work ethic during the time of Teddy Roosevelt. And he personally was the epitome of the tough, hard-charging, and gritty public servant and leader that we look for today. He often philosophized about life with statements like "speak softly and carry a big stick, and you will go far" (1901). And then there were his comments that same year about applying oneself to the task at hand: "The first requisite of a good citizen in this Republic of ours is that he shall be able and willing to pull his weight; do what you can with what you have where you are." Back to the drawing board. Truly inspirational.

CHAPTER 13
CREATING WIMPS

Have you seen many recent changes in rules around the American workplace? Usually when I hear about a new addition or restriction, I find myself scratching my head—wondering about what sort of challenges prompted the adjustment. I found this particular suggestion to be genuinely troublesome: banning "handshakes" in the workplace (pre COVID-19) as being inappropriate "touching" when one of the participants was uncomfortable with or intimidated by the gesture. Back when I was growing up, it was understood that many agreements between two or more parties were committed by a handshake as the equivalence of a written document with signatures. It was called a "gentleman's agreement" (sorry for the sexism here). It has also been an important part of greeting a client, customer, or friend, or a means of congratulating a person for an accomplishment, or an acknowledgement when meeting someone for the first time. We were taught by our parents that it was a positive attribute to have a "firm" handshake—a sign of confidence. In recent years many of those handshakes have been replaced with "fist pumps", possibly more sanitary than "pressing the flesh". Again, I may be incredibly old fashioned in hoping that the handshake will continue to be appropriate, at least between consenting adults.

As I am writing, an Ohio school district decides in its' infinite wisdom to eliminate the selection and recognition of

Valedictorians in order to decrease the competitive culture in schools and the resulting pressure to succeed. This example of a failing America could have been in many of the chapters in this book—the decline in real education, our loss of a strong "work ethic", and political incorrectness. Whatever happened to the days when we were being taught that "good clean competition" was a positive element in one's upbringing? And how about a lesson which encouraged us all to strive for success, with each of us to define what it would mean to succeed. Life here and around the world is filled with competitiveness and success, and any effort to hide them from the view of our children is a major error in judgment. Boomers were taught by the "great ones" to be tough, the opposite of the "coddling" of children which has been the new norm for thirty years now.

Every chance they get these days, those on the Left (especially the Liberal media) take "pot shots" with spitballs at the National Rifle Association (NRA) as the latest group of "domestic terrorists", often as the Liberals are lifting up groups like fascist Antifa as the protector of the masses or the Marxist group "Black Lives Matter". The NRA is considered by its' supporters as a leader in the protection of the Second Amendment to the US Constitution—the right of citizens to bear arms, whether through a militia or individually. The Courts in America have ruled that there can be reasonable restrictions on this right, and that is where the different interpretations come forward as to the meaning of "reasonable". The definition of a "reasonable person" can shift over time but must never be used to create and enforce confiscatory rules and regulations against the meaning and purpose of the Amendment. Pardon the use of incendiary projections, but such a development could be one of the catalysts for a second civil war in America. Even a hint of such actions by the US government would most likely result in an "arming of America" unlike what we have ever even imagined prior to today. We need to tread lightly when we even suggest taking firearms away from our citizens, even with those "red flag" laws designed to remove them from persons who are mentally ill or have otherwise shown erratic behavior.

Do you regularly hear the phrase "how lazy are we in this country?". Another example of this phenomenon came to light recently as McDonalds Restaurants announced that their culinary delights were now available for delivery by "Uber Eats". That means you are now able to have questionably unhealthy food delivered to you without leaving the couch. Well isn't that special! There is no question that overexertion can be damaging to one's body.

This item fits here or in Chapter 14 below. I chose this chapter. As the US Women's Soccer team in the World Cup beats Thailand by 13-0 in group play, there are those whiners out there who complained that this was too many goals—the US should have stopped scoring goals at some point short of the thirteen. I am sure that the team was sorry to have offended you. Or not! Anyone who understands the sport, and in this case the competition, realizes that those are the rules by which the sport lives. Goal differentials are the means used to compare one team with another and to place each team on a list of those which will move forward in the competition and those which will not continue. It may be time to "suck it up" and enjoy seeing excellence in action. More on that amazing team later.

Police officers in Tempe, AZ were recently asked to leave a Starbucks because another customer felt "uncomfortable"—most likely a "snowflake" or a victim of past unfortunate law enforcement interaction. If I were a manager of that coffeeshop, I would have requested the complaining party to vacate the premises.

We recently learned that Oregon has at least a partial answer to adolescent mental illness problems. They are adding up to five days every three months of "mental health days" to be claimed by their K-12 students. So instead of going to school for interaction with their classmates, they can sit at home and play video games or spend the day on their cellphone with social media. Perfect! This is just what young people need today—fewer days being educated to face the outside world. Our Pacific Northwest in the US does tend to come up with some "doozies" while thinking "outside of the box/universe".

"Snowflake" students at Northwestern U. complained on Veteran's Day (2019) that a Jeff Sessions visit/speech article in the local newspaper "traumatized" them with the facts. We must protect "free speech" from these Gen-Zers who have been educated by Liberal teachers that the only speech in need of protection is the "garbage" spewed on the Left. These are the same students who sought counseling the day after someone said "Boo!" to them on Halloween. #ProtectFreeSpeech #Snowflakes

In many parts of the country today, people are talking about school discipline, especially as it relates to violent and disruptive students. It does not appear that there are many clear and feasible answers. And then we hear of some of the program ideas which are being put forward for consideration, such as yoga, meditation, and "restorative justice"? Probably the only reason that ukulele lessons was left off the list was because the instrument is too often used as a weapon. The "old school" approach is still one of the best potential solutions, featuring separation, security, psychology, and science. There have been major developments in the effective treatment of violent persons, short of turning them into zombies. Let's be creative and cutting-edge in our vision and direction for this arena.

Not even seemingly innocent holiday advertising is immune from the PC police. They will "call a spade a spade" whenever they think they see it. The "sexist" Peloton stationary bike ad with a woman receiving one from her husband for Christmas? Oh, the humanity of it! How can that be allowed to reach the airwaves? Just another blatant example of the thin-skinned wimps we continue to create in this country. #GetALife

There have been some great quotes out there as we boomers were raised in the center of North America. For a number of these phrases, they were integral lessons for us in understanding the importance of being mentally and physically tough, the opposite of being wimps. One of the favorites that comes to mind was from poet Alfred, Lord Tennyson in his "Charge of the Light Brigade" (published December 2, 1854). The short version was "Ours [Yours] is not to reason why, Ours [Yours] is but to do or die". In other words, there is a time and place to deliberate, but then comes a time to focus and accomplish the mission. That abbreviated saying is not totally accurate though, and the real words cast an even more ominous shadow on the topic: "Half a league, half a league, half a league onward, All in the Valley of Death rode the six hundred…Theirs not to make reply, theirs not to reason why, theirs but to do **and** die." Now that is a wholly different matter. It was a suicide mission with death certain as the outcome. This writing embodies the thought of "War is Hell", as it reflects the dangers of being a soldier in armed conflict. Sometimes in life it is imperative to have reality thrust upon us so that we can be prepared for the possible cruel outcome. It does make us hardened and more mature if we survive for that next battle which is virtually certain to follow.

One of the new program developments these days is called "adult recess". As they are in the process of eliminating or at least reducing the amount of recess time in K-12, the workplace is seeing a surge in the "time out" for its workforce. From what I have read, this time is set aside mostly for nerds who weren't involved in sports in their school years—setting aside a few hours here and there for "personal reflection" and relaxation.

This might be an option that you would want to avoid even if it was made available to you. Or at least make sure that no one witnesses you using the benefit.

The millennials and Gen-Zers in America have turned the "*Brave New World*" into the "Weak New World", at least in the US.

Be warned that the airline industry and its federal regulators are moving forward to limit the ability of ticketed passengers to bring "emotional support" animals on planes. These efforts are long overdue as the misuse of this trend has left the fellow passengers at the mercy of a population that probably should be using and will need to once again utilize alternate forms of transportation for themselves and their "pets".

A local media story is about a female pediatrician speaking at a luncheon event called "Women Unite", encouraging parents to teach their children "soft skills". Are those lessons about the "self"? So, I do some online investigating. Those themes and topics include leadership, teamwork, communication, problem solving, work ethic, flexibility/adaptability, and interpersonal skills. Interesting, as those are the same skills the baby boomers were taught as we grew up in the Heartland. In this book as well as in "*AGG*", I address the decline in America which has led us today to little or none of this training for our school-aged children. Very disappointing that we arrived at this place and yet encouraging that some people realize the missing parts. My question remains: why isn't the session called "Parents Unite" as I would argue that both parents should be hearing these proposals?

CHAPTER 14
POLITICAL INCORRECTNESS

Many of us in a generation noted for compassion and benevolence are not believers in the whole concept of "reparations" in the sense of the descendants of an erring society paying damages to the descendants of persons injured by those faults. Why should we pay for the actions of others from a distant era in which their conduct may have even been lawful at the time in question? Many of the Liberals in the US today take the position that such payments are the politically correct way for someone to atone for earlier conditions which under today's standards were inappropriate, immoral, or unlawful. There are many additional questions which must be answered in preparing for payments: why, for what period, to whom, in what amount, from whom, who ultimately pays, and others? And the most important question of all is probably "when does this all end?" Such payments have been discussed for descendants of slaves, Native Americans for property "taken", Japanese and German Americans for "imprisonment" in the US during WWII, developmentally disabled Americans who were institutionalized prior to June of 1967, and the list goes on (with the latest being damages from China to cover world costs of those who died from or were economically injured by the Coronavirus pandemic). And how about those gays who were not permitted to marry until recent changes in the law? Many Democratic-Socialists believe there should be a blank check for each of the categories. I argue with many others that reparations were paid by the country for slavery. It was called the Civil War and was fought to end slavery, with the US losing 10% of its' entire population during that War. This battle over reparations will continue forever, with no one satisfied in the results.

News out of Canada: there is a movement to ban dodgeball from schools as some administrators deem such "elimination games" as a "tool of oppression" and a "vehicle for bullying". I could have placed this entry in Chapter 13, as it appears such actions to cushion the lives of some could turn them into wimps.

Fox News falls victim to their historic program of providing news which is "fair and balanced"—at least for this viewer. On October 7, 2019, I take a temporary leave of absence from the network programming, primarily a good portion of it. A problem arises from such a journalistic focus when even the mainstream and moderate politicians on the Left have become so poisoned by the insanity of those with whom they caucus, that they become a part of that PC madness. When there is such animosity and hatred between the opposing political camps as we see today, I personally prefer to listen and watch those with whom I basically agree. I will never succumb to the "resist" movement mentality but will always be active in moving forward with my beliefs and in supporting those with whom I agree at least in part. Our mission is to make this country better for all and not to push forward the agenda of those residents of the political swamp which threatens to engulf us all. I sent my first real tweet (on Twitter) today about this topic.

Just before the 4th of July 2019 celebration in America, Nike pulls the Betsy Ross flag tennis shoes that were being readied for release to commemorate the famous flag and the holiday. The obvious and brilliant reason for this move was that their rocket-science consultant on matters of race, Colin Kaepernick, determined that the design glorified slavery and racism?! Just what I was thinking without being paid all that money—or not! Suggestion to Nike: don't put all your eggs in the CK basket where everything that moves (or does not move) is "racist". On the other hand, there is something positive about seeing a supposedly smart company making a costly "bonehead" move based on the rantings of a "race monger". Good call.

I do agree with many of the Trump tweets which have made him the most transparent President in history. But I do not support some of them at all. There was no reason for his tweet on July 14, 2019, telling the members of "The Squad" to "go home" to their country of origin, solve the problems there, and then return to the US to educate the rest of the country about how they were able to succeed. This is as close as he has come so far in aligning himself with racism. Trump probably meant to say something like "many of our most recent immigrants have forgotten about how much better conditions are here for them in America as opposed to the situations they would face if they still lived in the country of their ancestry." But he did not say it that way. Each of "The Squad" members was born in the US, with the exception of Ilhan Omar. It is insulting to suggest that a natural born citizen of the US should go anywhere outside of the country to do anything they are not inclined to do. The tweet in question was "ill-advised" at best. Trump should have followed our old lesson: "look before you leap", and then decided to not take the plunge. This communication did not match Hillary's "deplorables" but came quite close—in the neighborhood. Memo to President Trump: Pray that the members of your base are not counting the possible "errors in judgment" you have made as POTUS—primarily in your tweets and definitely not in your policy decisions. #MakingAmericaGreat

Berkeley (CA) continues to lead the way in the US when it comes to political correctness and the "PC culture". Recently they changed a number of terms used by the city to describe things, places, and people. A "manhole" had now become a "maintenance hole"—makes sense. There were many more that were strange but acceptable. Then they lost me with this one. Many of us were members of a fraternity or sorority in college, and we lived in the fraternity or sorority house. Oh no, must not go there anymore. Now it is better to refer to them as "collegiate Greek system residences". Simple question: then how do you know if there are men or women living there? Here in the Heartland, we do not have members of both sexes living in such a "residence". My constructive advice to Berkeley: is this a productive way to use your time? How absurd. Maybe it is time to get back to work. "Real" work.

The emergence of the #MeToo movement has had some interesting companions. "Baby It's Cold Outside" (Academy Award winning song from Frank Loesser in 1949) is being rewritten by John Legend and Kelly Clarkson to be "politically correct" and in conformity with the movement. How pathetic are we becoming in America? The promoters of this need to get a life! The song was originally sung by Ricardo Montalban and Esther Williams in *Neptune's Daughter*, and later by several other duos. Those were obviously different times. This is a tendency by the "holier than thou's" on the Left—lose track of history in order to "grandstand" a "present" that will not offend anyone who does not know about the history that is being bulldozed into oblivion. Many of us boomers will never capitulate to those Liberals who want to totally forget the past in favor of creating a "plastic" society today at the expense of a yesterday from which we can learn and live a brighter future. #PCRunAmok

How many times do you look at or hear about something that looks harmless on the face, but turns out to be offensive in today's PC culture? In early-December of 2019, Michael Bloomberg calls fellow 2020 Democratic Presidential nomination contestant

Cory Booker "well spoken", to which Booker responds calling Bloomberg a "racist"? He drops the #RaceCard. Wha? Many of us consider such a description as a compliment, an indication that the recipient is intelligent and articulate rather than a demeaning racial slur against the Rhodes Scholar. What is serious misconduct in the eyes of some can be "much ado about nothing" for the rest of us.

When I was being raised during K-12, San Francisco was one of my parent's favorite cities. They and the family would travel there periodically as well as to their other favorites, New York City and New Orleans. The San Francisco we learned to love no longer exists. It is now a US symbol for "how to destroy a city" with homelessness, rampant crime/illegal drugs, sanctuary protection for illegals and criminals, and what remains of the rapidly disappearing "political correctness" mentality. One of their most amusing (in order to "laugh to keep from crying") additions to the latter category is the recent renaming of "convicted felons" to "justice-involved persons". Okay. So then what do you call the victims of the justice-involved persons? Aren't they also justice-involved persons? This will obviously get very confusing before it makes any sense at all. It is obvious that the SF Board of Supervisors is running on empty. Offenders released from custody are now "formerly incarcerated persons", while "juvenile delinquents" are now "young persons impacted by the juvenile justice system. "Drug addicts" or "substance abusers" are to be called "persons with a history of substance use". Isn't this all very special? None of this would have been possible when my friend and legal colleague Ed Johnson was involved with that city hall. I applaud the Supervisors for having the guts to handle these critical matters and in dealing with these past offenders and druggies in such a humane manner. I probably could have documented these matters in the "Creating Wimps" Chapter as well, as that is clearly a big part of what is being accomplished in the once great "City on the Bay".

I have never been a fan of tearing down historic statues when it turns out that there was something seriously negative about that person when they were alive. History should not be covered up, removed, or destroyed because of the "period" deficiencies of the subject. There has been discussion of changing historic places and commemorations of famous Americans such as George Washington because he was a slave owner, even the name of the "Washington Monument". There are similar efforts to change "Columbus Day" to "Indigenous People's Day", because the discovery of America by Christopher Columbus led to the persecution, displacement, and killings of hundreds of thousands of Native-American people. I personally buy in instead to the idea of keeping real history in front of us as Americans and emphasizing how we have learned from our "mistakes" in favor of making our country a better place. More later about these efforts by some to destroy US history rather than face it.

Here is a concept directly out of the playbook of the ACLU. Some people are concerned that doorbell cameras which have been used to locate and arrest trespassers or thieves are being used to violate the privacy OF THE CRIMINALS? Sounds like more positioning by the Liberals in our country, many of whom believe that those who break the law here are entitled to rights superior to those of law-abiding citizens. I wonder if this would extend to social media captures like the African-American woman who was taped by cellphones entering the lion and giraffe enclosure at the Bronx Zoo in order to get material for her Instagram page on which she is a "queen"? On second thought, that may be a better case to bring in the local mental health authorities.

Be careful what you say if you are traveling to or live in New York City. According to new guidelines from the city's Commission on Human Rights, you can now be fined up to $250,000 per occurrence for referring to someone as an "illegal alien", even though the person to whom you are referring is a non-citizen of the US and is in the country in violation of the law? Those are the "words of art" used in our federal immigration laws, by numerous courts in the land, and should be protected by the First Amendment. There is little doubt that this plan will be struck down by the courts, if it has not been already when this book is published. In a commentary written by Hans von Spakovsky of the Election Law Reform Initiative and Patrick Featherston of the Young Leaders Program of The Heritage Foundation, they referred to this idiocy as the equivalent to the propaganda, surveillance, and censorship of Big Brother in Orwell's "*1984*" having arrived in the Big Apple. That is probably being way too kind. This all goes far beyond poor judgment and enters the realm of lunacy or insanity, with those of us who are onlookers as the victims of such senseless drivel.

We continue to lose good and bad opportunities because of the "PC Movement". Some of them recently have been the Cold Play World Tour (because of "climate change"?), the Victoria Secret Style Show with Angels (prior to the entire retailer folding), and "pee wee' as the category of hockey teams with young kids in Canada. "C'est la vie" say the OKers.

In mid-June of 2020, the #Liberal "cancel culture" became the latest glaring example of PC run amok following the horrific George Floyd death in Minneapolis, starting with the preposterous proposals in many major and dangerous US cities to "de-fund" the police. The question that cannot be answered by these dreamers is "who will answer the 911 calls when they are made?" One can hear the crickets loud and clear. And then there are the solid business leaders being fired for saying things such as "all lives matter [instead of 'Black Lives Matter']" or "there are many good police officers out there"?! Many of those suffering from Trump Affective Disorder are in desperate need of mental health intervention—and hopefully they will get it soon. No one would deny that some serious challenges in America need to be addressed and rectified, but let's accomplish that with a unified effort to identify the problems and implement logical solutions to put teeth into "liberty and justice for ALL".

CHAPTER 15

EVERYONE IS CAPABLE OF LOVING
AND NEEDS TO BE LOVED

I ran across this anonymous quote which fits this topic very well: "Find someone who is proud to have you, scared to lose you, fights for you, appreciates you, respects you, cares for you, and loves you unconditionally." If you have one or more of these persons in your life, do all that you can to keep them there. If you do not have anyone like this, you are not alone. And it probably is not because you don't deserve it. My suggestion is to be this individual for a special person in your life, and chances are that you will become this person to them.

There are a couple of racial groups in America between which there is a fairly amazing animosity, somewhat of a "turf war". The African-Americans as the largest minority voting block in the US have been riding high, but that is about to come to an end. It is predicted that in 2020, the percentage of Hispanic-American voters among minorities will take over the lead. Meanwhile, the percentage of whites as a block that year will decline by 10% from 2016 (76% to 66%). Now that is pretty astounding. The composition of America is changing rapidly.

One of those questions raised by our greatest-generation parents when our conduct would not meet their expectations was: "What are we going to do with you?" Good point as they considered the appropriate discipline we would face for our mistake(s). When we were in grade school and junior high (middle school), minor to moderate corporal punishment was acceptable in those days. Once we were older (in our teen years), our penalties were generally "take-aways"—a reduction in our privileges and activities. It seemed that these reactions to our malfeasance were generally effective, especially toward the process of preventing similar future failures in judgment. The saying "spare the rod, spoil the child" may have been more accurate for our parents as they were growing up than it was for us. They had learned growing up that any physical discipline used needed to be appropriate and measured.

Baby boomers have had lessons in life about keeping things in a proper perspective. We learned how to separate the important aspects of life from those which were less critical and those which are immaterial. I remember growing up with a saying or quote which I have tracked down to "author unknown": "The happiest people don't have everything, but they make the best of everything." This sometimes preceded or followed the common proverb still used today: "When you are given lemons [bad or difficult things in life], make lemonade [a positive outcome]!" This same issue was addressed by German philosopher Friedrich Wilhelm Nietzsche who said: "That which does not kill us, makes us stronger." I was reminded of that many times while growing up. Our current climate of hatred and demonology on one side and happiness and joy on the other seems to indicate that we can no longer control our emotions when it comes to political outcomes over which we have little or no control. When I had something bothering me as a child growing up, my mother would say "get over it" or "get on with your life!" That nudging and prodding paid off over time, helping me to control my emotions and actions, and by letting love guide the way ahead.

The training I received in the Episcopal Church emphasized the power of being present in the lives of those in need. This was set forth beautifully in a writing by modern-day counselor Sheri Eckert, entitled "That One": "Be that one. That one who forgives when deep offense has been committed. That one who loves when no one else does. That one who gives kindness to those who are mean. Be that one who looks past the insult, instead seeing the pain that motivated it. That one who shines light upon those who sit in utter darkness. Because the impact of being that one runs far and wide. It brings healing to the wounded, joy to the sad, and hope to those in despair. Be that one." This concept cannot be said much better. It represents the antithesis of "low road". People who believe in these positive actions are around us today at this time of "inhumanity on steroids". It seems that the media today is simply not interested in accentuating the good in the world but instead dwells ad nauseum with the tenants of the swamp in which they are wallowing around. You are out there. Please continue to do what is right, fighting the good fight, even though those around you are often not aware of the results of your actions. Your service to others will eventually be judged and rewarded by a compassionate God who is watching and patiently waiting.

Many of us in our recent/later years have made a point to be with those members of our friends and family who want to be with us, and to ignore those who do not, while we help others in pain along this road of life. This is a calling to be positive about who we are, what we can do, and then are accomplishing to make this a better place in our own way. Such activities ring a distinct bell, the idea of serving rather than being served. Most of you know that of which I am speaking. We learned this at a very young age and will carry it with us to our grave.

The generosity of Americans is virtually without boundaries, but should it be? It is often shocking how much and how often our citizens are forking over their cash for people they never even knew. For fellow Christians out there, Jesus taught us to give to all others in need. Few of us have that ability and inclination. Why is it that there seems to be a "GoFundMe" page set up for virtually everyone who dies these days? One of the reasons appears to be that many out there do not prepare financially for death and thus cannot afford to die. It is a pretty expensive experience that the decedent doesn't even have a chance to enjoy—at least as far as we know. The fund-raising efforts that seem particularly surprising are when a goal of something like $3,500 is set and $35,000 is raised. This is normally attributable to the story behind the passing seeming especially sad or unfortunate, or when the deceased person was somehow well known. When the boomers were being raised, the financial responsibility for a person's demise was normally the responsibility of the family and was often planned for with insurance or savings. When there were shortages, it could be the effort by a church or group of family friends who would step in—rarely total strangers. Maybe this modern practice is an extension of the "love your neighbor" rule we were taught from a long time ago. Unfortunately, there are so many scam artists out there in our present world that the pages can be started by those who never intend to help anyone other than themselves. Another "one bad apple" situation. My parents always urged fact-finding in advance of giving and trying to assure that the donations would go to the intended recipient(s) and with little or no administrative expenses to reduce the positive impact. Good thinking.

Every once in a while, there are "civil" and positive suggestions for us which arise from former colleagues of our national or local leaders. This was the case recently from Former Trump Deputy National Security Advisor KT McFarland as she emerged from a hiatus, apparently in time to push a book she had coming out. "Sorry Mr. President: don't listen to Trump, look at what he does". That is just what many people have been saying. There is apparent consensus that President Trump is not the best speaker in the world (not smooth like Obama), but he has appeared to be getting a lot of good things done, despite the constant bombardment from the Left of garbage and grenades which started even before the 2016 election.

"Queer" (regrettably used in the past by some boomers in referring to "gays") is transitioning back from forbidden to accepted by the LGBTQ+ community, especially when used by millennials and Gen-Z'ers. Less "restrictive"? Another mystery of the mind. #LGBTQ+

On and after October 8, 2019, Ellen DeGeneres was the recipient of hateful mostly-Hollywood blowback from her statement that people with different politics "can be friends" in describing her friendship with former President George W. Bush and his wife Laura who were pictured together in a suite at a football game. She expressed the importance of "kindness" when dealing with good people of all persuasions. Salutes out to those of her fellow celebrities in LaLa Land who showed support for Ellen and her expansive mind and eloquence when it comes to being a truly nice person.

A warning to women and men who are in a relationship and consider encouraging their significant other to commit suicide/ telling them that the world would be a better place without them—the authorities and courts will come after you if that person follows through with a suicide. A woman in Massachusetts has been charged with manslaughter and failure to act in the successful suicide of her boyfriend after he plunged to his death from a parking garage on the day he was to graduate from Boston College. The allegation is that the 47,000 text messages she sent to him during the two months prior to his death constituted undue control over the boyfriend, and psychologically drove him to take his own life—with her present.

Rest in peace, Kobe & Gianna Bryant. Nobody on this planet is perfect, but Kobe was about as close as one could become on the basketball floor. Both were far too young (on January 26, 2020) and will be missed. May God be with their family and close friends left behind. #KobeBryant

Tweet on 3-21-20: Be more aware of your family, friends and neighbors over the coming weeks while practicing separation, as the mental health care system will be totally overwhelmed by the isolation, job losses, and resulting feelings of desperation. We cannot let suicides take more than the #CoronavirusPandemic (as I have predicted would be the case in the US).

CHAPTER 16

LOSING OUR RELIGION
AND PROMOTING PERSECUTION OF BELIEVERS

The "war on religion" continues to rage with the April 21, 2019 (Easter Sunday) bombings of three churches and three hotels in Sri Lanka, killing at least 250 people and injuring over 300 more. Islamic radicals were suspected from the beginning, and sure enough ISIS eventually claimed responsibility. Some of the detractors from what I write remind me that killings in the name of God are not new and indeed have been going on for many thousands of years. In my mind, that does not provide justification for the murder of innocent others simply because they worship a different God, or the same God in a different way. In a bastion of religion located in the Northern Plains of the US, it is highly unlikely that persons of any faith will take up arms against any other faith community, other than those rare instances in which mental illness drives a person to commit acts which are not taught nor condoned by their beliefs. Are we moving toward armed camps at our places of worship around the world? There is no question that such a situation has emerged of late in many places around the globe. Such a waste whenever it happens.

With every serious tragedy in America today, we hear from those on the Left: "don't bother the victims and families who are affected with your unwanted 'thoughts and prayers', but rather do something to prevent such an occurrence from happening again." These speakers are obviously not people of true faith to say such a thing, because those of us who are "believers" have seen the miraculous and healing power of communal prayer. My parents and our church always emphasized the importance of daily and other regular prayer to our God. And do such prayers infringe on the rights and lives of the naysayers? Obviously not. These detractors are simply bored with the constant bombardment of the fact that there could indeed be a "higher being" in this universe who listens to the prayers and supplications of others. What is there to lose by asking an almighty spirit for their positive intervention in the lives of others who are in pain? This is another example of an old saying and one we continue to use today: "out of sight, out of mind". I and my religious ilk will continue to pray for those we deem to be in need of heavenly grace as well as for those who deem such activities as "humbug".

The latest attack on religion in America as of this writing was the shooting at the Chabad of Poway Synagogue in California on April 27, 2019. The attack was perpetrated on the final day of the Jewish Passover holiday which fell on a Shabbat. One woman (60-year old and 33-year synagogue member Lori Gilbert Kaye) was killed and three other people were injured, including Rabbi Goldstein, who visited the White House on the National Day of Prayer (May 2, 2019). The other two people injured were Israeli Nationals. The shooter was "strangely" a nursing student at Cal State — San Marcos. Democratic California Representative Eric Swalwell, in response to President Trump's appropriate response to the pathetic shooting, said "spare us your thoughts and prayers!" This was totally unprecedented and inexcusable, especially for a member of Congress. This is not unusual for Swalwell, a 2020 candidate for the Democratic nomination for President (until he wisely withdrew). He is obviously not a Christian nor a believer in God. Who do you think you are, Mr. Swalwell?! The pathetic Left criticizes those who are religious and send their "thoughts and prayers" to those who are in pain or who have suffered loss. What is your answer in response to victims of crime, violence, sickness, and death? Do you have compassion enough to be "sorry"? Some Liberals who are not religious are accused of replacing faith with passion for their causes—climate change, abortion, or open borders (or all of the above).

Democratic Representative from Michigan, Rashita Tlaib, once again spills her anti-Semitic guts: "The Holocaust calms my soul—a calming feeling". Pardon me for being such a "devil's advocate" in taking a different slant on this thought, but I can honestly say that, for me anyway, there is no comfort in contemplating the extermination of six million Jews and the murder of another 11 million innocent people at the hands of the German Nazis. And the response to her statements by the Leftist leaders of her party and the Liberal media? You are correct if you guessed "crickets chirping".

Ronald Reagan had the ability in many instances to use his words to place things in proper perspective. One of the favorite quotes from him was this one: "Live simply, love generously, care deeply, speak kindly, leave the rest to God." Wouldn't this be an even better country if more of us were taught this sentiment and lived by it in our daily lives?

In our local paper on June 22, 2019 there is a "Letter to the Editor" from one of the regular opinion page contributors who happens to be a Muslim and a good person. He says: "respect people of all religions." Many of us were taught about this in a different way, such as: "respect those people who deserve your respect no matter what is their faith or lack of faith." Big difference.

There is a Biblical reference that ties into US nuclear negotiations with Iran. Proverbs 29:9 has been interpreted to mean that "a wise man who argues with a fool will never be satisfied." I leave that to you to match the parties with the titles.

A Baptist church in Birmingham, AL displays a sign out front: "A black vote for Trump is insane, a white vote for Trump is 'racism'". This proves it is possible to be Christian and dead wrong at the same time. And so much for churches as being non-political.

A judge in the United Kingdom has ruled that the firing of a doctor for refusing to use female pronouns for a male patient was justified. The court ruled that the reliance of the physician on *The Bible* to oppose alternative sexual lifestyles is "incompatible with human dignity" as well as in conflict with the fundamental rights of transgenders. Is there anything today for which you can rely on your religious beliefs to justify your behavioral choices? In many situations this does not appear to be the case any longer.

China has detained over one million Muslims in the western part of that country in "retraining" facilities. There has always been a fear of Islam by Chinese leaders. #ChinaHumanRights

On December 11, 2019, the POTUS issues an Executive Order to eradicate anti-Semitism at our US colleges. The rise of anti-Semitism throughout America and including our college campuses is shocking and unacceptable. We cannot let this continue. The Order would permit the withholding of certain federal aid to colleges which are determined to be permitting anti-Jewish and anti-Israel rhetoric and activities on campus. I have some First Amendment concerns with the Order, but it seems to be a good start toward addressing this hateful and dangerous trend among our young people and their college instructors and administrators.

The recent increases in anti-Semitism in the country appear to be centered and most apparent on the East Coast, including Pennsylvania, New Jersey, and especially New York state and NYC. Late in 2019 there have been numerous attacks on Jews in those areas, resulting in significant injuries and deaths. Everyone seems to be asking "why now" and "why to such a population of gentle people"? Recently in a response to a FB post that "Anti-Semitism is Un-Christian", I retorted that my position goes beyond that thought. My post was speculation that "the God of us all and Jesus for Christians would believe that it is impossible for a 'true Christian' to be an anti-Semite". It is not compatible to hate anyone (let alone an entire religious people) when we are told by our faith to love even those who are our enemies—no matter how they became such. One of the latest acts of religious violence was a shooting by two African Americans who killed a police officer earlier and then three others before being killed themselves after they attacked a kosher Jewish market on December 10, 2019 in Jersey City, New Jersey. The shooters were later linked to an anti-Semite and anti-police group known as the Black Hebrew Israelites.

Keep your eyes open and focused on the Miftaah Institute headquartered in Warren, MI. Many of us first learned about this entity as the unusual sponsors of a Congressional trip to Israel including "Squad" members Omar and Tlaib, who were both denied visas to enter Israel. Maybe the country is a little too thick skinned about blocking people from entering the country simply because they hate Israel and openly support groups that want to destroy it.

The Reverend Doctor Martin Luther King, Jr. had "a dream" which remains unfulfilled. As we commemorate and celebrate Martin Luther King Day 2020 in America on January 20, 2020, may the passion and power of his spirit empower us all to continue his work over the coming year for religious freedom, justice, and equality. And one of his quotes hit me hard today, applying here as well as in several other chapters of this book: "We must learn to live together as brothers or perish together as fools." For those of us who are Christians, many of us were taught from a very young age that we are all brothers and sisters who have evolved from a common source. Thank you, Dr. King, for showing us how to bring about change by firm but non-violent means. #MLKDay

We are hearing more and more every day about eschatology, the branch of theology dealing with "end of life", the "judgment", and any "after life". This is a topic that is covered very well in many books and should take up that much space for a thorough study. Much of it ties in with Christian "hope". I suggest *Things to Come* by J. Dwight Pentecost (great name for a writer about Christianity).

Holocaust Remembrance Day on 1-27-20 and the 75th anniversary of the liberation of the Auschwitz Camp. We will never forget these heinous Hitler/Germany atrocities which remain unmatched in the history of the planet. Remembering all who died or survived. #Auschwitz #Holocaust

One of my favorite Bible verses (from The Gospel According to Matthew), part of the liturgy on this Fifth Sunday After the Epiphany: "…let your light shine before others, so that they may see your good works and give glory to your Father in heaven." #Christianity

An actual answer on last night's (2-11-20) "Game of Games" with Ellen Degeneres: What do you call animals which eat only plants? Answer given: Presbyterians. Some considerable laughter followed. At least she did not say "Episcopalians"! #humor

A current survey/study from Pugh Research documents a drop in the number of Christians in the US from 78% to 65% during the ten years from 2009 to 2019. The decrease in the numbers for Democrats was even more precipitous from 72% to 55%. This obviously has had a major role in the decline in civility in America during that same period. The rates for "unaffiliated Christians" increased over those years from 17% to 26%, which is very understandable as younger Christians in many cases prefer to not connect with a single church congregation/facility in favor of having flexibility to "play the field" without making a financial commitment to a single place. It is no longer "hip to be square".

@realDonaldTrump is a President who stands up for freedom of religion in America, ordering states on May 22, 2020, to make sure places of worship are being permitted to re-open safely during the pandemic. #Liberals complain that POTUS cannot do that. Of course they do. #ReligiousFreedom

Some personal preaching here about the power of two words that are the basis and foundation for my religious beliefs and faith — "grateful" and "thanksgiving". I was recently asked by a FB friend (as were his other friends): "which do you prefer — going to sleep or awaking in the morning?" I had no hesitation with my answer. Although I sure love to sleep, it is the morning and awaking for another day on this earth that is the highlight. I immediately thank the Lord for providing me with another day among those whom I love. I express my gratitude for being able to be a positive light to shine my faith among all the people I will encounter for the day. Shine your light.

What better way to complete this chapter than with a practicing and proud Christian to share positive thoughts about life, not from *The Bible* but instead from ManilaPapers.com: "Hate no one, no matter how much they've wronged you. Live humbly, no matter how wealthy you become. Think positively, no matter how hard life is. Give much, even though you've been given little. Forgive all, especially yourself. And never stop praying for the best for everyone!" Amen, Brothers and Sisters.

CHAPTER 17

THE DEATH OF TRUE JOURNALISM

Our local newspaper in Fargo came up with a headline as we were awaiting the release of the Mueller Report: "Speculation grows over Mueller Report". DUH. This represents more of the factors which create "fake news". The Left-wing feeding frenzy which we call the current mainstream media is eager for even a hint of information that can cast negative light on the Trump administration and/or Republican party. We have seen this lead to fabrications of events or statements by political pundits disguised as news reporters, either directly or through the wording of articles which implies actual or probable issues adverse to their opponents on the Right. This is now the age of "speculation" becoming "fact". Not only is Liberal America guessing about what will be in the Mueller Report, they are already actively preparing in the Leftist House of Representatives to bring impeachment proceedings against the POTUS, hoping that the Report will somehow support their efforts. Such a frivolous waste of time and energy all in the name of hatred. Most of the OK Boomers were instructed that there was no room for "hate" in life, especially disguised to represent valid disagreement. These are desperate times for the Left, leading them to embrace hatred as a focal point in their platform.

Also in that newspaper, which provides me virtually every day with a source of smiling or confusion (or both), there was an article about an interim replacement for the position of President of the University of North Dakota. Former Republican US Representative from Minnesota, Mark Kennedy, had served in that position for three years and was accepting the Presidency of the University of Colorado. The writer opined that the "obvious" choice to replace President Kennedy was former Democratic US Senator from North Dakota, Heidi Heitkamp?! That constituted the best joke of the year that I had seen or heard anywhere, despite the fact that the liberal faculty at the University would strongly embrace such a suggestion. Recommendations in North Dakota to replace a Conservative Republican with a moderately liberal Democrat generally do not gain much traction. Instead, they replaced Kennedy with the very capable head of the University's Medical School. Prudent. After all, we are talking about "higher education" rather than "lower education".

You cannot help but watch and listen to political stories in the media and see or hear mistakes in language and content. It seems that even the best talents in the industry make significant errors. The "bastion" of Conservative news, Fox News, is not immune from such "flubs". I witnessed Fox anchor Bret Baier make such a blunder as the redacted Mueller Report was released to America by Attorney General William Barr. "There's no evidence that no American colluded with the Russians in the 2016 elections." Ouch—zapped by the proverbial "double negative"! The second "no" should have been, for instance, "any". In the Report, there was no evidence of collusion by the Trump campaign, and no "corrupt intent" to obstruct justice. But the mistakes can confuse and mislead.

A "miracle" in the media has occurred on April 24, 2019. Nine and one-half weeks after President Trump declares a national emergency at the US-Mexico border, "commentator" (according to Google) Thomas Friedman of the *New York Times* becomes the paper's first member of the news staff to agree that such a serious situation exists. I must admit that I never saw that coming. And I plead guilty to my own claim that the misuse of the word and meaning of "miracle" is rampant, an affront to all those performed by Jesus of Nazareth and the saints of the Roman Catholic Church.

More local newspaper "incest", as two lazy reporters write about area rock concerts that they once covered elsewhere and for the paper. Lazy AND boring. They just do not get it. This world does not rotate around you. I am thinking that our predominant paper needs to be renamed the "Hick City Journal" to better describe its' content.

George Orwell, author of the famous predictor of the future in "*1984*", was once quoted as saying: "The people will believe what the media tells them to believe." How frightening is that commentary, particularly in the face of *The New York Times*, *The Washington Post*, CNN, MSNBC, and the rest of the Left-wing media. That is even scarier than the actual year of 1984 which turned out to be quite tame and not at all cataclysmic.

American journalist and educator, Thomas Byrne Edsall, who is 78 years old as of this writing, once wrote: "The Media is Liberal. We are all on the Left." It can be refreshing to hear from intelligent persons who will tell things like they are rather than as they want them to be or want others to believe. Granted, however, that there are Conservative writers and other commentators who do not fit this mold. Edsall is obviously referring to what we sometimes call the "mainstream media", rather than all the news generators out there.

There were some enlightening moments recently in late-May of 2019 that would suggest real journalism is not totally dead yet. The ultra-Liberal *New York Times* "blasts" the Leftists in control of virtually every major city in the US for destroying the inner cities over the past many decades. The newspaper was correct, but was behind in its' news gathering as the Trump administration had been working over the previous six months with Secretary Ben Carson and the Department of Housing and Urban Development, for the new Opportunity and Revitalization Council to spearhead unprecedented public-private initiatives to "save" the inner cities as had been promised but not delivered by the Democrats in charge for over 50 years. This could be the most significant and successful program in history to turn our big cities in America around—Finally! And it will be joined by Trump's infrastructure funding plan to make these cities more livable. Awesome. Big-city Liberals in control of those places have claimed for decades that they want to "lift up" the lives of inner-city residents and the homeless populations in their midst but have been a clear AWOL. And those of us on the Right are still not tired of "winning" (for America).

Periodically, my spouse and I are forced to watch one of the "Big 3" networks for nightly news, especially on the weekends. We recently turned over to NBC News and saw an excellent story on 100 years of the National Grand Canyon Park. Then all turned south when substitute-anchor Kate Snow blew lunch in chunks in "Her Take" with the line "and I will take my family there this summer". Well aren't you special. Believe it or not, this world is not about you and does not revolve around you. Use your brain to think. Do you realize that there are people watching who can never even dream of going to the Grand Canyon, or even to their neighboring state? Are you trying to express your superiority which allows you to do this? Many of us are simply interested in the "news", as opposed to what is happening in the life of the news reporter. How about saying instead: "Hopefully someday you will have a chance to visit such a magical place if you haven't already." Words are very powerful, and potentially destructive in the wrong hands.

So much of network advertising these days is "incestuous"—providing coverage for the shows and celebrities who are featured in the programming of that network. Fox News joins this practice by reminding us on May 28 that the FIFA Women's World Cup will air on Fox beginning in 10 days. NBC used to be the biggest player in these efforts, beginning coverage of the Olympic Games to be televised by them more than a year before the opening ceremonies. I guess that you can't blame the networks for doing this as the competition for viewership is so much greater today than it was in the 50s when there were three stations from which to choose as opposed to the hundreds of choices today. Why pay someone else for publicity when you can DIY? We see this all the time in our local market as the hometown newspaper also owns the ABC affiliate. They are constantly "tooting their own horn" as we learned to call it in the old days. And then there is special coverage for those who are the major advertisers. They must know that all of these occurrences are very visible and obvious.

Virtually all news programs today are staged. When the boomers were growing up, there were so many times when the newscasters were "flying by the seat of their pants" as news was breaking, and without social media to propel it. It was fun recently to see Fox News scrambling after being "blindsided" with a report that Robert Mueller would make an impromptu appearance in front of the media in just 90 minutes—so little time to speculate about what he would say! It was very entertaining!

"Laziness" in local news exposes itself quite often in one way or another. A recent example occurred in our area when the "Fallen Soldiers" motorcycle group traveled during the summer of 2019 through the region. Among their stops were those in Bismarck and Fargo, approximately 200 miles apart. A Fargo television station was invited to cover the extremely emotional and somber stop here in their backyard, but instead opted to skip that opportunity and run footage from a sister station in Bismarck—just not the same. Others from the local press corps did a wonderful job with their features. In life "you win some and you lose some". That one was a definite loss.

Is there anything that the "showboating" media won't do to get attention for their stories? I am thinking more and more that they will do and say whatever it takes to get their adoring viewers to notice them and their story du jour. "Ag is king" in my corner of the hemisphere. Some "newbies"/"cub reporters" will go so far as to report from the fields of crops, even as spray planes are applying their chemicals on the immature produce. Advice from an experienced observer: do not breathe the air for a while after the plane has drenched you, and shower/change your clothes as soon as possible. I don't believe that any "scoop" is worth getting sick from the hazards, but then again I am not experienced in that industry. Follow up: I describe in both books some of the media gimmicks thought to make them look tough in the trenches. As we are dealing with the COVID-19 pandemic in the late-winter and spring of 2020, the macho thing is for these media hacks to wear a fancy facial mask while making their report from the "middle of nowhere"! I get the idea of a mask if they are close to some other people in addition to their crew, but not when there is no one except the camera operator within a mile of them. It doesn't make you look cool, but rather foolish as your viewers are astonished by your lack of common sense.

But then there is that article from which you figure that anything is worth the damage or injury to bring on the "news". A great example is the article which appeared in our local newspaper on June 4, 2019: the "business" feature about four female employees of retirement age who will stay on the job? Wow. Whatever it takes to bring home that bacon is certainly justifiable. What could be news for a few is also a boring waste of space for the masses.

In early June 2019, NBC Nightly News hosts the program from the American graveyard at Normandy—what a disgrace, and disrespect for that sacred ground.

We find ourselves on Monday, August 5, 2019, following the weekend shootings at El Paso, TX and Dayton, OH. NBC and their commentator Lester Holt spend the first 18 minutes of the "Nightly News" criticizing President Trump and the white supremacist El Paso shooter and ZERO minutes on the Dayton shooter who is a devout socialist and Liz Warren supporter. I expected nothing less. Holt has officially graduated and received his diploma as a media prostitute. I want to drop the "W" bomb in describing the NBC anchor, but will once again aim higher. Let's try this again and give you another chance to "come clean" the next day, Leester. Again, NBC blocks the truth about the Dayton, OH shooter—a socialist, and supporter of Warren, Sanders and Antifa. Are you kidding us? How dare you keep this from the American people? But it does not stop there. Those on the Left jump at the opportunity presented by their media leaders in blaming the POTUS and his followers in Texas for the mass shooting deaths in El Paso. And out on the frontlines is Democratic US Congressman Joaquin Castro from San Antonio who is responsible for the release to the media of the names and addresses of Texas Trump supporters. Maybe a few days in jail would have taught Rep. Castro about the dangers of inciting violence.

The New York Times comes under criticism and scrutiny following the leaking of an internal memo outlining the need for the newspaper to shift its primary focus from Russia/Trump to "racist" Trump, thus promoting class warfare in the country. Isn't *The Times* supposed to be a respected media outlet and not an arm of the Democratic Party in America? It is long overdue that we call a spade a spade and no longer provide the radical Liberal media with camouflage to hide their true intentions from the consuming public. I long ago decided to stop reading articles written by that publication, and this revelation will not soon lead to a reversal of that position.

The ultimate "journalistic incest" in our local newspaper on September 12, 2019: the frontpage lead article is entitled "Light, Camera, Fargo", about a film crew setting up locally to produce a movie here. There was not much of a problem there. Then I see a photograph of the screenwriters in front of one of the filming sites—the building which houses the newspaper? Couldn't they have used one of the other filming venues? Yes, and that would have made much more sense. Dumb. And that does not end the intoxication with "Tankhouse". It continues for a week of swill. It would be wonderful if they would replace their self-serving ego trips with time spent correcting typos and mistakes in the paper. And they never met a newspaper insert they did not like, as they are usually the company which does the printing—and best friends of the newsprint recyclers.

As the Democrats in the US House are moving toward an investigation of Trump "hush money" payments, we have a real calamity on our hands on the Eastern seaboard of the US. Reminiscent of required junior high reading by the boomers of Charles Dickens' classic novel "Great Expectations", those words and thoughts take on new meaning in early-September of 2019 as Hurricane Dorian veers east from the Atlantic coast of Florida abruptly leaving dozens of eager beaver "cub" reporters high and dry, dashing their hopes and dreams of being taped by their network in torrential rains and being buffeted by hurricane-strength winds, thus becoming media heroes and icons. It will never be too soon for this meteorological "showboating" to come to an end. It has been absurd for decades that these commentators preach about the advice of local authorities to stay inside as they are being pummeled outside in those very dangerous conditions. Put an end to this before someone is seriously injured or killed based on the media desire to prove their toughness. We believe you.

This week (October 6, 2019) I came close to cancelling my local newspaper subscription and delivery after an article about teen Climate Change "experts" Thunberg and Iron Eyes at a Standing Rock Rez presentation, one about a local reenactment of the "*BIG*" piano dance scene, and a pork cutlets/"National Pork Month" recipe feature on Yom Kippur (the holiest day of the Jewish year). And then there is the local opinion page contributor who calls the present days as "the darkest times under the Trump challenge" and that "out of darkness comes 'hope'". Give me a break! I consider that an attempt to attract mutineers on the Right to come to the Left and pandering to any "snowflakes" out there. Very quickly I changed my mind as I realized that the typo-riddled newspaper is an irreplaceable source of material for my books on a daily basis. What would I do without it? This is the same formerly Conservative newspaper that recently replaced its' national news contract from *USA Today* to *The New York Times* and *Washington Post*?! What does that say about its' current leaning? It is time for our local newspaper to dump its' arrangement with the *Times* and *Post* to provide their "urban east coast" idea of "news", as the product from those tabloids does not reflect the morality and political makeup of our region. This was a huge mistake in judgment by the newspaper. But I will attempt to no longer "rant and rave" in these writings about a newspaper in Fargo (please hold me to this!) that you do not care about. I will use the material they provide but will not identify the source unless somehow required to do so. (Update: I later retract the promise as this source of material for me heads off the rails. Alas I tried but failed miserably). My parting shot—the paper used to have maybe a couple of articles per month regarding Native Americans, and these days there are probably at least three in each edition (Update: then two as the paper shrunk to virtually nothing amid COVID-19). You do the math (90 v. 2). Madly obsessed. Another Update: news from North Dakota State University in Fargo in April of 2020 that they will draft a resolution acknowledging that the college occupies former "Indigenous Lands"? No, the campus rests on the former lake bottom of Lake Agassiz, while the Indigenous Lands in question were in Wisconsin. The whole idea for this resolution reeks of Liberal pandering, PC culture, and "snowflakeitis" (a new word I made up).

The New York Times occasionally gets something right. The baby boomers are old enough to remember when the newspaper had a positive reputation in the industry. They come out in late-October, 2019 to declare that Hillary is a "master troll" for the Dems based on her treatment of Tulsi Gabbard. Is it time for HRC to go back into her "troll hole"? This is pure evidence that even the solid base of the party is starting to become annoyed with the antics of this relic of a "bygone era" during which she and the "womanizer-in-chief" built what is now the modern Democratic Party. "All good things [in life] must come to an end". Then the paper (*NYT*) gets into trouble for the headline: "Trump Urges Unity vs. Racism"—it is too positive for the POTUS. Needless to say, the headline was changed to "Assailing Hate But Not Guns". That is how thin-skinned the Left is these days—not even a single headline about the President should be capable of a complimentary interpretation.

As of the end of October 2019, NBC News "usetowaser" Tom Brokaw states to fellow septuagenarian Andrea Mitchell that there is no "hard" evidence for a Trump impeachment—old but wise (and observant). He was a "rock star" in the news industry, while she has been a disappointment. It may have something to do with Brokaw having started his life and career from South Dakota (not "God's Country", but just south of it).

Hot off the press in early-November, 2019: Be wary of local news. People do not trust the national media anymore, so foreign countries are now focusing on undermining local news sources. Will we ever again be able to believe what we hear on the "news"? #DoNotTrustMedia And on top of that, failing newspapers are attempting to impose "subscriptions" on the users of their online editions and appear to be failing miserably in that effort. Our local paper is no exception. They try to have one of their writer wannabes cover it up, but that attempt falls flat on its face. #Gotcha #ToughToCompete

There is a serious question about the integrity of the "mainstream" media at that same time. It is and has been very exciting for many of the boomers over the years to see one of our newspapers or television news groups get that "scoop"—the first in the media to "break a story", an important one. One can only be skeptical if not miffed when news outlets uniformly block important information from the public. Such occurrences are a sharp contrast to their efforts via the Freedom of Information Act (FOIA) to uncover someone's or some group's improper or illegal conduct. We understand that there are certain topics which are not discussed nor revealed, such as the name of a minor or sexual assault victim or the story about a young child of a politician or celebrity. There must be some "privacy" in the world of fast-paced social media despite the sicknesses of the society. During the Trump Impeachment Inquisition, it becomes common knowledge (long after some of us took the position) that the identity of the Ukraine whistleblower is not protected, as opposed to their job security which is. So why did the #LiberalMedia conspire to protect the name reveal of the partisan complainer when they discovered who it was? Hmm. Could it be that the whistleblower was "one of them", a fellow comrade on a never-Trump mission? This is all unprecedented, which apparently occurs when a biased population reveals their communal insanity. #BackToRealNews Added to the mix is the fact that everyone who cares knows who the whistleblower is. Social media sees to that. There were those hints which made it obvious—part of the Obama administration, still working in the Trump administration, worked with VP Biden in Ukrainian matters, possible connection to the CIA. We have a "BINGO"! It was comical to see people dancing around the identity of the whistleblower once his name became public knowledge. The "fake news media" insisted that it was a crime to even print the name of this secondhand knowledge perp. What a dazzling charade. More throughout the book.

Bloomberg "News" announces in late-November of 2019 (immediately following the former NYC Mayor entering the fray) that it will not investigate "the boss" nor any other Democratic candidate during the Presidential run while continuing an "open season" on Trump. Not journalism, but pure and simple fascism or communism. Sickening. #FakeNews POTUS reciprocates by banning members of the Bloomberg news coverage team from attending Trump political rallies, at least as "legitimate press". I am personally not a fan of such prohibitions, but it is apparent that the President is attempting to make a point: "if you are not acting like your profession dictates, then you will not be treated to the courtesies of the position." Seems fair during the extreme times we are experiencing today.

Retweeting a Tweet which criticized MSNBC's Nicole Wallace and Andrea Mitchell for blaming Trump for the Ukrainian deaths in their battles with Russia while the US aid was withheld: We should not waste any of our precious time listening to these Leftist #FakeNews commentators—of course they would stand up for King Obama and Prince Biden.

Liberal #FakeNews *Washington Post* small staff party following the inquisition vote…a "Merry Impeachmas" party. It sounds like a great gathering for the anti-Christ media ilk.

Our local newspaper front-page lead article on January 8, 2020 in a quick reporting of a non-lethal Iranian military response to the assassination by the US of their top General—"IRAN STRIKES" from the pathetic *New York Times*. Fox News likened the military response to a moderate "fireworks display". Advice to that paper and others seeking to get the early "scoop": do not get caught with your pants down. The attack was obviously an intentional "whiff" by Iran which wanted to keep their oil industry and nuclear production capabilities. They smartly realized that a deadly and significant missile barrage against US troops and equipment could be met with a devastating counterattack that would debilitate Iran for decades (and possibly take out their terrorist regime).

@RushLimbaughEIB announces he has advanced-stage lung cancer. God bless you, friend of the American #Conservatives. Please get back to better health as soon as possible!

An area Tribe in the Northern Plains claims that they have been protecting their people and land. How is that working out with drug use and distribution, human trafficking, sexual assault, domestic violence, assaults, murders, and MMIP on and from the Rez? They want people to believe that the DAPL protests came to an end because of actions by the Trump administration. No. The protests ended abruptly and the participants from around the world were sent home when the Tribe realized that their casino had been trashed and their money machine probably irrevocably destroyed because of regional bridges burned by the Lakota Sioux Nation. It was readily apparent that the protests needed to be stopped when it was disclosed that the proposed route for the pipeline near the North edge of the Reservation was not over and through sacred burial grounds, but was instead planned underground on the same path as numerous other pipelines. All of this was disastrous strategic planning for the Tribe. Sad indeed.

A local "journalist" (actually an opinionated Liberal media commentator), who will go unnamed, is recognized in the slanted "Best of the Red River Valley" competition sponsored by his employer, as the "Best Newspaper Columnist" in the area. I haven't read one of his articles in years since he long ago burned the bridge of this Conservative a number of times with his Leftist mumbo jumbo. I did decide to read his "thank you" in the paper to all of his voters/fans, and I am so glad that I did. In the short single-column article he mentioned "I/me/my" 36 TIMES! I should not have been surprised, as it has always been about him and his ego the size of Pelican Lake (seven miles long and one-two miles wide). And he will not see this entry as he would not touch a book like this on a bet, probably for the fear that it would burn his hands or brain. God still loves you, Jim! Oops!

It is important to often express how important words are. This may be trivial to some but is very important to others. I read locally on 12-20-19: "Traynor appointed to federal judgeship." No! That happened months earlier. The headline should have stated: "Traynor confirmed [by the US Senate] for federal judgeship." Big difference that the author and editors missed by a mile.

Made a mistake today (3-20-20) watching NBC & media distorter #chucktodd following the Trump administration COVID-19 update. He belittled the plans to defer tax returns and expedite refunds…what good are they [the refunds] if there is nothing to buy? Like all products will disappear from the virus? Pathetic excuse for #RealNews! #Liberals

The local yokel tabloid newspaper today (3-22-20), while we are in the throes of an international pandemic, chooses a frontpage lead article about the installation of a photograph of Greta Thunberg on the outside back wall of a downtown tavern? AYKM? Who has commandeered that suicide train? #MSM

Ben Smith and the *NYT* again "blow lunch in chunks". They claim that @FoxNews is responsible for COVID-19 deaths because they deny there is a pandemic. NO! Fox calls the virus the latest #Liberals "hoax" for the way the Leftist Media is criticizing the Trump admin response! #COVIDIOTS! (made that one up too!)

#FakeNews CBS is milking the negative alarmist COVID-19 media with former @FoxNews commentator Catherine Herridge who has transitioned to the dark side of the virus "news". They are bent on inflaming the fears of the general public. Despicable. #Liberals

Sadly (called this one a couple of years ago), our local award-winning newspaper ("*The* [Dying] *Forum*") of Fargo-Moorhead has reached a milestone today (4-6-20) in my nearly 70 years — it is moving to a 5-day printed and delivered publication, while trying to force their remaining subscribers at least for the other two days to the online product. They blame the pandemic (No!). It was caused by deteriorating content over the past ten years, a shift from Conservative to Liberal (in the Heartland?), the abdication from print to electronic news, and their obsessions. It is tough to witness the destruction of a once excellent newspaper. Just five days later as we prepare for Easter, a local Left-wing "*The Forum*" writer wannabe tears down others in an op-ed. No surprise here. That is what the #Liberal "destroyers" do. How pathetic, and shame on you (you know who you are).

"*The* [Failing] *New York Times*" takes off on POTUS for a claimed slow response to the #CoronavirusPandemic, even though the administration closely followed the WHO in the pandemic declaration in March. No mention of the lack of preparedness for any pandemic by the Obama-Biden administration? Go figure. How embarrassing for them! What a poor excuse for a newspaper.

Newspapers can die because of "lazy journalism"—like our local "*Forum*". My daughter is mentioned in a COVID-related article on 4-12-20. "No"—she has not been laid off, she lives in ND (not MN), and they use her maiden name although she has been married for 8 years? Ouch! The batter is out after 3 whiffs. And it is time for them to lose the reporter photos they post and replace them with written copy. Fortunately, we know what these people used to look like. #DyingForum

@FoxNews reporters in NYC this AM (4-18-20) break the law by not wearing a facemask outside as people with facemasks walk by them! Dangerous media "showboaters"!

Decided to give Liberal media ABC/CBS/NBC another chance and watch the Global COVID Concert last night (4-18-20). That soon became an obvious mistake as it became a propaganda platform for the WHO which colluded with China to hide the #CoronavirusPandemic. #Liberals

#FakeNews #Liberal media reporting on COVID-19—everything is "grim". Time to leave behind the laziness and angst with words such as "serious", "alarming", or "significant".

#MorningJoe criticizing @realDonaldTrump while interviewing #AlSharpton. The credibility factor lost me at "morning". #FakeNews

On April 28, 2020, #FakeNews #WaPo claims @realDonaldTrump "allies" are inflating the #TaraReade assault charges against #JoeBiden2020? Meanwhile, it is "no-show Joe" in the #LameStreamMedia! #MeToo

Question from during the entire Trump administration(s): why is the #LameStreamMedia not concerned about finding the leakers on the #Left? Many of those offenses are felonies! Could it be because these individuals are the ones who provide most of the "news" to that media? Hmm.

I listed a number of our former true journalists in "*AGG*" and learn on July 2, 2020, that another one of the great ones had passed away. Rest in peace, Hugh Downs (who died at 99), formerly of *The Today Show* and *20/20*. He was always factual and believable.

Another "duh?" moment from Howie Kurtz of Fox News during "Media Buzz" on July 5, 2020: "far more Democrats than Republicans trust the media"? This confirms what all of us have known for decades!

CHAPTER 18

"TRUTH" CANNOT BE FAKED

In 1739, Voltaire opined in *Sept Discours en Vers sur L'Homme* to "Love truth, but pardon error." And, of course, error is never intentional but can be negligent. Later (1761) in *Letter to Cardinal de Bernis*, he wrote that "There are truths which are not for all men, nor for all times." So some truths are not for everyone, and can change over time. We are charged with being diligent in our determinations about truth as we journey through life. In our current difficult times, we are called upon to make these decisions (a lot of them) throughout a regular day. Many of those determinations are a matter of interpretation—what is being said, what does it mean, and is it backed up by facts. That is a lot of work!

One of the new mantras on the Right relating to the leadup to the 2016 national elections and the aftermath: "The Democrats lied and denied surrounding Hillary, her secret and illegal server, and her collusion with the Russians and others, and Obama spied on the opposition without transparency and truth." Those are my words in summary rather than the statements of others. What a sordid period in our history, a time of incredible corruption and deception. Will these appalling violations of law and trust ever be addressed by the legal system and courts, or will they continue to be ignored as simply aberrations of truth and justice? I am suspecting and expecting the latter. The deep state will never permit these instances of malfeasance to be judged by a system designed to do just that. Leader on the Left, Senator Chuck Schumer: "if you mess with the intelligencia, they have ways to get back at you." Very scary!

As I write here today, we are awaiting an appearance in two days by former Special Counsel Robert Mueller before a couple of US House Committees. The *NY Daily News* in an AOL article addressed how President Trump "trashed" Mueller today in a tweet (not true) and claimed the upcoming testimony would be "blockbuster" (speculation). Funny thing as this "fake news" all looked so real! But I did not get sucked into the trash. I do hear and read that the most expected question to be asked of Mueller is "when during the two year/$25 million investigation did you and your team decide that there was no collusion between the Trump campaign and the Russians." This is an appropriate inquiry as it reflects on whether the delay in disclosing such a determination had any impact on what could be considered a "stealing" of the 2018 mid-term elections. This could be somewhat analogous to the affect all of the lack of transparency by the Obama administration (the least transparent of virtually any Presidency in history) and intelligence community had on the 2012 Presidential election.

Breaking news from the scinewsreporter.com: a report from scientists indicates strong evidence that the earth is endangered by a new strain of fact-resistant humans! Pardon me, but that deduction did not require much investigation.

Former Vice-President and 2020 Presidential hopeful, Joe Biden, is noted as much for his "gaffs" as his words of wisdom. At least he admits (much to the protestation of some of his Liberal colleagues) that some Republicans are good people! During a recent presentation he said that "China is not competition for the US." Wha? He apparently has forgotten that they were once a fraction of the economy size of America, they are now approximately tied, and will soon pass us by [the situation prior to the #ChinaVirus]. They have stolen much of our weapons, communications, and artificial intelligence technology. China is also doing very well against the US in cyber-espionage. They have a population six times greater than we do. Not a threat, huh? Biden is obviously not a "bean counter".

The New York Times strikes again. A story in early June of 2019 reports that US/MX border arrests have surged to a "7-year high". No. It is a <u>15-year high</u>. "Fake news" can simply be a numeric mistake caused by laziness or intentional deception.

On August 7, 2019, MSNBC's Nicolle Wallace apologizes (somewhat) for a statement she made on the air the previous day, a major lie that Trump had called for the "extermination of Latinos". Conservatives are wondering how such a blatantly-biased idiot still has a job with that Left-winged network. At the same time, Twitter blocks Senate Majority Leader McConnell's feeds which showed a Leftist mob outside of his personal residence while spewing foul, hateful and dangerous language. This type of censorship by social and the Liberal media must stop as it is a threat to "free speech" in America.

A dubious record was set during the first two nights of the 2020 Democratic Presidential candidate debates — the largest number of "Pinocchio's" made from a single stage in history. For those of the participants who believe that Trump lies more than any other President ever, they are apparently getting ready for their term of office a little early. And the Dems are facing additional "Pinocchio moments" with their 2020 nomination seeker, Joe Biden. Are any of you concerned like I am with his memory? Our Vice President during the Obama regime, Biden seems to have forgotten all of the disastrous things that happened to him and the President from 2008 through 2016. And he goes further at the present time to call for "rebuilding America"? Curious, and really quite disturbing. As of the end of October, 2019, "Hidin'" Biden is a current "no show" for the Presidential nomination of his party. #HidinBiden Into November, he peeked out from behind a wall and was quoted as saying: "Trump has squandered the outstanding Obama economy"? Like the fact that about then a statistic was revealed that 5.2 more Americans were working at that time compared to the end of 2016. I finally figured it out: this Biden is not really the former VP but is instead a newly arrived alien from outer space. That must be right! #CrazyBiden Update: In five more months, Biden would become the presumptive Democratic candidate to take on President Trump.

Those on the Left in America took a major trip to the truth during the first half of 2019. In January, they were not buying Trump's declarations of a "crisis" at the MX/US border, and instead were declaring that any problems there had been the fault of and manufactured by his administration. Only 23% of the Liberals believed the crisis was real. Turn the calendar ahead to June. At that time, 70% of the Democrats/Liberals had become believers that there was, in fact, a true challenge at the border. How could it have taken that long to realize the truth. And what has the majority in the House done since that time to address the situation? Zero, zilch, nada — approximately. Shortly after this, Trump diverts $10 million in FEMA funds which were unavailable for preparedness or damages, in order to improve needed housing for single men on the Southern border. The "FakeNews media cried "foul" and claimed that the funds were being used instead to separate families (like Obama did?). More egg on the face of the Liberal press that they will never be able to successfully remove.

There was a saying that we boomers learned from the greatest ones: "the chickens have come home to roost". This was loosely translated as an "I told you so" when the truth presents itself after someone has done wrong and it comes back to haunt them. A current analogy occurs when the media presents "fake news" which later blows up in their collective faces. There was considerable speculation on the Left that Trump would use an executive order to return the "citizenship question" to the 2020 Census forms after being initially (and improperly) turned down by the courts. But instead of doing that, he simply ordered several federal departments and agencies to provide similar data and facts which would lead to the same information being accumulated. Brilliant, and very messy for those in the mainstream media. A definite "Gotcha!" moment.

The strategic leaks by the Impeachment Inquisitors (Democrats on the House Intel Committee) in October, 2019 are leading to more #fakenews at NBC News (as well as on other Liberal media sources) from Lester Holt, who has turned into a manure spreader. That becomes very messy and extremely stinky! Holt is a good guy working for an employer "on the ropes" from numerous scandals.

During a Congressional appearance, the Dems lambast Zuckerberg /FB for not "fact-checking" political ads. And who exactly would want FB to do that? I would not trust them to determine truth in grade-school essays. #FBTooBig #BreakThemUp

A "quote of the day" on October 29, 2019 was made by Sen. John Kennedy (R-LA): "If you held Nancy Pelosi upside down and shook her, Adam Schiff would fall out of her pocket." When it comes to this kind of stuff, you always watch Kennedy with the sense that he could come up with one of his "zingers". On this occasion he certainly did not let us down. We have realized for a very long time that these Californians were close, but I believe few of us realized it was this connected. Together they will make every attempt to assure that the results of the 2016 Presidential election are overturned by the US House, that

President Trump is totally humiliated and brought to his knees, impeached, and put in jail—at least for a start. If capital punishment was an option, they most certainly would be seeking it with their fellow Democrites. And all of this to vindicate Hillary, America's "shoulda, woulda, coulda" Presidential candidate. Oh, the humanity of it all!

In late-October, 2019, a poll claims that 51% of Americans support the impeachment and removal of President Trump. I am personally not buying that any more than the I did the 2016 Presidential election polling. #FlawedPolling

Biden says: "He and Obama brought a strong economy to Trump in 2017". Later that day, he was injured when he tripped over his nose.

Twitter moves to ban political ads and those addressing controversial topics such as abortion or immigration. Back when the boomers were growing up we used to call that "censorship". Will FB follow? Not good for reasonable political discourse in America.

Why are we still seeing articles in early-November of 2019 about Greta Thunberg? Hasn't she already received the 30 seconds of fame she deserves?

The Liz Warren "Medicare-for-All" plan will only cost $52 trillion and 2 million lost jobs over 10 years. Does this seem reasonable (?) albeit possibly underestimated? #MFASucks Advice to seniors: be wary of Democratic Socialists who want to raid the Medicare System and Fund which you created to protect you and your fellow retirees.

I will not spend much time in this book writing about "Climate Change" and "global warming", even though I believe we are currently in a cyclical change with a myriad of causes, including the worldwide levels of carbon emissions. Our local newspaper tries to subtly push their Climate Change agenda, but the frequency of their nudges makes it obvious what they are trying to do—change the position of many area doubters. This has become a very serious dilemma in North Dakota, as we are now one of the largest producers of fossil fuels and sit on some of the world's largest deposits of shale oil, natural gas, and coal. At times it has made our state the richest in the US, per capita. We also have reputedly the most fertile farmland in the world (eastern 40-mile wide edge of the state) and are the largest producers of about 20 different agricultural commodities (like malting barley, soybeans, honey, flax, rye, and sunflowers). This is all in the context that we have also been one of the most religious-conscious states in the country, learning from a very early age that we have a responsibility to be "good stewards" of the environment and what it produces. The US cannot solve the climate issues on our own, but must do our part to lead in developing and using new and innovative sources of renewable energy. Countries such as China, India, North Korea, and Russia must also share in the solutions. We all have a desire for our children and grandchildren to inherit as clean an earth as is practical and must work with the rest of the world to accomplish that goal. This is another of those instances in which the bad apples can spoil the barrel.

"Speaking truth to power" is a very convenient cop-out for the arrogant and elitist Liberal/"fake news" media. Many if not most of them would not know "truth" if it hit them in the face. #NotMyNews #FakeNews And that includes Joe Biden at the 2019 Iowa State Fair when he was quoted as saying: "We [Dems] choose 'truth' over 'fact'!" Keep talking, Joe, and you will never be President of the United States.

As I am writing, "Christ the King" Sunday arrives on November 25, 2019! It is the last Sunday after Pentecost and the Sunday before Advent in the Christian church. According to the *Gospel of John*, Jesus said to Pontius Pilate at the beginning of "the Passion": "You say that I am a king. For this I was born, and for this I came into the world, to testify to the truth. Everyone who belongs to the truth listens to my voice." This is certainly one of the most famous quotes ever written relating to "the truth". Amen. #ChristIsKing

The whole status of truthfulness can be tested by the release of certain facts and the omission of other information which could place the original correct information into proper context. Hopefully, I did not lose you with that concept. Let me explain my thoughts further. When the facts came out about the weekend shootings in El Paso, TX and Dayton, OH on August 3-4, 2019, might it have been important to mention also the significant bloodshed on those days in Chicago—7 dead, 50 injured, 219 murders so far in 2019? Of course it would have. But remember that the Liberal media is not interested in having to constantly report that the gun laws in the "windy city" are among the strictest of any major city in the US, and yet it remains one of the bloodiest. It may be a cliché, but "weapons do not kill, people do." "Sad but true" as we learned growing up in the Heartland. At this same time, potential gun violence reared its' ugly head in neighboring Moorhead, MN (across the Red River of the North from Fargo). A Chicago man was arrested there for possession of an armor-piercing weapon and bullets (a very serious offense) but was only required to post a $100 bond to be released. Wha? Another flaw in our justice system. I will admit I was wrong if and when the man charged shows up for his court appearance on the charges. Apparently the court deemed that he was not a flight risk to return to Chicago and just stay there?

An area "journalist" on October 20, 2019, has a piece published on the front page of a local newspaper which should have been on the "opinion" page. There is no place for supposedly serious writings which are attempted to be passed to the public as fact when instead they constitute fiction. That is the very essence of #FakeNews. Such shameful efforts are a disservice to all those people who strive for the truth and expect it in return.

In early-December of 2019, AOC claims the new Trump food stamp (SNAP) rules would have starved her family—hard to imagine these restrictions could have endangered the Congresswoman and her life with a struggling single mother when the change only affects able-bodied adults under 50 and without children. Can you say "grandstanding"? Or "showboating"? It is terrible these days how politicians on both sides of the aisle as well as Hollywood "celebrities" need to be so careful about what they are saying. It just does not seem to be fair.

Thankfully, the Inspector General report on FISA abuse will be unveiled today (December 9, 2019) and we can reduce the rampant speculation from all sides. Breaking News: The Inspector General Horowitz Report says the Obama/FBI spying on the 2016 Trump campaign was not "politically motivated"(?) and then follows with 17 mistakes in the implementation of the search warrants relating to the campaign. It is extremely difficult to believe that a program of spying by Party A against Party B using fake information from a report paid for by Party A was not formulated on the basis of partisanship. Heads need to roll. Only time will tell if this scandal rises to the level of the Nixon Watergate "dirty tricks". #FISAAbuse #ObamaSpying The Report sets forth that FBI Director Comey violated Bureau rules and procedures as well as his employment agreement, but as with Hillary and her private servers there will be no prosecution. These are dangerous double standards when basically law-abiding citizens of our country are charged and convicted of minor violations of the law while the most egregious abuses of power in history by our government leaders are treated with harsh words of admonishment. Two days later, IG Horowitz testifies before the Senate Judiciary Committee. It appears impossible from what he says to buy the "no political bias" finding based on all of the "Trump Haters" involved with the FBI surveillance of that campaign and with the use of the Steele Dossier by the FBI in FISA applications for months after they knew it was fake. #FakeNews The GOP basically claims that the Obama FBI tried to overthrow the Trump presidency in a bloodless coup (AZ Rep. Andy Biggs). It is extremely apparent that no one among our government elite will ever be prosecuted for even intentional actions, except possibly President Trump after leaving office (as no doubt someone with legal clout and TAD will take a shot at bringing him down for something—anything)! What a tangled and demented web they weave. (Loosely from Sir Walter Scott in 1808).

Separate "facts" from "fears" in response to the #Coronavirus Pandemic and follow the former. We will be fine. (3-18-20)

Our household attempts to be fair and balanced for our news with @FoxNews in the AM and NBC Nightly News in the PM. This will probably end soon as the Leftist #FakeNews on the latter becomes a clear and present danger to the truth. #LiberalMedia

Leave it to the #FakeNews #WaPo as we approach the end of April, 2020, to turn "difficult" into "devastating". Huge and obvious difference, morons! #Liberals

Evidence is uncovered on April 29, 2020 that General Flynn was entrapped to lie. The FBI had no intent to secure facts and justice for the American Hero! Heads must roll and a pardon issued. #FreeFlynnNOW Update on May 7, 2020: Blockbuster Development. No pardon will be needed as Gen. #mikeflynn (ret) will not be prosecuted by the DOJ for lying to the Feds after the FBI is accused of unlawfully entrapping him and his testimony. The world of the #Liberal elitist #Democrites continues to disintegrate in real time. #NotYourParentsFBI Update: the Liberal federal judge assigned to the case refuses to follow the decision of the government to end the Flynn prosecution in a virtually unprecedented move supported by legal analysts on the Left and decried by those on the Right. "Is nothing sacred anymore" as my generation was taught to expect. Update in late-June of 2020: A three-judge panel of federal judges has ruled that renegade Judge Sullivan MUST dismiss the Flynn prosecution. Will he now seek an en banc (full court) review of the dismissal decision? This is "nuts".

On July 5, 2020, ABC News complains that President Trump in holiday speeches called the far-Left protesters "fascists". "Truth" is the defense here.

CHAPTER 19

TAKING HUMAN LIFE RATHER THAN PROTECTING IT

We are bombarded these days with all the anti-2nd Amendment/anti-NRA advocates who yell and curse about the senseless mass firearms deaths around the US (except in big cities like Chicago and Philadelphia). There is a glaring double standard throughout these protestations. What is the position of this malcontent population about the 1,700+ killings each day in America of helpless unborn infants in our abortion mills? We fly the Stars and Stripes at half-staff to remember the victims of mass shootings. What do we do to honor the victims of abortion, living and dead? Some states have passed laws to require the burial or cremation of aborted fetal remains while other states permit disposal in the garbage. Legal abortion may be the "law of the land" in the US, but that doesn't mean that all of us need to support the "right to choose", at least after the first trimester, or when a heartbeat can be detected. And every American should be abhorrent and disgusted at those who go so far as to support infanticide—the termination of human life immediately following a live birth that some on the Left openly condone. This is one of those significant issues that could lead with others to armed civil insurrection in the future of our country.

As I write this entry, US Senator Kristin Gillibrand of New York is a former Democratic candidate for the 2020 Presidential election nomination. She used to be a moderate member of the party who has apparently "seen God" at the Left edge of the spectrum and thus bolted in that direction. Over the past five years she has flip-flopped on many issues—as one would expect during such a dramatic ideological sprint off the grid. I will leave you with one of her many insane policy positions. "Pro-life" is "racism". Is it now? That is not how many of us were taught to consider abortion as we were growing up. But this is how she views the killing of the unborn today, no doubt learning it in "her place of worship" (if she even has one). This does follow the Democratic and "Squad" bullet points that everything supported by Trump and Conservatives is "racist". And that goes for those who do not support Socialism and anti-Semitism. A recent poll as I write had 51% of Americans believing that the President is a racist (the Left) and 45% saying "no" (Right). This has become very predictable. Even an "alleged writer" in the local newspaper of my sleepy community has decided to label our POTUS as a "racist". He did have a valid excuse however as he (the writer) is an idiot. In other words, when in doubt drop the "R" bomb just as President Obama was known to do during his reign. Nancy Pelosi is the "poster child" for this Liberal tendency, declaring that Trump "wants to make America white again", and is a "racist". Shame on you! And just how long ago was America "white", Nancy—approximately? It is obvious that she is trying to prolong her lack of leadership in the fractured party of Democrites. The most blatant racism which has emerged in the middle of 2019 has come from the mouths of the intolerant Left at pro-impeachment rallies around the country. The truth can really suck when the discrimination you are trying to expose rears its ugly head in your backyard, like Pelosi's walled-off neighborhood in San Francisco.

It is not just the big cities and coastal states that are seeing an increase in their assault and death numbers. Recent figures released for North Dakota revealed that in 2018 there were 48 thousand crimes against people in the state (an increase of 15%), and a rise in murders by over 25%. These trends come in part from the state attracting a lot of people from around the country and world for high-paying work.

San Francisco boycotts 25 American states based on pro-life laws in place. This is more modern-day "McCarthyism" by a fascist regime. And it is interesting to see more Liberals calling out such behavior by their cohorts as "crazy", so much so that it becomes somewhat reassuring that one is not alone in those perceptions about the absurdity of such radical conduct.

When there are three or four deaths reported at the US/MX border, immigration activists who are "open-border" advocates come unglued and blame Trump personally for these unfortunate circumstances. Most of the time, the illegals who breach the border bring their sickness and poor health with them. As a factual matter, the number of deaths at that border have been fewer under Trump than they were until George W. and Obama, even with the seriously increased number of illegal crossings.

In late-July of 2019, two American students from the San Francisco (CA) area are arrested for and admit to a killing of a newlywed police officer in Rome. This apparently occurred during the course of a drug deal gone bad. The officer who may or may not have identified himself as such was off-duty and stabbed eleven times. There is much of this story that does not seem to "add up". One thing is for sure, it would have been better for the students to be more engaged with their packing than with a drug transaction. And what is it with our society that is turning our young people into murderers?

There had been no thought about completing this chapter in this manner until we reach this point in the history of America while battling the Novel Corona Virus pandemic in May of 2020. The issues are when and how do we re-open the US economy with as few deaths as possible, or is it with as few deaths as practical? Like everything else in our country these days, the questions clearly separate us by political ideology. Most of the Conservatives seem to believe that we need to "get back to work" as a country as soon as possible, which will result in more deaths from the inevitable "community spread" of the virus. The Liberals (who hate our POTUS and do not want even the chance of his success) appear to favor delaying the process of "getting back to normal" as long as possible so that our economy and citizens are still suffering when the 2020 elections arrive in November. "Every life" is suddenly precious to them even as the abortion providers are being deemed "essential" services for pregnant women. On the Right, there are expectations now of at least 100,000 deaths in the States, while the Left is convinced that opening the country too soon (before July) will result in at least 250,000 deaths. My personal concern has always been (from Day 1) that we cannot make the cure worse than the disease. People are going to die. We need to protect the elderly and vulnerable populations and continue to live our lives. Instead, we stopped our incredible economy that was running on all cylinders with a brick wall—from record low unemployment to over 30 million jobs lost and an unemployment rate of probably over 18% when the numbers come out next week. Suicide and overdose deaths are at atrocious highs as people lose their businesses, jobs, and livelihoods that they have been building during their life. There is despair all around us, and it is continuing to get worse by the day. May God be with us and bless us as we try to extract our country from the brink and return to some sense of normalcy. And I hope I do not strangle the next person who tries to explain to me what they call the "new normal" as where we are today. I and my ilk will not be buying into that plan. We will not settle for less than the best no matter how long it takes.

An addition as I sign the contract to publish this work: our country has been thrust into chaos during the COVID-19 pandemic when African-American George Floyd is brutally and senselessly murdered by a white police officer on the streets of Minneapolis after being detained and restrained for suspicion of passing a counterfeit $20 bill. Protests and (in some cases) riots follow in most of the major cities around America. Yes, "Black Lives Matter". I will not go into the debate now about whether all lives matter, leaving that up to each person to decide individually. The officers involved in the Floyd killing are charged and will presumably proceed to a trial. Then as those protests continue, Rayshard Brooks (a person of color) in gunned down by white police officers in Atlanta with two wounds to the back after a stop for a possible DUI infraction. The shooting officer is charged with felony murder and will face the possibility of a death sentence. Calls come out ranging from de-funding or reducing funding for the police, eliminating jails and prisons, to improving training for law enforcement personnel and demilitarizing police forces. Two things are certain from my eyes: we need policing reforms in the US including the identification and removal of bad officers, and by far the majority of all police officers are continuing to serve and protect everyone in a fair and non-discriminatory manner. Just imagine what America would be like without our faithful law enforcers—anarchy. A portion of the debate in the future must attempt to address related issues of "systemic racism" in the US, the breakdown of the traditional family in minority communities, de-escalation of confrontations between citizens and police, use of healthcare professionals in appropriate law enforcement situations, and the cataclysmic proliferation of black-on-black violence in our inner cities, among many other factors.

CHAPTER 20

RESPECT FOR ELDERS AND FOR THE PERSON AND PROPERTY OF OTHERS

It appears that Starbucks is past due for another "day off" for barista training. Their most recent educational day was caused by open racial profiling and hostility. The topic this time is "respect for constituted authority", our officers in blue and brown. This hotbed of hatred must be stopped now. As a large percentage of the employees of this coffee chain are millennials, I probably could have placed this into that chapter; but as there are enough of the staff members in all of the older generations, it appeared more prudent to place the entry here. There is a striking stench that this company has developed an elitist culture that shows little if any tolerance for anyone in authority who does not fit into their "clicky" genre. I would personally choose to not patronize their establishments, but I do not consume their caffeinated fare and use them instead for my spouse when we travel and find their use to be convenient, especially in hotels. If I were management for the coffee purveyors, I would probably plan for a day of some sort of attitude adjustment every six months or so.

Notoriety has been rising over the past year for the movement to face and combat MMIW ("Missing and Murdered Indigenous Women"). These efforts have been stifled for so many decades by a "code of silence" among Native peoples. It is almost as if there has been an effort by various Tribes to ignore or even cover up problems amongst their members. Maybe they are embarrassed to admit that there are problems at home primarily of their own creation which need to be met head on and solved. Is there some sort of inherent disrespect for women in the Native culture and teachings? If not, then what is causing these dangerous and abhorrent activities to continue. If the problems are perpetrated by outsiders, then who are these offenders and what must be done to stop their plundering? We will see these efforts to protect indigenous women increasing significantly in the years ahead, with success in stopping the destruction as the only option for meeting the problems seriously. In a case from the Fort Berthold Reservation in North Dakota, the recent headline questioned that there had been no developments reported by the FBI in the death of Olivia Lone Bear in the year following the discovery and recovery of her body. The 32-year old mother of five had been found nine months after her disappearance, in the passenger seat of her vehicle submerged near the shoreline of a bay in Lake Sakakawea on the Reservation. Did she simply lose control of her vehicle and drive into the lake, or was there some "foul play"? She had been drinking on the night she went missing, and we should probably assume she ended up in the water by her own mistakes when there is not enough evidence to the contrary. There is no question that a good portion of the MMIWs met similar fates of their personal making. This was simply another instance of "news by speculation" in the case of a death of a MMIW. That definitely misses out on the "truth" meter and in no way diminishes our respect for the woman she was. Then there was the saga of a Standing Rock Rez mother of three who disappeared on 11-8-19 (reported to authorities a month later). We were given the impression by local authorities and the media that she was most likely a victim of human trafficking! Wow! All of a sudden (poof!), she is found alive on January 22, 2020 in the Dallas-Ft. Worth area, and now it seems that she was there on her own to avoid being arrested in North Dakota on multiple warrants? What is going on in the

Native-American community? You can only get by with so many lies before the general public will disregard even the important truths, sending your valid concerns and complaints down the toilet into oblivion. It is long since past the time for demanding transparency regarding the myriad of challenges faced by every-one of Native heritage on and off the Reservations—before it is too late.

Much work needs to be done to educate our US population about how we treat our elderly citizens as well as the property and business rights of others. This came out loud and clear following the Floyd and Brooks murders and the looting, destruction of property, and blocking of livelihoods that ensued. One of the most egregious of these incidents occurred in broad daylight along a street in Manhattan on 6-12-20 when a 92-year old woman using a walker was clearly pushed to the ground for no reason (hitting her head on a fire hydrant). This was all captured on video. The attacker was later identified as a 31-year old man who had been arrested in the city over one hundred times in the past. What is in the mind of such a person who would injure an elderly person (or anyone else) in such a callous and cowardly manner? This could have easily been included in the chapter about the current increases in mental illness throughout the US.

CHAPTER 21

THE REPLACEMENT OF CAPITALISM AND FREE ENTERPRISE WITH SOCIALISM

One of the pillars of the world Bolshevik revolution, Vladimir Lenin, said it very succinctly: "The goal of Socialism is Communism." Those who are arguing against that philosophy are either trying to actively pull it off or are too naïve to know where their efforts are guiding them and their puppets.

The baby boomers were educated with a phrase that "you get what you pay for". This can be translated today as "if you are not willing to pay for what a product or service is worth in the marketplace, you will probably end up with an inferior product or service." When we remove private ownership of a business and the companion profit motive in a conversion to socialism, there will be a parallel decline in the level of quality caused by the emphasis instead on the quantity produced. This tendency results in reduced demand for the crappy widget, procedure, commodity, or benefit. Whether it is in manufacturing, medical care, professional or common services, the arts, or otherwise, the effect is to diminish the value and nature of the desired sum and substance. This would only continue the "dumbing down" of the United States at a time when other countries are already speeding past us toward the 22nd century. We as Americans need to continue to demand the best from ourselves and our efforts in order to maintain the position as a world leader and power. Socialism will only destroy all that we stand for and have built up in the past. Included in this decline would be the Democratic Party itself which is on the verge of a split between the moderates in the center and the Socialists on the Left edge. We may very well be on our way to a five-party system in the US—Republicans, Libertarians, Independents, Democrats, and Socialists. More about this later.

Bernie Sanders continues his "war" on wealth and corporate business in America—and Elizabeth Warren is onboard in those battles. Yet, for each of the past two years, Sander's spouse had income over $1 million and they donated 1% to charities in 2017 and 3% in 2018. We do not judge this, but merely share the interesting facts. And Sanders as a 2020 candidate for the Democratic nomination, runs into a "buzz saw" from his campaign staff. Bernie advocates for the $15 per hour federal minimum wage while his workers complain about their pay and request a raise from far below that level! When pressed about this, he agrees to pay his staff more, but requires them to pay more for healthcare coverage and then reduces their hours?! BS makes his Democratic Socialist Party very proud, but he has fallen out of the running for the 2019 political "boss of the year". If Bernie had shown this compensation plan on the old "Gong Show", he would have been "Zonked"! Bernie and side-kick AOC then blast Bloomberg for attempting to "buy" the Democratic 2020 Presidential nomination. Most of the rest of the "Squad" has also joined in the support for BS. Fun to watch the Socialists "at war" with the middle-of-the-road in the Democratic Party. That itself should be enough to scuttle his ambitions. And that schism continued and was blown wide open as Sanders came up with his $16 trillion plan to address climate change, as he claimed it "would pay for itself". Right. #DividedWeFallDemocrites

The Democratic Socialists running for President in the 2019 primaries are all supportive of "Medicare for all" (MFA). Does that make any of you who are baby boomers or planning for retirement nervous? Well it should. Many of us have paid into the federal government for future Medicare benefits for as many as 47 years or more, and such a program of using our health care resources for universal health coverage for the masses could easily bankrupt the entire retirement system. Not only that, but the United Healthcare CEO recently stated that this ill-conceived proposal "would destroy the entire US health industry"—from benefits for all to benefits for none. We cannot buy in to such madness by those who suggest that the federal government should pick up the tab for everything medical we need.

More news from the Socialist Mayor of NYC, Bill de Blasio: "There is a lot of wealth in New York City, it just isn't distributed 'fairly'." The next thing he will tell us is that he has set up a wealth distribution police force to make such determinations and to enforce a solution. Story at 10 PM.

There is not enough wealth to take from the wealthy to pay for all of the Socialist Democrat programs. This is very similar to the statements made decades ago by British PM Margaret Thatcher, to the effect that the main problem with Socialism is that you will at some point run out of the money to take away. In another one of her "hair-brained" programs, Native-American wannabe Elizabeth Warren is suggesting that the US impose a "wealth tax" to raise the funds necessary to forgive $50,000 of the student loan debt of applicable millennials who make less than $100,000 per year. So, this would require people of means to not only pay for the education of their own children, but also that of the young people across town and throughout the country who overspent themselves on a worthless college education. That just does not seem to be fair to this fiscal conservative.

Democratic Presidential candidate Elizabeth Warren has never met a tax she did not fully embrace and support. She wants to reverse all the tax reductions of the Trump administration which have resulted in an astounding economic climate and more disposable income for virtually all employed Americans (pre-COVID downturn). Our current individual and family tax liabilities would be virtually doubled under her current Socialist platform, and who knows how high our tax bills would go before she runs out of new government handouts? Not to worry though, US billionaires. Liz only wants a wealth tax on you totaling "two cents" each? Warren also warns in the fall of 2019 that an impending economic crash in the US can only be stopped with a $15 per hour minimum wage, strengthening unions, and putting workers for large corporations on the Board of Directors of those companies. I do not believe that she has any sort of degree in nor experience with economics, nor with ever having employed anyone. #LyingLiz Follow-up: instead, it took a virus from China five months later to bring down the American economy.

A Monmouth poll during the summer of '19 has Bernie Sanders and Liz Warren in a "dead heat" at 20%, and Biden closely behind at 19%. The Republicans are chanting "Bring on the Socialists!"

Another random factoid for all of those Liberal crazies out there who are pushing for free college tuition for all. A recent study found that college grads have a $1 million advantage in lifetime earnings over high school graduates. Wouldn't you think they could afford some of that extra income to pay off their college loans? Wishful thinking, I guess.

Kamala Harris and several of the other Democratic 2020 Presidential Candidates are calling for an end to "right-to-work" laws which have helped to reduce the power of Unions through-out the country. That is most assuredly wishful thinking as 27 of our 50 States (54%) already have such laws without much visible dissatisfaction. As long as non-Union employers treat their employees fairly, it would seem that Unions will continue their precipitous declines in popularity and membership.

Many of the largest companies in America, especially in the tech and social media industries, are facing a considerable appetite in Congress for anti-trust intervention by the US Department of Justice. Some would say that these companies have become too large, dominant, and anti-competitive, with a few of these entities even having been permitted to acquire companies which simply added to their market share. Among those discussed for action have been Apple, Google, Amazon, and Facebook. This is not like the old days when it seemed that the federal government was much more aggressive in these threats to competition. Two recent examples of questionable actions by these corporate giants were the Facebook acquisition of Instagram, and the addition by Amazon of a new division called "Pill Pack" to presort medications and provide them to customers with little or no shipping costs.

Capitalism clashes with Socialism in Venezuela with an attempted people's revolution and coup on April 30, 2019. Usually in such an effort the tyrannical head of the country is ousted or the opposition leader is arrested or worse. In this case, dictator Maduro is still in place as newly-elected President Juan Guaido remains on the scene to continue as the face of the opposition. Weird! This confrontation will continue until Maduro is eventually removed or departs. Someday, he will move with all of his stolen assets to one of the countries which supports him and is propping him up—probably Cuba, Russia, or China.

One of the things that gives Capitalism such a bad rap today is the extremes in wealth and poverty, and there are few places in the world where this is more pronounced than in the State of California—the collision of Tinseltown with shantytown in Los Angeles, and that of Silicon Valley with the putrid filth and squalor of what used to be the beautiful City of San Francisco. The politicians of this state are constantly claiming to do so much for their residents, while millions of them are leaving every year for greener pastures. Can it possibly be true what has been said recently by the media of this situation: California is now the "home" of 49% of the country's homeless population — huddled masses yearning to breathe free. The state blames this on the great weather and a shortage of care for the mentally ill. Why don't you do something about the situation with the billions of dollars of surplus which you claim to be sitting on? As a sanctuary state, the illegal immigrants there are treated far better than those who are our legal neighbors and living on the streets. That is not the Christian way of treating people that we were raised to support and facilitate in the 50s and 60s.

"No pain means no gain" has been a mantra for entrepreneurs (and body builders) for decades. I use it in the case of "business builders". These individuals forging a future need to have "skin in the game", risking their personal resources to create success. A variation has always been: "no risk means no reward".

Based on a Christian upbringing, many Conservatives and some Liberals consider Socialism to be "anti-Christian", contrary to the Biblical passage of "reaping what you sow". With Socialism, people are reaping the finished product from what has been sown by others, basically stealing (another "no-no") from those who "have" by those who for one reason or another do not have. On the Left they refer to this as "wealth redistribution". Not much of an incentive for those who are hard and successful workers to continue doing that.

Conservative radio host, Rush Limbaugh, proposes a slightly different take on the common bedfellows of "Big City Liberals" and homelessness in a segment of his show on September 12, 2019. He believes that these Liberal Socialists embrace homelessness as a crutch to which they can conveniently point as a tool in their box—"See. Capitalism doesn't work". Very clever on the Left.

Capitalism is not a perfect economic engine. Sometimes it can assist in the creation of mega-companies that test out our disdain for and laws prohibiting monopolistic practices. The Sherman Antitrust Act was created in 1890 to set forth a structure to meet the anti-competition threats of some large combinations. The primary corporate giant which met the anti-trust axe in front of the boomers was AT&T (American Telephone & Telegraph Co.) in 1982. Some of the "baby bells" created in that breakup and still in operation were NYNEX, Bell Atlantic (now Verizon Communications), BellSouth (now again part of AT&T), Southwestern Bell (also back as a part of the current AT&T), and USWest (which was bought by Qwest and later by CenturyLink). Probably the next companies to meet the wrath of the Sherman Act will be Facebook (FB) and Google. FB's Mark Zuckerberg was back for testimony in DC on October 23, 2019, touting the company's new crypto currency, Libra, which will probably never happen (at least in my mind not to the extent envisioned by the FB "money grubbers"). One of the fears related to Libra is that FB would attempt to use it to pay off a $5 billion fine being assessed against the company. It would probably be wiser for Zuckerberg and the company to focus instead on avoiding a breakup of the behemoth company. #FBTooBig Apple is probably the only reason why Microsoft did not meet the anti-trust knife, and there is no company in that position to cushion the punches against Facebook. And Amazon probably won't be far behind FB and Google.

Another day, another amazing idea from Socialist "Squad" member Ilhan Omar: "Homes for All". That seems pretty easy and inexpensive? #CrazySocialistDems #SquadStrikesAgain Not to be outdone by a relative political "newbie", Bernie Sanders has a proposal to forgive $81 billion of medical debt, to be paid from the same source as the bank bailouts following the Great Recession. The debt in question was caused in large part from those people who refused to sign up for health insurance under the Affordable Care Act (ACA—Obamacare) or who had the large deductibles ($8,000-$15,000) which came from that program (like not having any insurance at all). His health debt payoff would fit in there well with his suggested plan to confiscate assets from the wealthier Americans, one of the most dangerous aspects of Socialism and Communism.

The US House passes a Bill for a $15 per hour minimum wage, which will be another "lost in action" in the Senate. If you are curious about what the effects of this legislation would be, one needs to look only as far as Washington State ($16 there) to see the catastrophic results in job losses and business failures.

As we approach December of 2019, NY Governor Cuomo is getting blasted for being played by AOC in the loss of the Amazon Center for NYC. Nothing boring about watching a flyweight beat up on a heavyweight (only because of his weight). #OutAtTheBell #Democrites At the same time, AOC says she does not want to hear that people are receiving "free stuff" anymore (such as college at no cost, payment of past student loans, no-cost housing, Medicare-for-All, and guaranteed minimum income for starters). So, then all of these benefits are "entitlements"? Now that is incredibly disturbing. #GetOutYourWallet #DemocraticSocialists

The government of Communist China should fear capitalism with over 324 billionaires in the country, including 10%+ of the world's 200 richest people.

Some Democrats, especially those in the portion of the party that will become the Socialist Party of America, favor lowering the federal voting age from 18 to 16? This makes sense for the proponents as they believe that this segment of the population (more Generation Zers) are more idealistic than any other portion of the potential voters. Is it possible this came from their K-12 education which preaches the power socialism? This is suggested as it is shown that less than 40% of the 18-year old's vote based on recent statistics. And then take into consideration that this segment of the population knows less about government and civics than legal immigrants and any of the older generations. This idea of expanding our potential voter ranks is one of those "thanks but no thanks" ideas.

As the Dow backs off (at least temporarily by -280) on 1-3-20 due to problems with Iran and higher oil prices, the Liberals exclaim: "The Sky Is Falling!" Where were they the previous day for Dow +330? Over the past couple of years since Trump was elected, we have heard endless speculation about an impending "recession" for the US and dragging the world with us. Nothing has been further from the truth and reality (pre-COVID economic collapse). The scariest part of the Liberal predictions is that they seem to be wanting the economic downturn as a mortal wound to the Trump presidency and legacy. One of the primary offenders for such a bent is Liberal media "whore" Bill Maher. This is a first timer for me, that Americans would actually hope for troubled economic times for virtually everyone in the country and extending around the world all because they do not like (and in fact hate) the President of the United States. That is a total afront to the way the OK Boomers were raised and is about as un-American as it can get.

As the 2020 Presidential election heats up, Democratic Socialist candidate Bernie Sanders is creating a major disconnect with a portion of the traditional foundation of the Democratic party—Unions. His proposal of "Medicare For All" (MFA) is a slap in the face of these mostly blue-collar laborers who enjoy some of the finest negotiated healthcare programs anywhere in the US. I have personal knowledge about that industry as I represented many Taft-Hartley (Union-Management) employee benefit plans for 24 years. Such "Cadillac Plans" are the envy of the health coverage industry with all of the bells and whistles and very little in out-of-pocket costs for the union members. A transfer to MFA would be like replacing a Ferrari with a used Ford Taurus (sorry Ford as I definitely like their vehicles). Sanders attempts to mask this rip-off with his support for the repeal of "Right-to-Work" laws and jurisdictions which promote a worker's protection from having to join a union in order to be employed in those trades. That sounds great for unions but is seen by many as contrary to the rights of individuals to make the personal decision to work for union or non-union companies based on what fits best for their goals, financial circumstances, politics, and personal needs. The ability of Sanders to be a viable candidate for his national party would be fatally destroyed without the support of laborers. Wealthy Democrats are also in a full sprint away from the Sanders-led party as it continues to shift quickly toward Socialism.

#KimJongUn is rumored to be dead or near death (on April 25, 2020). Would his sister, #KimYoJong, be more likely to lead #NoKo away from the brink? Chances are good that we will find out fairly soon. #NorthKoreaNews Update as this book goes to press: as there is virtually no information nor intel available regarding the young dictator, it appears that Chairman Kim is indeed alive and continuing to personally run his country into the ground.

CHAPTER 22

DO YOU CONSIDER YOURSELF A "PATRIOT"?

Now Teddy Roosevelt was a real patriot, he and most of the members of his "Bull Moose" Party. Here is the way he proclaimed it: "We have room for but one flag, the American flag. We have room for but one [official] language, and that is the English language. We have room for but one sole loyalty, and that is a loyalty to the American people" [interpretation of the author added]. We are proud in North Dakota to have adopted Teddy as a "native son". He loved this state, especially in the west where we have a National Park bearing his name, and where we have decided to build a Roosevelt library (in Medora) commemorating him. Bully!

What does it mean to be a "good citizen"? This is something we were taught as baby boomers by the greatest generation. That makes sense as most of them were. If you want to list the lessons we learned, you can pretty much look at the Scout Oath & Law many of us learned—Oath: honor, do my best, duty to God, help others, stay physically strong, mentally awake, and morally straight; Law: trustworthy, loyal, helpful, friendly, courteous, kind, obedient, cheerful, thrifty, brave, clean, and reverent. Should I just end my writing here, as that just about sums it up?

"Patriot Day" 2019 is here as I write this today. It will always bring tears to my eyes as we hear the old stories and new ones about those who died that day and since that time from the terrorism perpetrated by evil and misguided fools. That day and its' aftermath cost America dearly and also serves to unite us in the pledge that this can never be permitted to happen again on our soil and to be diligent in our efforts to identify those around the world who are truly our allies and those who are disguised as such, what can be referred to as "vigilant and compassionate realism" (VCR). We are proud in Fargo that the first name read each year from the list of 911 victims is "Gordon Aamoth, Jr." who was raised in Minneapolis by a father who was from Fargo and was a member of a family who were pillars in our community during the early decades addressed in AGG and in this follow up. We dare not ever forget the faces of those enemies from around the world with whom we have battled as long as our country has existed. And we will remember those who died in close proximity of time and space to the three "killing fields" and directly from their wounds of that day, as well as those who have died since from the fallout of those attacks and the destruction which resulted. More than six million brave Americans have joined the voluntary armed services of our country since that day.

There are those on the Left side of our country who hate President Trump more than they love America—and it is killing us!

There is a new Gallup poll out at the beginning of July 2019 measuring "pride in America" from the month of June. The numbers of those who are proud to be an American have reached the lowest point in the eighteen years of the survey. Seventy percent of all US adults say they are proud, while only 45% say they are "extremely proud" (with Democrats at considerably lower levels than Republicans). The highest rates of patriotism occurred following the 9/11 terrorist attacks, between 2002 and 2004. Extreme pride by Democrats has plummeted to 22%, less than half of what it was only months before the Trump election in November 2016. Extreme pride for Republicans has remained quite stable, 76% at the present time and never lower than the 68% during the Obama Presidency. Independents with extreme pride is between the major parties at 41%. At the lowest levels of Democrats are women, Liberals, and younger adults. No shockers in any of those figures.

It appears that the level of patriotism in the city council of St. Louis Park, MN, is not particularly high, at least at the present time. They decided to eliminate the "Pledge of Allegiance" from the beginning of their council meetings. I was pleased to hear at least that it was not done to save time, as the "Pledge" is only about eleven to twelve seconds in duration. The "logical" reason was because "we have become more diverse [in our city]." Okay. So those people who have made the city more diverse are somehow offended by the idea and words in the recitation? I want to understand all of this. If we decided in the US to not do anything that would offend non-citizens, there would not be much we would accomplish. Is this a matter of not being proud to be Americans? We may never know, as the decision of the council was reversed after two weeks of considerable local and national uproar and the pledge reinstated.

During the period of July 12-14, 2019, Congresswoman Ilhan Omar claims that she is a "bigger US patriot than most natural born citizens." "Americans are not living their values." This becomes the funniest joke of the year so far. Many are urging Omar to leave her position in the government to become a standup comedian. It is not such a laughing matter however when we learn that she is under scrutiny for the improper use of campaign finances and deceptive marriage activities such as marrying her brother to help him stay in the country.

Failed Kamala Harris calls Trump "criminal". Good thing she lives in the US rather than Iran, NoKo, Russia, Cuba, or China, where she would have ended up in prison (or worse) for making such statements about the leader of the country. #HarrisLostInCalifornia

About once per week now, a random factoid is revealed that helps to define just how much hatred the Democrites, "never-Trumpers", #SwampRats, #Swampsters, "deep-staters", and others on the Left have for President Donald J. Trump, and for how long it has been going on. Did it begin when then-businessman Trump and Melania came down the escalator in Trump Tower, or from the first 2015 Republican debate, or during the Presidential debates between he and Hillary, or Election Day, or the night of Election Day, or between then and Inauguration Day, or on Inauguration Day? It really does not matter much does it? None of these anger-filled zealots can claim to be "patriotic", by definition. True patriots in America support their country, and the President of their country. They are able to transcend political bias in favor of "one nation", "E Pluribus Unum", and "indivisible". On November 7, 2019, the "Day One Conspiracy" (which terminology started with this writer that day on Twitter) begins to unravel. It is reported that whistleblower attorney Mark Zaid announced the beginning of a POTUS "coup" and "impeachment" as Trump was being inaugurated (January 2017). #Gotcha #SwampCreatures #DayOneConspiracy Everything that has transpired since that day to bring the President and country to our knees has been orchestrated by this traitor and other conspirators who cannot accept the "will" of the American people. They will not stop until POTUS is forcibly thrown out of the White House. Then even if the old English traditions of hanging, disemboweling, quartering, and incinerating were carried out, it would still not be enough to satisfy the "bloodlust" of these pathetic pagan partisans. May God help us and be with us as this disgrace continues to unfold before our very eyes.

In a speech to the UN on September 24, 2019, President Trump makes a simple yet profound statement: "Liberty is only preserved by the devotion of patriots...The future belongs to patriots and not globalists." As a highlight, the POTUS also related the Micron chip story in which the Chinese stole the chip technology and then prohibited the use of that technology in the country. Craziness.

Great News of the Day (on January 21, 2020): a US Navy aircraft carrier is named after African-American Doris Miller based on his heroic actions at Pearl Harbor and WWII which followed. May God Bless the Soul of This American Hero and Continue to Bless America. #USMilitary

As I prepare to submit this finished manuscript to the publisher, happy 244th birthday for America on July 4, 2020! With anarchists and fascists from the Left on the streets attempting to destroy some of our US history and as COVID-19 cases are again on the rise, this is one of the scariest times that I have ever experienced in my nearly 70 years. These criminals are using the crutches of racial division and law enforcement reform to create chaos in the place of what should be calm and cooperation. What challenges we have in our country have been blown totally out of proportion in order to justify their calamity and carnage. We patriots need to be vigilant and prepared as there are those in the US who want to take away the positive institutions we have built up over the years. We will not succumb to those who would tear our country apart rather than work together to improve conditions and raise up those in need. My suggestion is for us to celebrate what we have every day as we strive to be better! #ProudToBeAnAmerican #GodBlessAmerica

CHAPTER 23

SINCE WHEN IS "RESIST" A POLITICAL PLATFORM?

It appears today that everyone on the Left is attacking President Trump and his followers on the Right, especially in DC. This is to be expected as many of these assailants are a part of the "swamp" which Trump was elected to drain. Most of us would feel the same way if war was being waged against us for our beliefs and actions (or inaction). It has not been difficult to predict the dilemma of gridlock in which we find ourselves today, caused by those brilliant minds who decided in 2018 that dividing the national government by electing a Democratic House of Representatives would somehow improve an already fractured governing structure. These voters on the Left of center have created a monster with a voracious appetite for division and inaction, making it virtually impossible to get any legislating done with the exception of an occasional bipartisan bill that no one could ever logically oppose. My advice for 2020 is all or nothing. Either reelect President Trump and replace the House with a GOP majority (my preference) or throw the Republican bums out and roll the dice that the Democratic Socialists do not destroy the Republic during their "reign of terror". Any outcome between these two poles will simply continue the partisan madness which has become too familiar since the 1990s and especially after the 2016 election.

The Democrats are being trained to learn and repeat the same "fake news" bullet points. There are few things as humorous in our society today as listing to several clips from the liberal media stories for a particular day and learn about the fact that many interviewees and their Leftist commentators are repeating exactly the same thing—word for word. This is what I refer to as the development of their "clone script". Many of these "dog whistles" are set forth and discussed elsewhere in this book. Here are some of the other uniform bullet points that we hear day after day from Liberals (followed by the facts (as necessary) in parenthesis):

1. Trump is unique as a President in separating illegal immigrant families at the US/MX border. (This has been going on since the Civil War. Someone needs to give the Liberals a quick history lesson on this one.)

2. Trump is trying to build a wall/barrier along the ENTIRE US/MX border. (The real plan is to replace effective and well-positioned old barriers along the border, and to build new barriers only where they are necessary to stop illegal crossings according to the Customs & Border Patrol.)

3. The Trump administration is anti-immigration. (There is record or at least near-record legal immigration into the US under Trump. This is contrary to the record deportations during the Obama years.)

4. The GOP will not support health coverage for "pre-existing conditions". (Republicans are in favor of "pre-existing conditions" coverage, with the costs to be passed on by the insurance industry through increased premiums.)

5. Release of less than all the unredacted Mueller Report constitutes a Republican cover-up. (It would be a violation

of federal law to release the entire Mueller Report without required lawful redactions.) A copy of the Report which was supposedly 99.9% unredacted was made available to members of Congress. Many Republicans went to review it. How many of the whining Democrats do you think went to view this document—approximately. If you responded with a "ZERO", you are correct.

6. US capitalism is leading to a Russian-like oligarchy. (It is socialism and communism which lead to Russian-like oligarchies.)

7. Republicans are fascists. (Antifa is fascist, with the Democrats in the lead trying to justify and condone the group.)

8. Attorney General Barr is biased. (Twice Attorney General, Barr is one of the most highly respected and trusted lawyers in US history.) Democratic Rep. Jerry Nadler: "The Democrats did not relish bringing a contempt citation against the Attorney General of the United States!" In North Dakota, we call that statement "bull crap"—or worse.

9. Trump is a compulsive liar. (Like Hillary Clinton was and is? I agree that Trump has been known to embellish a bit. Okay, a lot!)

10. The GOP is using illegal immigrants as "pawns". (Republicans believe in legal immigration and overall in the "Rule of Law".)

11. Rep. Nadler and the Democrats/Liberals regularly claim that the Republicans and President Trump have thrust the United States into a nonexistent "Constitutional Crisis". These are the same people who site the Constitution for a particular position and then ignore it for others. Is this more

of a Constitutional Crisis than proposed by many on the Left that we abandon the US Constitution as a governing document for our country? US House Majority Leader (since the 2018 midterms) Nancy Pelosi often states that criticism about an inactive Congress is not really about them, but rather about the destruction on the Right of the Constitution and the American people. She is joined by Texas Congressional "madman" Al Green who demands that the Conservatives "honor the Constitution". His personal conduct in calling for Trump's impeachment because of and since his 2016 win would suggest that Green would personally substitute "ignore" for "honor". More of those "cattle feces".

12. The position of the Republicans is "holding [some group] hostage". The Left just uses the phrase but changes the name to fit the topic.

13. The Democrats continue to take credit for President Obama regarding the current [pre-COVID] successes in the US economy. Meanwhile the Trump administration remains on course to reverse virtually everything which the previous administration put into place and thus creating a sluggish economy and the worst effort ever to recover from a recession. (It appears certain that those on the Left will continue to take the curtain calls for our vibrant economic conditions until the explosive growth falters [which it did from COVID] or until Trump leaves office, whichever occurs first.) Hint to Liberals: there is a reason why America elected an experienced businessperson to lead our country and to drain the cesspool of Washington, DC.

14. Trump believes and acts as if he is "above the law" (do they mean like those Democratic nihilists on the Left who espoused Hillary's right to have her own Internet server, or who support "sanctuary jurisdictions" and the abolition of

ICE in order to protect illegal immigrants who have committed serious crimes in the US, or who favor open borders and unlimited migration into the US (including DACA) in violation of our current immigration laws (we could go on for hours), or the Liberals who support eliminating the US Constitution as a governing document of our republic, or who support the partisan "packing" of the SCOTUS—like that?).

15. And how about the claim by the Liberals that any position by the Conservatives on the Right constitutes an "existential threat", such as Joe Biden exclaiming that "Trump is an existential threat to our democracy!" (Please give us all a break on this one.) And I will categorize in here those who are constantly barking that Trump's conduct "is a threat to our national security". This was prevalent when the POTUS put a temporary delay on 2019 Ukrainian aid. No. Nothing he does in any way lessens our national security, but instead enhances and strengthens it. Speaker Pelosi even attempted at one point to use "NS" as fuel for extortion against the POTUS. Pitiful.

16. If Trump loses in 2020, there is a good chance that he will not voluntarily leave the White House and Oval Office. (In the law, we call this point "moot", as the chances of it happening with the way the Democrats are acting is probably slim to nothing.) There are even those "crazy Lefties" like Rep. Maxine Waters who refer to POTUS as merely the "occupant of the White House", the ultimate position of those who never accepted the 2016 Presidential election and who have always declared "not my President".

17. Trump, Dem. Tulsi Gabbard, Senate Majority Leader Mitch McConnell, and other GOP national leaders are "Russian assets". (No. Many Republicans would like to normalize some appropriate relationships with Russia.) In McConnell's

response to these claims by the *Washington Post* and MSNBC, he referred to those lazy idiots as practicing "modern-day McCarthyism".

18. Liberals/Democrats claiming that Republicans do not take responsibility for their actions. And those on the Left do all of the time? As we were brought up to learn, "life is a two-way street".

19. Trump on the Ukraine call was acting like mob boss Don Corleone in *"The Godfather"* movie—we support you, so please do me [us] a favor. Loved the movie. The analogy amuses me. The Left is desperate.

20. The Dems amid the Novel Corona Virus pandemic: First it was "ventilators, ventilators, ventilators" until it became clear there were plenty. Then it changed to "testing and tracking" until it was made clear that those were the responsibility of the individual states. The "lamestream" media and their mob of #Liberals throughout the country try to twist the knife they have inserted into POTUS every chance they get. It must be embarrassing and tiring to constantly lose in their efforts to inflict blame and pain.

Accusations abound from the Left about the Republicans "slow-walking" the release of information about an important topic. This is from the Democrats who were considered by many as the kings and queens of slow-walking during the Obama administration from matters such as the Clinton email scandal, the IRS scandal relating to the granting of tax-exempt status for conservative causes and entities, "Fast & Furious", Benghazi, and now during the Trump administration the Congressional approval of Executive Branch nominees and appointments.

There has been much division in the Democratic party lately, much of it caused by "The Squad" made up of four new and progressive female members of Congress—Ocasio-Cortez, Tlaib, Omar and Pressley. They have been and continue to be a thorn in the side of Speaker and caucus leader Pelosi. The members of "The Squad" certainly are loudly vocal (albeit vocally wrong), and their comments are prompting calls from their Conservative colleagues for censure, apologies, retractions, and occasionally resignation. To many on the Right, "The Squad" represents an asset for them which will help to assure the reelection of Donald Trump as President in 2020. The hateful rhetoric of this fearful foursome appears to foment unity among the patriotic Right, center, and mainstream of America. But it does appear that AOC has solved the mystery of the increased immigration surge of Central Americans to the Southern border of the US—Climate Change(?). I must admit that I did not see that coming. AOC does appear consistent however in her calls and those of many of her buddies on the Left to end Climate Change as well as the US Immigration and Customs Enforcement (ICE) agency and Department of Homeland Security (started in November 2002 as a response to 9/11). More serious action was taken to end ICE on July 13, 2019, by the Liberal anarchist and "enforcer" Willem van Spronsen when he attacked the Northwest Detention Center in Tacoma with multiple weapons and firebombs. The Left apparently takes the lawful holding of illegal immigrants quite seriously.

Following the 2018 elections, the US House controlled by the Democrats has become a "circus of clowns"—a "theater of the absurd". America spoke clearly, and we are all paying the price.

And the Left is behind this "Green New Deal" that would eliminate the use of fossil fuels within the next 12 years—or else we die! Mayor de Blasio is on board with this plan and supports NYC eliminating the future construction of steel and glass skyscrapers as well as retrofitting the current ones to reduce the city's carbon footprint. Such a program would sure change the landscape we saw on shows like "The Jetsons", "The Orville", and "Minority Report"!

Democrats have recently claimed that they want to be "aspirational"? There is no sign of that today, and where were they during the Obama years? That would be AWOL. The party as a whole does excel at something, however. I refer to it as "unison head wagging"—often staged. Just make note of the next time you watch a Democrat speaking with a planned crowd behind. This phenomenon reminds me of "bobbleheads", you will witness it (if you have not already) either vertical or horizontal, depending on the topic presented.

The call from the Left for the impeachment of Donald Trump continues loud and clear during the summer of 2019. Michigan Congresswoman Rashida Tlaib (of "I'm not going nowhere" fame) vows to introduce a resolution for the impeachment of the President, and fellow "Squad" member Ocasio-Cortez says she will support that effort. In the wings are House members Al Green ("we must impeach Trump to prevent him from being reelected") and Maxine Waters ("impeach, impeach, impeach"). The Democratic leadership states during this conversation that "it is time to move on" from such discussions. The "mainstream" Liberal media did mention the "I" bomb at least 309 times in the 24 hours following the release of the Mueller Report. The split in the Democratic Party which I have predicted for twenty years is starting to develop and widen. The Democrats claim that they can "walk and chew gum" at the same time, but there is virtually no evidence of that. On that front they seem to be fairly consistent. There certainly have been only negligible signs of their ability to get anything constructive and non-political accomplished during the past two and one-half years from the beginning of

2107 to the middle of 2019, even now with a Democrat majority in the US House since the beginning of 2019.

There appears to be Democratic hypocrisy from others relative to the impeachment madness. Speaker Pelosi said in 1996 that the Clinton impeachment (for a clear violation of the law) was based on Republican hatred of the POTUS. Congressman Nadler said back then that impeachment was "bad for the country" and an attempt to reverse an election and take away the votes of the people. Today these leaders on the Left are whistling a different tune.

California Congressman Eric Swalwell becomes the first Democratic candidate for the 2020 Presidential nomination to pull out. That is no surprise, as based on his positions I would refer to him fondly as "Swillwell". Despite his Liberal bent, I actually sort of liked the guy for a period of time until he turned sharply to the Left to follow the young branch of the party. Few people like a political chameleon, which is what he became. Blame it on something in the air out West.

As the 2020 Presidential campaign is in full swing, that brings some "shockers" (topics that are surprisingly not being used for campaign purposes). One of the most glaring omissions is what may be the most significant efforts in history to address the ignoring of inner-city problems over the past 50 years by their Democratic leadership. President Trump's "Opportunity Zone" Program is using public-private partnerships to bring hope to these populations. This is totally unprecedented! The days of letting our most vulnerable citizens languish in these hellish neighborhoods is hopefully a step closer to the grand finale. And to think that Trump was mocked when he announced this initiative as he told this forgotten segment of society "what do you have to lose by supporting my efforts?". The answer is that whether they support Trump or not, he will be moving forward to improve their lives, like no one has ever done before—EVER!

2020 Democratic Presidential candidate Kamala Harris has some skeletons in her closet, as she has a history of being very effective as a prosecutor (or is it more correctly "persecutor") in California, even serving as the Attorney General for that state. Now she has some advice for her entire party: "Democrats must put country above party" and impeach President Trump. Many of the knowledgeable Republicans respond with a hearty "bring it on!" There is pretty much a consensus on the Right that an effort at such would assure the reelection of Trump in 2020, to which I concur.

Some things are very predictable in life, while others are not at all. At this moment, we expect that virtually every statement from anyone on the Left side of the aisle is "anti-Trump" and evidence of the speaker being part of the "swamp" that America sent Trump to the White House to "drain". Even the most moderate of the Democrats, Joe Biden, is not an exception to the rule. He recently stated that Trump was the first President in history to be "there for his base but not for all Americans." Au contraire mon frère. There has never been a better friend of the common American as our current Commander in Chief. He is focused on making this country fairer for all, especially those who have been traditionally forgotten by our leaders in Washington, DC as well as the government representatives of their state. Trump is viewed by many as the "liberator of the masses", acting for everyone rather than those convenient partisan electorates which serve to perpetuate our system of only benefitting the elitist minority throughout the country. This is becoming more apparent as his first term continues.

Democratic Senator and 2020 Presidential hopeful, Amy Klobuchar of neighboring Minnesota, was heard in front of a crowd saying: "I am a progressive [apparently meaning a 'non-Socialist Democrat'], and we get things done." And in what period of time was that? This cannot be stated with accuracy about the Trump Presidency beginning in January 2017. In fact, this is a pretty laughable thought in this current "Era of Division". As I write in September of 2019, the Democrats in Congress claim in their script that they are actively working for infrastructure projects, to reduce prescription drug pricing, and healthcare (among other things). There has been no evidence of that over the past 2.5 years, except for some lopsided pieces of legislation in the US House which have no chance of passage in the Senate and would not be signed by the President. This is not exactly a diligent bipartisan effort on the Left to move the country forward.

As the US House of Representatives and many of its' Committees (all controlled by the Democratic Left) move with "contempt of Congress" proceedings against President Trump and his administration, it often appears that large portions of the electorate are not only not supporting these efforts, but are instead holding Congress in contempt for the time wasted in these pursuits. Those who claim that the Congressional Democrats are not getting anything done in Washington are obviously not considering all of these partisan hearings and subpoenas as constructive accomplishments. GOP House Leader Kevin McCarthy put it succinctly when he declared that "the United States has many problems, but the Democrats care more about subpoenas than solutions".

One of my favorite political cartoons in a while was published by Tim Campbell on May 14, 2019. It suggested that the Democrats should hire all of the record-low 3.6% of the unemployed US population to criticize the US economy. Just a passing thought as the Democrats are still taking credit in September of 2019 for the incredible current economy. Sorry, Charlie—it has been the rollback of regulations (Obamalations) and the corporate/individual tax cuts which have made most of the difference. And the economic tariff wars have not hurt as much as I expected, with the Trump administration rolling back the trade injustices which were perpetuated and increased during Clinton, both Bushes, and the Obaminator. Update: we now have NAFTA replaced with USMCA, Phase One of our trade agreement with China, and new trade agreements with Japan and others in the works. These agreements will continue to make a significant difference in our American financial successes. Update: then the Novel Corona Virus pandemic hits and the blazing US economy is shut down! Wha? Totally unprecedented.

Earlier in this book we addressed the possibility of a second civil war in the United States, resulting from a governmental program to disarm the American people. There are other factors which could contribute to such a national calamity. There are signs of many of these factors all around us today. Serious divisions can form from religious persecution and discrimination, a disappearance of law and order/appearance of rampant crime, free abortion on demand at any time, exorbitant "spending and taxing", open immigration and borders, and others. And we are not the only powerful nation in the world to be vulnerable to a war between factions—just look at the challenges today in China, Russia, India, and the Koreas, in addition to less-powerful countries such as Iran, Turkey, Afghanistan, Venezuela, and The Ukraine. For third-world countries in trouble, just look throughout Africa and you will find a number of them. The world is seemingly on the edge of destruction. With those of us who are eternal optimists, we are hoping and praying for clear heads and thinking to prevail—the challenging task of keeping the "crazies" from the controls. Update: Then the COVID-19 pandemic arrives throughout the world. Many knew this could happen at some point, but no one expected it now.

Climate change is one of the next issues that has become political. A recent survey showed that 84% of Democrats believe it to be an "emergency", with only 18% of Republicans considering it as such. Basically, most of the scientists and citizens on the Left believe that without a major addressing of this challenge and necessary action within the next 11-12 years, the world will be irreversibly on track for an end date shortly thereafter. That is why this issue has become the prominent talking point for the 2020 Democratic Presidential hopefuls. The remaining scientists and those people on the Right admit that there is climate change but only partly caused by industries and our environment (with the major offenders being China and India), that there is little which can be done to help the earth with so many of the offenders unlikely to do anything to change emissions over the next thirty years, that climate change is cyclical, and that we should take all reasonable steps to change the use of fossil fuels over a period of the next fifty years or so (with America as a leader as it has during the past thirty years). Recently I viewed a "*NOVA*" segment on PBS that was quite enlightening. Over the history of the Earth, the planet was totally covered with ice 716 million years ago and had no ice whatsoever about 90 million years ago. The temperature of our planet seemed to be controlled by the fluctuating levels of carbon dioxide which depended on the amount of volcanic activity — the higher the activity, the greater the level of CO_2 and less the amount of ice, and vice versa. Where I live in Eastern North Dakota, this area was covered with a glacial lake (Lake Agassiz) ("yes", covered with an ice sheet) from approximately 30,000 years ago until the ice sheet disappeared about 13,000 years ago. Now there is some climate change. That is why the farmlands around Fargo are the most fertile in the world, as they were at the bottom of the vast lake where silt (plant and animal matter) settled for those thousands of years. Those of the baby boomers like myself who were raised in Christian homes learned from *The Bible* about our responsibility to protect the environment as one of our most sacred missions. And probably to an even greater extent, the Native American tribes of our region have been committed through their indigenous teachings to respect, love and nurture the land. It appears to this writer that the major problem which has resulted in the politicization of Americans regarding climate change stems from all of the predictions about catastrophic climate changes which have come and gone without the expected results. Some of the most recent scientific warnings of "imminent global cooling" occurred in the 1920s and 1970s. And those expectations did not become reality. Democratic Presidential hopeful for 2020, Elizabeth Warren, has said that "climate change is a bigger problem than World War II"? This is music to the ears of millennials as this is their #1 issue for 2020. Among the countries not reaching their emission reduction goals is Germany. Do you think it has anything to do with their elimination of nuclear power? DUH? The climate change "terrorists" are hurting the cause with their extreme and misleading rhetoric. The issue of fossil fuel emissions has a monumental impact on the economies of all countries and regions with large amounts of oil, natural gas, and coal—like North Dakota. As the US has become the largest producer of fossil fuels during the past 10 years, energy independent, and a "net" exporter of natural resources, incredible wealth has been created in the backyards of Western North Dakota. With the plan of the Liberals to destroy all of this wealth and dominance in the next eleven years as well as to increase the taxpayer costs for energy, some economists have suggested that the unemployment rate in our country could be increased from 3.5% to over 10%. We are told that the alternative is to face the end of the Earth. There needs to be a continuation of bipartisan discourse and action to do what we can (again within reason) to address changes in our climate. And that will be one immense order! Update: Then suddenly the "oil war" arose between Russia and Saudi Arabia, followed shortly thereafter with the Corona Virus pandemic, resulting with the US oil industry in shambles. This disaster could take many years to be rectified, if that can happen at all. Ever! The unexpected collateral damage of a world health epidemic will change the face of the earth forever.

Inaction and malfeasance by Congress for 2018-19 is a national disgrace. This is simply evidence of the swamp which needs to be drained as you who have participated in this are the predatory members of the deep state. Democrats talk about "serving all of the people and not just the affluent." And how is that working with "resist"? In all fairness to the Left, there is something that they are very good at and practice often—"labeling". They seem to have a category for all their enemies and anything that bothers them.

In early June 2019, Liberal pundit Mary Ann Marsh says "the problem with Joe Biden is his lack of support for women and their issues". And she is not the only one who is disappointed in the Ukraine-China loving former Vice-President. At nearly the same time, CNN predicted that Biden would "eviscerate"Trump in a speech, but the candidate for presidential nomination "whiffed" (or forgot the scalpel). How often our expectations or perceptions do not match with reality.

When John Stewart became a celebrity spokesperson for the bipartisan effort to extend and grant a virtual "blank check" to the 911 Victims Compensation Fund, I was amazed at how calm he seemed and I therefore supported his efforts—which was very unusual as I had seldom in the past even listened to the nonsense he espoused. Growing up, we baby boomers were taught that "all good things must come to an end." And this "bromance" was not an exception to the rule. Just about on cue, Stewart became incensed when a couple of fiscal Conservatives on the Right questioned the advisability of passing legislation with such an uncertain financial exposure over the next 10 years and beyond. In this he was joined by US Senator from NY, Kristin Gillibrand, who was "grandstanding" with him by saying that this legislation should not have been so difficult (and it was not). It did not take many of us long to turn away as fans of Stewart as he became a blithering imbecile even though the legislative probability of the extension was somewhere in the 99% neighborhood. It is not and was not pretty when someone with supposed intelligence becomes unhinged for the sake of trying to make a mountain out of a speck of dust. It is better to not put new supporters to the test over insignificant matters. Sorry, John.

Is anyone else concerned about the influence of our own social media companies on the elections in 2020 and in the future? There are reports that leaders of Google have said that they will "hack" the 2020 elections if necessary, and will not ALLOW Trump to be reelected? BIG BROTHER! This appears to be more of the "Trump Termination Effort" (TTE).

One of the least agreeable/understandable candidates for the 2020 Democratic Presidential nomination (at least from my eyes) is Massachusetts Senator Elizabeth Warren…the poster child for lying to enhance your opportunities and life position. I do find some amusement in her efforts with a couple of new hashtags she has been given—#oldyeller and #screamingmimi. Liz—we can hear you without your loud and angry rhetoric! That does not mean that we like you, because we do not. Good luck in becoming the first female POTUS and Socialist one at the same time.

Question: how is the Impeachment "Inquisition" handling of the Trump/Ukraine call in October, 2019 different than the dispositions of the Obama/investigation of the Trump campaign, Hillary/illegal server and evidence destruction, McCabe/lying, Lerner/tax-exempts blocking, Lynch/Clinton "plane-gate", Hillary/Trump dossier funding, Holder/"fast & furious" contempt, Obama & Clinton/Benghazi, Comey/leaking, Rice/lying, FISA Court Applications based on Hillary's Trump dossier?

Answer: the hypocritical "no-one-is-above-the-law" Trump-hater Democrites want to reverse the 2016 Presidential election by ousting their "Tormentor-in-Chief" and ignore the illegal conduct of their comrades on the Left and anti-Trump friends. Do I correctly sense a double standard here? Naw, couldn't be.

The first debate for 2020 Democratic Presidential nomination hopefuls was held on June 26, 2019, and was hosted by NBC. I learned from others that probably the highlight of the evening was when the microphones failed, and the network was forced to speedily take a break. We always seem to learn important facts from these staged events. One thing that was important for our Northern Plains voters was that Minnesota's favorite moderate daughter, Amy Klobuchar, announced her alignment with the "no-borders" Left in supporting the de-criminalization of illegal border crossings, definitely not one of the common positions in our "law and order" border-compliance region. This is the same Liberal candidate who called the Trump impeachment bases "a global Watergate"—apparently though without the illegal break-in. And all of the participants favored providing medical care for every illegal immigrant as a matter of right, a slap in the face of our US citizens who work hard every month to provide healthcare coverage for their family. Immediately following those two nights of debating, Joe "it is all about me" Biden suddenly comes up with all of these great ideas (at least in his mind) about how America needs to be led and operating. Where were you during the period of 2008-2016? AWOL/downstream without a paddle. On July 4, 2019 his quote was "where there's faith, there's hope". And that has what relevance with your party and its' vision for America (or lack thereof)? Skip ahead to June 30, 2020 and a tweet by me that day: "Law + Order + Security = @realDonaldTrump while Lawlessness + Chaos + Insecurity = #JoeBiden. You do the math. #Conservatives protect and #Liberals create anarchy".

"Commentator" Julie Hirschfield of *The New York Times* as of late-July, 2019: Virtually all of the Democratic House bills passed have been blocked by Mitch McConnell, and the few bills which have reached Trump's desk have been vetoed by him. No! #FakeNews Four out of the five bills were joint resolutions opposing military sales to our allies or to troops in Yemen. Lies will get you nowhere. At the same time following a 2020 Democratic candidate debate, US Senator John Kennedy (R-LA) ripped off one of his classics: he had heard a "job-killing, soul-crushing agenda" and "the only thing I [Kennedy] did not hear was the Cuban national anthem!" I wish I had his writer! Moderate candidates from the party seem to agree with Kennedy, calling the policies of the Left "fairytales" which would destroy Union "Cadillac" health plans.

In early-September of 2019, President Trump announces that "secret" peace talk meetings scheduled with leaders of Afghanistan and the terrorist Taliban at Camp David were being cancelled following the deaths of US soldiers in Afghanistan admittedly at the hands of the Taliban. Politicians and media on the Left (and a few on the Right) immediately pounce on the President for his efforts to settle America's longest war in our history on the "hallowed grounds" of the Camp—like those grounds had never been walked on by evil people such as Nikita Krushchev and Yasser Arafat. Get over it, Amy Klobuchar and Liz Cheney. History should not be shunted by unreasonable personal distaste and bias which they displayed.

Kamala Harris is just getting started in the 2020 campaign, and she is already playing the "race card" just like her hero Barack Obama ("Divider-in-Chief) did. He must be so proud of her efforts. And she has been asked about how she intends to pay the $40 trillion price tag for Medicare-for-all without raising taxes for the middle class, to which she responds: "there is no other option"? That certainly is not very comforting for those taxpayers.

When we boomers were starting to be out of the house on our own (in the late-60s), we were taught a concept that is inconsistent with "resist". The saying has been attributed as a misquotation of Eldridge Cleaver, an American writer, and early leader of the revolutionary Black Panther Party. Our generation was never supportive of his politics nor methods, but he probably had some thoughts at the time that were inspirational toward positive change. The quote was: "if you are not part of the solution, you are a part of the problem." The apparent correct quote from Cleaver was: "There is no neutrality anymore. You're either part of the solution, or you're part of the problem." There is a subtle difference. What appears to be relevant is that as Americans we need to be engaged at all times in seeking and working toward solutions to the ills in the country. If we are instead "sitting on our hands" without a plan and active effort to make things better for everyone, we become a part of the problem(s) at hand. "Resist" simply does not crack it when evaluating how well we are engaged in improving our lives and those of the masses. No one ever said it would be easy to help make things better, but it certainly is more fulfilling to be actively a participant in building things up as opposed to tearing things down.

House Judiciary Chair, Rep. Jerry Nadler (D-NY), announces that his Democrat-lead Committee has approved procedures for a Trump impeachment inquiry. During the announcement in a press conference, the women behind him are "giddy". This is not a good look for what is claimed on the Right to be a partisan hoax supported only by Trump-haters on the Left. It is obvious that the reactions shown tell a clear story of what is about to transpire. And this has become the first such Presidential impeachment inquiry in history which did not follow an authorizing vote by the House of Representatives.

It gets nauseating after a while when the Democrites continue to call for an effort to "heal the country". My but aren't we becoming medicinal about a problem in America caused by the immense hatred they have created within themselves following the angst and tears they experienced on Election Night 2016. They were already despising Trump during the campaign leading to that day and were now coming to the realization that the new President would be with them for the next four years at a minimum. This was the point at which the earlier speculative talk of impeaching Trump started to rapidly ferment in the hearts and veins of the Liberal elitists, even before there were any plans for an inauguration and smooth transition from blue to red at 1600 Pennsylvania Avenue. For the deep state, this was also a time of excruciating pain and intense sweating as a great American builder would begin the process of excavating the "swamp" beginning with clearing off the scum which covered it. The "party" was coming to an end with a "new sheriff in town". We have been witnessing the uncovering of the "DC cesspool" since that momentous day, as different predators in the mire are identified and extracted. The process has begun and will take decades to accomplish, even with the implementation of the employment limits discussed in *AGG*. "Resist" does not have a chance to stop or even slow the progress of the "urban renewal" which has been embarked upon in the District to clean up our government and remove layer upon layer of our bloated and ineffective bureaucracy. We will need many different means of disposal available as we reduce the waste that is sucking the lifeblood out of America.

During a "news" conference by Nancy Pelosi on September 24, 2019, she states "it's a sad day!" as numerous reporters in the background are openly chuckling. There seems to be somewhat of a disconnect between the Dem leader and the press about the solemnity of the moment. That same day, the Impeachment Inquiry/Investigation begins for the Congressional Left wing. We will see where this takes them and us. Liberals and other never-Trumpers like Fox News commentators Shepard Smith and Judge Andrew Napolitano are as giddy as schoolgirls. The Judge talked of Trump committing crimes in the Ukraine call without Napolitano having even seen the transcript? Odd. The Inspector General had found the Ukraine call whistleblower to be politically motivated for ties to and support of the Democratic party and one of the party leaders. Yet the whistleblower claim was found to be credible? All of a sudden, Trump releases the transcript of the call…with NO QUID PRO QUO! Many of us are getting ready for twelve months of nothing accomplished in Congress.

With "Witch Hunt II (The Sequel)" going on as October 2019 arrives, the GOP is asking itself "whom from a foreign country can you or do you accept information from in a political campaign?". It might be well for all persons with national exposure to get a clarification on this. Joe Biden probably needs to get a consult for this based on his dealings as VP and those of his son, Hunter, in Ukraine. I should consider writing a book based on Biden's campaign gaffs, with the latest from the trail being to a mostly minority group of voters in Iowa: "poor kids are just as bright as white kids!" And I would let that book be made into a full-length movie!

Huge backlash and national protests from an announcement that ICE will be making raids to gather up and deport approximately 2,000 illegal immigrants for whom there are valid deportation orders from a court. Seems pretty routine to this writer. Much of the opposition (if not all) is from bleeding-heart Liberals who are the soul of the "resisters". Such a position to ignore the law and regular legal process results in the coddling of the immigrants and the endangering of our lawful citizens and first responders. Where were these activists on the Left when the "Deporter-in-Chief", Barack Obama, was removing 200,000 more people (and separating families) from 2014-16 than the

Trump administration has sent home during the same period of 2017-19? The answer: snoozing hypocritical crickets. No Democratic member of Congress nor their Liberal media and citizen supporters should be able to criticize the current immigration and humanitarian crisis in the US until the lawmakers come up with a bipartisan and comprehensive solution to the archaic asylum laws in our country.

In late-October of 2019, the "Impeaching Democrites" are nervous that the inquiry into the cause(s) of the Russian "hoax" investigation has turned into a criminal matter, and that the investigation of the FISA warrants to spy on the Trump campaign is about to conclude—as they should be. There are even some beliefs that one of the possible original sources of this hoax was the CIA with John Brennan at the helm. #DeepState

Dems are now complaining about needing to add more candidates for their 2020 Presidential nomination. Nearly 30 was not enough. This bodes well for Trump-Pence. I predicted in October of 2019 that NY businessman and former NYC Mayor Michael Bloomberg would come out of the woodwork to enter the race. That has still not happened as I write here. Others discussed have been Hillary (and it is not even April Fool's Day!), Michelle Obama (who is still not proud to be an American), and Oprah (who probably would be qualified to run for a local dogcatcher position). As we used to say: "the more the merrier"!

On October 27, 2019, President Trump authorized a successful US Special Forces raid in Northern Syria to "neutralize" ISIS leader Abu Bakr al-Baghdadi. What a thrilling time for the US to take out such a notorious murderer and international war criminal. Speaker Nancy Pelosi criticizes Trump that Russia did but Congressional leaders (on both sides) did not have advance knowledge of the al-Baghdadi raid. Duh? And have it "leaked" by the Dems and shot down by the Russians? It is time for her to use that grey matter between her ears for more than filling her head. That same day the Leftist Washington Post referred to al-Baghdadi in their headline as an "Austere Religious Scholar" rather than the terrorist thug and inhumane butcher he was. That had to be changed to "Terrorist" following imaginable public uproar. As we used to say: "you cannot make a silk purse from a sow's ear!" The Post ended up with three different headlines for that single story. Embarrassing to say the least. The entire United States (except for terrorists and those who believe there is never a justification for killing anyone) celebrated the killing of Osama bin Laden under Obama in 2011. Today the Liberals do not support the death of Abu Bakr al-Baghdadi as they were not "invited to the party". Any questions?

The Nancy Pelosi meltdown continues on October 29, 2019 as she succumbs to bipartisan pressure for a House vote backing the Impeachment Inquisition. It will happen on 10-31-19. Ooooooooooo. I must say that I did not believe she would cave in this way. There are unquestionably forces behind the scenes with her caucus that helped bring about this wise decision. Update following that vote: Pelosi claims the Impeachment Inquisition is "not partisan" after no Republicans vote in favor of it, and two Democrats vote with the Republicans (sometimes even leaders among the Democrites show glimpses of sanity)—but that deaf, dumb, and blind gal sure plays a mean pinball! Still, the resolution for the formal Inquisition passes and we are "game on" again. The next time I hear her mention the "Constitution", "Democracy", "prayerful", "sadness about the Inquisition", "impeachment is patriotic", or "no one is above the law", I know that I will need to puke. It would indeed be a "sad day for our country" if everyone on the Left wasn't so "elated". #PelosiMeltdown #Spooky

At the same time as Pelosi is unhinged, Liberals in the Congress and media proclaim: "It is not proper for POTUS to ask a foreign country to investigate a US citizen." This is even asserted at a time when there is an ongoing US Department of Justice probe to determine how, when, and by whom the Russian collusion story started. Question for the Left: So then how was it possible in 2016 for the Obama administration to investigate the Trump campaign in foreign countries? Answer: hypocrisy. Apparently on the Left "you can have your cake and eat it too".

Democrites running for the 2020 Presidential nomination are calling for a "political revolution"? Response: and what is it exactly that you think happened with the Trump election in 2016? When was the last time (approximately) that a candidate elected as POTUS had called for America to "drain the swamp"? From the eyes of this political scientist, there has never been a greater "revolution" in US political action than that which was started in 2016. Not even close.

And "Showboat" Joe Biden is on the loose as well, not willing to be outdone by anyone. He talks to a group and the press about his dangerous trips to Afghanistan. "We can lose a Vice-President, but we can't lose many more of these kids [US soldiers]!" Interesting thought. And his other remarks went south of reality from there. "The honest to God truth — as a Biden." That pretty much says it all.

The Dems campaigning for the 2020 Presidential nomination are also busy embracing the non-religious electorate while they alienate persons of faith. This is all done as they criticize Trump for his divisiveness. Hmm. At the same time, the Dem hopefuls are "cursing" their way during the process, pandering to the millennials who are foul-mouthed. Is there something wrong here? Nasty people.

A former Yale Law School classmate of Brett Kavanaugh has come forward with a new allegation against the SCOTUS Justice, as set forth in a *New York Times* article. This person claims that he witnessed Kavanaugh exposing himself to a woman while they attended a party. There was a slight problem with the article, however. The newspaper failed to mention that the alleged victim of the incident was not interviewed by the paper and did not remember that it happened, at all. They blamed the Editors for the omission, forgetting apparently that Editors do not change content. The *Times* later apologized, its' sixth correction relating to Trump articles since 2016! I see a potential lawsuit in the future between Kavanaugh and the newspaper.

Fox News anchor, Shepard "Shep" Smith, needs to be separated from his employment there based on his anti-Trump bias. This has been my position for about a year now as we are in mid-September of 2019. He wasn't always this way, but it seemed like all of a sudden the worm had turned against the POTUS. My belief is that the animus arose following Smith's admission on May 9, 2017 that he was gay, presumably from a perception that Trump was homophobic and anti-LGBTQ+. Smith has become another victim of the decline of true journalism which follows a downward slope based on the commentator's personal selfish motivations—an example of no longer being able to see the forest from the trees. At this point I declined to continue watching his "my-life-as-a-Trump-hater" monologues. UPDATE: Less than a month after I wrote here about Shepard Smith, he announces on October 11, 2019 that he has just done his final show with the network. I happened to be watching his show in "real-time" that day. This was a "bombshell" which reverberated around the entire cable news universe. His settled departure from the $15 million per year position was purportedly due to his feeling of an ethical dilemma, and followed his being critical of colleague Tucker Carlson for his allowing a guest to criticize Fox Contributor Judge Andrew Napolitano, another "never-Trumper". The management of the network apparently sided with Carlson following the kerfuffle. I hope that Smith lands another position in the industry, which most likely would be with a network which is not as Conservative. He is articulate and believable, albeit susceptible to political interference from his own personal pathways. Good luck to you, Shep, and "Go Rebels"!

The media reports on September 17, 2019, that it is not clear from where approximately 20 missiles were fired in an attack on an oil refinery in Saudi Arabia, setting it on fire. That is total "BS". Let's just say that the CIA and US government are not revealing the point(s) of launch. Suffice it to say that anywhere in the world where a missile is launched, our country can track and trace the trajectory of the weapon from departure to impact. Our military satellites are orbiting and positioned all around the planet to do just that.

On October 1, 2019, Fox News commentator Howie Kurtz and former House Speaker Newt Gingrich agree that the "Pelosi impeachment effort" is an elitist effort to take control of the country, another bloodless coup d'état attempt!

It does not help race relations in America when persons of color get caught in a lie about being the subject of racial profiling and/or hatred. I wrote in *AGG* about the sad saga of Jussie Smollett claiming that he was mugged and beaten in downtown Chicago by white men wearing MAGA hats. It didn't help that he paid off the real staged perpetrators with a check. Sickening. There was a recent episode in which a young black girl claimed that white male classmates at her Christian school attacked her and cut off some of her dreadlocks. She later recanted and admitted she lied about the allegations of racial assault and battery. The only positive thing about this damaging story was watching the Liberal media cleaning the egg off their faces as the dream story that they believed was real had turned into a nightmare.

With a year to go until the 2020 election, "Squad" member and Representative Pressley (D-MA) breaks with her sisters by passing on "Quack" Sanders in favor of "Jerky" Liz Warren for the Dem 2020 nomination. Good luck with that one. One Socialist is just as bad as another. #Democrites #JerkyLiz Meanwhile, there are some nervous politicians on the near Left who are not buying what their Liberal colleagues are trying to sell. I predicted in April of 2019 (seven months ago) that gazillionaire and former NYC Mayor Michael Bloomberg would enter the 2020 Dem Presidential nomination fray because of the weak group of candidates being offered. He is now knocking on the door. I will follow up on this and let's see what happens. Update: Later in the month it is done…he is in. On November 24, 2019, former Republican and Independent Bloomberg says "yes" with a $30 million ad campaign. Without question he will not be the nominee. What an unconscionable waste of money, albeit all his own loot.

As groups of Congressmen and Congresswomen visit Israel, there is much consternation that the country has blocked the admission of Ilhan Omar into the country. "She has that right!" No, she doesn't. That country has a law which prevents her coming in. Why would a place like Israel allow a person who calls for their destruction to enter their sovereign nation? There is no good reason in my mind.

Sen. John Kennedy (R-LA) is a constant source of great quotes, and he did not disappoint today as I write in early-November of 2019: "Nancy Pelosi is trying to impeach President Trump! It must suck to be so dumb!" There is something to be said about "being short and to the point" (like this paragraph). #PelosiMeltdown

For those of you who ignored the Open Impeachment Inquisition (starting November 13, 2019 and continuing through December 9, 2019), which was not exactly bi-partisan (no House Republicans voting for it and all but two Democrats voting to proceed (one of those voting "no" for the Dems was neighboring Rep. Collin Peterson (D-MN) representing "twin city" Moorhead, MN)), here are some highlights which I had "tweeted' about during that time:

Highlight 1 in Day One of the Open Impeachment Inquisition (OII): Following the testimony, Chuck Todd of NBC Snooze says that he has heard enough to interest him in watching on Day Two? Wow. Now that is alarming! #FakeNews #NBCSnooze (incidentally, it was I who came up with the #NBCSnooze).

Highlight 2 in Day One of the OII: Joe Biden says he did not watch any of it, but "heard it was devastating for the President"? That sounds as inadmissible as the hearsay testimony we heard and saw during the day! #SleepyJoe #FakeNews

Highlight 1 in Day Two of the OII: This is a definite "yawner" with former US Ambassador to The Ukraine, Maria Yovanovitch, testifying. She was apparently fired because she had preferred working with former Ukraine President Porachenko (weak on corruption) rather than SCOTUS favorite and new President Zelensky (who ran on cleaning up corruption).

Highlight 2 in Day Two of the OII: No question that Yovanovitch has been a good public servant, but she is a "poster child" for my *AGG* proposal of US civil servant employment limits in a single Department or Agency. #DeepState

Highlight 3 in Day Two of the OII: While Republicans are treating 33-year veteran State Dept employee Yovanovitch with "kid gloves", Trump tweets critical of the job she did over the years. The Dems cry "witness intimidation" as she "chuckles" at it. She is not as easily intimidated as the #Democrites had hoped. #ChooseYourBattlesWisely

Assessment of the Inquisition following the first week of "open" hearings and the continued "secret" Star Chamber depositions: The divided Democrites have not destroyed themselves yet, but they are well on their way. #Democrites #HearsayHearings

Highlight (or Lowlight) 1 in Day Three of the Open Impeachment Inquisition (OII): Yawn, is it over yet? The Vindman and Williams AM session was a cure for insomnia, dubbed as the "speculation circus". Where's the meat? #ImpeachmentInquisition

Highlight 2 in Day Three of the OII: "Shifty" talks about uncorroborated "extortion", "bribery", and the "Three Amigos", and blocks any question in front of his House Intel Committee which would name an intel community employee, as that could expose the identity of the "whistleblower"? Schiff is just making up the rules "by the seat of his pants". And everyone who has a computer or a cellphone knows the identity of the "whistleblower". Remember the key words: CIA, worked for Sleepy Joe Biden in Ukraine, Never-Trumper, current #Democrite operative. We have BINGOs everywhere! #ShiftyStrikesAgain

Highlight 3 in Day Three of the OII: Ambassador Volker and Morrison appear. MAAN ("Much Ado About Nothing"). There was no quid pro quo. Devastating for the Inquisition/#Democrites and positive for the POTUS. Score so far: POTUS—3, Inquisition—0.

As the Inquisition moves along, the #Democrites yell: "BRIBERY"! The Republicans respond with: Cattle Feces! Law 101 lesson: In order for there to be bribery, there must be at least an offer for a required exchange. Look again at the transcript! The Liberals will eventually realize that the focus groups they convened to create a new moniker for the Inquisition was an astounding mistake. #FakeNews #FocusGroupFailure

Highlight 1 in Day Four of the OII: EU Ambassador Sondland testifies amidst speculation of a "bombshell" day. The witness "presumed" a lot. After much of the AM testimony, "Shifty" declares to the Liberal media that the Trump withholding of security assistance was now tied to the Burisma/Biden/2016 investigations. Not So. Sondland never heard "Biden" mentioned and assumed that everyone understood this reason for the withholding although he never heard it directly from anyone. WHA? #FakeNews

Highlight 2 in Day Four of the OII: Lawyers are taught on day one of law school that they are to assume nothing. The law is based on facts. Sondland would have flunked out, or not presumed anything re Ukraine. Instead, he chose to presume that everyone was "in the loop" in presuming what he presumed. Score as the day ends: POTUS—3.7, Inquisition - .3.

Highlight 1 in Day Five of the OII: "Lifers" Holmes and Dr Hill appear under subpoena for the State Dept. Holmes has a 40-minute opening for a short telephone call, and Hill came to answer questions. Both did not appreciate Giuliani and Sondland "meddling", and Yovanovitch firing. Wow.

Highlight 2 in Day Five (Final) of the OII: Tale of two cities. The Dems are mockingly excited as they believe they have perjury and obstruction. The Republicans know that the Left has an empty plate with no dessert on the menu. Final Score: POTUS—4.5, Inquisition - .5.

As of the middle of November 2019, many of us are wondering when will "twitchy" Liz Warren be disappearing from the Dem 2020 stage? I admit I was wrong in thinking she would have been long gone by now. I guess I had too much faith in the level of intelligence in her party. Dummy. #Democrites #LyingLiz At that same time, Attorney General William Barr: The "resist" movement on the Left has been and is an effort to sabotage the Executive Branch of the Government and an affront to the US Constitution. #ResistIsUnAmerican

A note on how insane the Liberals in America have become. On November 15, 2019, their US House "leader", Speaker Pelosi, called Trump an "imposter". Wha? Has an alien from outer space taken over his body? As one of the "rats" in the "Swamp", Pelosi should know better. And they call her a "leader"? I would label her as an anchor around their necks. #PelosiMeltdown

There is an occasional element of humor as the Inquisition drags on. We are exposed to "Fart-Gate" as #Democrite CA House member Swillwell (as I call him) is interviewed on "Hardball with Chris Matthews". One of the two of them "let one go" during the interview (no, Mr. Matthews, it was not one of your anniversary mugs being dragged on a desk). Who doesn't enjoy occasionally hearing a hearty "fluff" on the air, i.e. passing air on the air! #FartGate

California tries to block President Trump from the 2020 primary election there unless he discloses five years of this income tax returns. What do they not understand about federal laws governing the conditions for candidates to be on that ballot? Then later, Trump indicates that he will release his returns in 2020.

As the Impeachment Inquisition winds down, US House member Brenda Lawrence (D-MI) announces she favors censorship of Trump rather than his impeachment. The Conservative media is intrigued. Then she flip-flops the next day. There must have been a Left-wing "hit" on her during the night. That will leave a mark. #Democrite

Google/YouTube have announced the removal of 300+ Trump campaign ads. Get ready for the DOJ antitrust action to break you up. We are ready. Can you say "monopoly"? And later in the week the "founders" of Google step down from their corporate leadership roles? Do you remember Larry Page and Sergey Brin? They are the same people who took to the stage with tears in their eyes after the results of the 2016 election of Trump over Clinton and vowed that it would never happen again—like they could do something about it? This is starting to get interesting. #LunacyOnTheLeft

Round Two of the Impeachment Inquisition starts this week with Rep Jerry Nadler at House Judiciary. POTUS and the GOP will not participate, nor in any way validate the most partisan political process of its' type in US history. #ImpeachmentInsanity

Day One of Illegitimate Inquisition Phase 2 (IIP2) as the proceedings move where they should have been from the beginning (House Judiciary): Back to Law School for some of us to re-study Constitutional Law and Parliamentary Procedure. Yawn. And with three "never-Trumpers" (Feldman, Gerhardt, and Karlan) and one moderate non-political (Turley) instructors. Please wake me when it is over. GOP Rep. Lee Zeldin watches the madness in DC and exposes the charlatan academicians who are testifying. What a waste. Questions for Law Professor Pamela Karlan (regarding her invoking the name of the minor son of POTUS before House Judiciary): 1. How dare you? 2. Who do you think you are? Answers: 1. Gall and hatred; 2. Nobody who matters. You would probably be better off venting in a padded room somewhere instead of in front of the American people.

Day One of IIP2: The three "brilliant" Liberal law school professors each misquoted POTUS on the Ukraine call: "do ME a favor" instead of the actual "do US a favor". BIG DIFFERENCE, IDIOTS! #ImpeachmentInsanity When the dust settled for the day, the three professors on the Left (is that being "redundant"?) outweighed the moderate (Turley) who warned them what our generation has always been taught: "be very careful what you wish for."

Day Two of IIP2: The Inquisition "Circus" reaches the strangest day yet as legal counsel for each side of the Judiciary Committee present the "facts", supported by staff members — and then they question one another. Time to move this farce on to the Senate.

Nancy Pelosi on December 5, 2019: "With a heart full of love" and "this is not political" directs House Judiciary to draft Articles of Impeachment. This is a "fait accompli" from what started the day following the 2016 election. #LiberalLunacy She later says (at the same news conference): "I do not hate the President…I am praying for him". Bull Feces. Here is a prayer for the comrades on the Left: Dear Lord, please bring sanity back to the Democrats in DC. ASAP. They need to get work done for America. In your name we pray. Amen.

On December 10, 2019, House Judiciary Chair Nadler presents just two fraudulent Articles of Impeachment with a fatal mistake in the intro — Trump did not interfere with the 2020 election, but rather wanted answers regarding The Ukraine support for Hillary in 2016. Ouch. That will definitely leave a scar. During the rollout of the Articles, we hear again from House Intel Chair, "Bug-eyed" Adam Schiff: we must impeach the President to prevent him from AGAIN colluding with foreign players to steal an election. Question: Did he sleep through the Mueller Investigation and Report? Probably — or else he is lying again. Hmm. #FakeNews #ImpeachmentInsanity Then, following a year of delay, Pelosi and the #Democrites report just minutes after announcing Impeachment Articles that their version of USMCA (which is "INFINITELY BETTER" THAN THE TRUMP PROPOSAL!) will be voted on. Nancy just inserted a knife into her target and gave it a twist! Is there anything good on the face of the earth for which the elitist Left will not try to take credit. It does not seem so from this vantagepoint. #LiberalLunacy

The fascist #Democrite-led "debate" of the Inquisition Articles on December 12, 2019 in the Senate Judiciary Committee is as close as we have come to Russia in the last three years with the exception of the Hillary-DNC funded #FakeNews dossier. #ImpeachmentBackfire On the following day, two Articles of Impeachment go to the full House of Representatives from a partisan "showboat" vote in the House Judiciary Committee which was postponed from around midnight on a Thursday night to Friday morning for the cameras to be present. Only a couple of weeks earlier, Speaker Pelosi had promised the Liberal media and American people that there would be no impeachment unless it was bipartisan. The only thing bipartisan about the whole "sham" Inquisition will be some House Democrats bolting to join the Republicans in opposing impeachment. How is that working for you, Nancy? During that week's Inquisition bull excrement, these matters and more were lost in the impeachment "haze": FCC approves 988 for a suicide prevention number (this is one of my favorites as I have worked for years in efforts to reduce Veteran suicides)(this comes on the heels of a report from the US Department of Defense that 541 active military members took their life in 2018); Carter Page was a CIA informant as the FBI was spying on him through FISA; Phase One of the US-China trade agreement is reached; 266,000 new jobs in November blew out the projection of 188,000; the Boris Johnson and Conservative Party landslide victory in Britain to further mandate Brexit! And there was plenty more. I continue to be shocked at what this President can do while he has a very heavy anchor and chain around his neck.

'Twas a week before Christmas when all through the US House, the impeachment insanity was stirring exposing the louses. The Articles were hung by the dais with care in hopes that the POTUS would soon join them there. To the Liberal Lunatics in Congress: there is nothing you can do to spoil our faith-filled holiday season. Merry Christmas and Happy Hanukkah. Go Home and hopefully you will "Get a Life" as a present. The Liberal members of the US House are all nestled in their chairs, while visions of a Trump-less White House dance in their heads. Out on the House floor there arose such a clatter; we sprang to our TVs to see what was the matter. When what to our focused eyes should appear but a partisan coup led by 8 #Democrites. More rapid than eagles her coursers they came, and Grinch Pelosi called them by name: Now Shifty, Now Nadler, Now Hoyer and Omar, On Waters, On Green, On Swalwell and Engel. The Inquisition Left in the House summon the same Constitution they threaten to replace and say "no one is above the law" while ignoring Hillary and the other Obama "thugs". Pitiful. The Star Chamber Impeachment Inquisition in four words: "The 'Swamp' Fights Back". How embarrassing for these "creatures of the DC lagoon". The #Democrites have their rushed baseless impeachment and now Speaker Pelosi is foot dragging turning it over to the US Senate. Early New Year's Resolution: TRY TO IGNORE THOSE IDIOTS ON THE LEFT AND THEIR GAME PLAYING. Our local "rag" ("*The Forum*") headlined on December 19, 2019: "IMPEACHED", with a disturbing photo of the POTUS. We call that blunder "premature headlineulation" as there is no such thing until the Articles are turned over to the Senate. Remove egg on face. #FakeNews One of the best descriptions of the Inquisition Insanity has come from Tucker Carlson of @FoxNews: "A flaming bag of dog bombs" as the "sadness" and "solemnity" of Leftist #Democrites turned to "glee" while they prepare to place the Articles on the doorstep of the US Senate. #Impeachment

Merry Christmas and Happy New Year (with prayers) President Trump! There is no impeachment until the Articles/Resolutions are delivered to the Senate, which #PelosiMeltdown failed to do prior to the end of 2019. She instead chose to extort the upper chamber in an attempt to control the methodology of the Senate trial. We always knew that "Crazy" Nancy had it in her, and now she has proved it! Prediction (as of 1-9-20 @ 9:15 AM CST): #Pelosi will send the Inquisition Articles to the Senate within the next 24 hours as her own party joins the GOP in calling out her senseless delay. FOLLOW UP: Missed my prediction from yesterday that Pelosi would pass the Impeachment Articles to the Senate by now — 24 hours later. "Should" was the correct word to use. Breaking News: Nancy has been hired by a regional circus as a clown, the company citing her vast Congressional experience in that capacity! Cool silver lining.

Retweeting POTUS Tweet about how the Liberals had been all over him since the Inauguration in January of 2017. Really? IDTS ("I don't think so" for you non-millennials). The mocking from the Left started when Donald and Melania took the golden escalator ride down in Trump Tower on June 16, 2015 and will not end until he is gone! #FakeNews

Minority Leader Schumer and the Dems in the US Senate have forced 81 cloture votes so far during US District Court Judge approvals. This compares to one such vote at this point in the final Obama term and ZERO votes during the previous five Presidents. You cannot make this stuff up. It is obvious that the national leaders on the Left think Americans are stupid — that we do not see this #Resist charade for what it is. If the Republicans are not put back in power in the US House in 2020, we need to get used to a maximum and unprecedented level of inactivity in Congress at least until early 2025.

Here is a project for you. Go into your online dictionary and look up "creepy". It will take you to a Democratic Socialist Convention or gathering in the US—a great example of disfunction in the middle of our country. You will witness gender confusion, compulsive chatter, and the offensive use of gender terminology, all leading to PTSD. What I saw was extremely disturbing. My advice for those of you who gravitate to these events is for you to come back to the mainstream and work with those of us who embrace inclusion in order for us all to work and grow together.

The #Democrites/Pelosi change less than 5% of the USMCA trade agreement (negotiated by the Trump administration to take the place of the disastrous NAFTA program) and try to take credit for it all. Sorry to say we on the Right are not insane enough like you to believe that. Trade Advisor Navarro: "she [Pelosi] put a coat of polish on the Ferrari". #FakeNews

Dems believe that Trump will lose in 2020 if the POTUS continues to Tweet—or is that just wishful thinking? The bottom line is that they want the most transparent Presidency in history to end in a "cloud of dust". How ironic that this term has followed the least transparent Presidency in history.

The 2019-20 holiday break for Congress has resulted in the year-end regurgitation of '19 stories, and a temporary respite from the hate-filled Liberal displays. During the first week of the new decade, we are getting ready for that to end abruptly. Too bad, as it has been quite refreshing.

The "leaking machine" Liberals in Congress wanted to know in advance of the deadly Qasem Soleimani drone strike on January 3, 2020. Trump had followed through on the opportunity to "take out" the top Iranian Quds Force General along with Abu Mahdi al-Muhandis, deputy head of the Iranian-backed

Iraqi Popular Mobilization Forces (PMF) in a convoy near the Baghdad airport. Two points: 1. There was no advance; and 2. Review the story of the "Scorpion and the Frog" (which originated in Russia). If you are not familiar with that story, be sure to google it. It is an enduring lesson about "trust" and predictability. There is also an element there about trusting your "gut" to steer you in the right direction. Smooth talkers will try to convince you to act in a certain way, leading you to use common sense and "a feeling" to guide you in the right direction. Following the assassination, those on the Left are going ballistic in criticizing Trump for escalating tensions in the Middle East and especially the poor relationship between the US and Iran. Reminder to them: we have been "at war" with Iran for the past 40 years. And "warning" for the #Democrites: Be careful that your support for Iran following the Soleimani attack is not "giving aid and comfort to the enemy"—as doing such is still treason and not protected by the First Amendment. When POTUS ordered the termination of Soleimani and it was carried out with a drone, the #Liberals questioned what the Trump "plan" was for Iran. They learned it again during the AM of January 8, 2020—maximum pressure leading to negotiations. When will the "pro-terrorists" on the Left understand Teddy's "big stick" philosophy? Sure enough in that message from Trump: the US is ready to embrace peace with all who seek it, "no nukes" for Iran, and continuing maximum pressure against the regime. It has always seemed like a clear "plan" to many of us on the Right.

As the #Democrite controlled House votes on a non-binding Resolution to limit the POTUS "war powers" relating to Iran (January 9, 2020), Ayatollah Ali Khamenei is fondly gazing upon his #Liberal "allies" in the US Congress. Isn't that sweet!

On January 14, 2020, #Pelosi claims the delay in sending the Inquisition to the Senate has delivered the desired results. Breaking News: Nancy has become an expert in successfully "spinning" garbage. Query: Was part of her delay in delivering the Articles of Impeachment to the Senate an effort to slow or block the rise of Sanders in the Dem 2020 race in favor of Biden? A Senate "trial" now will have that result. Interesting thought. The next day #Pelosi names the Inquisition Managers and says, "this is about the Constitution". No, Nancy. This is about #TrumpAffectiveDisorder #TAD. The #Democrites are the poster children for the need of better mental health treatment in the US. What a CRAZY juxtaposition today—the historic signing of Phase One of the US-China Trade Agreement as the House sends the pathetic #Inquisition to the Senate. Thrilling and Embarrassing. You decide which is which. #Winning versus #Losers.

As the Senate impeachment trial preliminaries begin on January 16, 2020, here are some observations from the Right. #Pelosi says that the #Inquisition will show the world that the US voters determine our President, not Donald Trump and Russia/Putin? Doesn't she know about the "Mueller Report"?

The #Democrites showboat the delivery of the #Inquisition Articles to the Senate with smiles, souvenir pens on silver trays, and selfies. Disgraceful. The better news is that this partisan charade is almost over. #Pelosi states that Trump will always bear the stigma of #Impeachment. Okay. But there will always be an asterisk to correctly reveal his acquittal and him being a victim of Left-wing hazing and bullying which resulted in a branding. What do the House Dems not understand about the POTUS request for an inquiry into why a rogue Ukraine government actively supported Hillary in 2016, as Hunter Biden was receiving $66K (or more) per month from corrupt Burisma while his VPOTUS father was the country's supervisor for the Obama administration? And at the same time the son was serving on dozens of other corporate boards around the world. This is going to get uglier (if that is believable) as the proverbial excrement hits the fan. #LiberalsHypocrisy

On January 17, 2020, Trump announces the "Dream Team" to present his defense in the Senate Impeachment trial (Pam Bondi, Pat Cipollone, Alan Dershowitz, Eric Herschmann, Jane Raskin, Robert Ray, Jay Sekulow, and Ken Starr). Suddenly the House Managers do not seem so formidable. Okay, the "Shifty"-led House lawyers never did appear to be very impressive. Prepare for a fast break and slam dunk by the POTUS to end the Leftist coup attempt.

"Quote of the Day" as we reach Day 1 of the Senate Impeachment Trial (SIT)—from Rep. John Radcliffe (R-TX) on FoxNews: "This [Senate Impeachment Trial] will be like killing a fly with a sledgehammer!" CliffsNotes of the forthcoming SIT—no "high crimes and misdemeanors" charged means no conviction and removal from office. Period. The ship to provide new evidence has sailed based on the House rush to judgment. Chuck Schumer: we cannot let foreigners elect our President. AYKM? Take a quick look at the Leftist Google and Social Media impact with international players. Duh? And it is impossible to "cover up" a sham now that it is in the open for all to see. #Impeachment #Liberals

Part 1: Day One of the Senate #Impeachment Trial (SIT) with the POTUS Dream Team up against the House "F Troop". "A partisan impeachment is like stealing an election" (our "Founding Fathers")(Cited by White House Counsel Pat Cipollone). Part 2: This trial is so important that our local NBC affiliate replaced their coverage at 1 PM CST with reruns of "Judge Judy". The charade must end quickly. Part 3 of Day One of SIT: The rules are adopted following a marathon session and a Justice Roberts admonishment to both sides—follow US Senate decorum.

Day Two of the SIT: the opening statement by Shifty for the Dem House Managers was two hours of useless information and no HC&M followed by Schumer's repetitive "that calls for documents and witnesses". With Nadler following, it is a guarantee of gagging and sleep without any assistance. Wake me when it is over. #Impeachment

Pelosi: Impeachment is a permanent scar on Trump. Is it really? Query: Could POTUS sue the House for the #Impeachment based on unconstitutionality as there was no finding of the required "high crimes and misdemeanors" (HC&M)? Hmm. #Liberals

#Hillary is all over the "news" on January 22, 2020: a day after "no one likes Bernie", she will support him if he is the nominee. And Tulsi #Gabbard sues HRC for $50 million—defamation for calling her a "Russian asset". That could not have happened to a nicer person!

Day Three of the SIT as it starts: "in a nutshell—different day, same Schiff!" Advice to the Dem House Managers: move away from the chalkboard and use your other presenters as well. Schiff has the credibility of a Clinton, i.e. zero.

Day Three of the SIT continues: reminder to the House Democratic Managers—you cannot "make a silk purse out of a sow's ear". #Impeachment

Hawaii Sen. Mazie Hirono appears with Sen. Schumer in a press conference on Day Three. Message to Sen. Hirono: wipe that sh _ _-eating grin off your face. Who do you think you are? Schumer: the word is "fairer", talk to the House about "witnesses and documents", and POTUS did not pledge to cut Medicare and Social Security. #FakeNews Listen with your ears, not with your mouth. Sen. Chris Murphy (D-CT) responding to a question about his "open mind" in the SIT: he is not expecting to hear anything positive about the POTUS? How not open can a person get? He is a "true" #Democrite (reminder: Democrat + hypocrite), as they claim the GOP Senators are ignoring their "facts". #Impeachment

Day Three of the SIT concludes with House Democrat Manager Nadler claiming Trump's actions were worse than Nixon's? Then why didn't the House charge a HC&M? You cannot make this stuff up. #FactIsStrangerThanFiction

Day Three Claim by Shifty: we are seeking the "truth". Seems a bit hypocritical when it comes from a compulsive liar, but that is what the #Democrites do.

Schumer: you can see that we are getting the attention of the Republican Senators [in the SIT]. Yes, you are, Chuckie. You are unifying them like never before with the outrageous performance of the Democratic House Managers.

Day Four of the SIT is ready to begin: the topic will be Article 2, Obstruction of Congress. What is it exactly that you do not understand about "executive privilege"? #Impeachment

At the same time as the #Inquisition "sleep-fest" is going on, Trump makes history as the most "Pro-Life" President in decades and the first to attend and speak at the March For Life! Dems claim he is trying to distract. No, he wants to #MAGA for all Americans, including the unborn. #AllLivesMatter

Day Five of the SIT begins following the House Managers delivery of groceries to the Senate Chambers: the Dream Team engages the "F" Troop. The House case against POTUS is indeed overwhelming—"overwhelmingly flimsy, lopsided, and incomplete". Cipollone, Sekulow et al shine! #Impeachment @ realDonaldTrump

As we prepare for Day Six of the SIT, will a leak from John Bolton's upcoming book push us closer to witnesses in front of the Senate? It should not. That would be the work the House failed to do. And I will pass on that book, as I do not read "kiss & tell" stories.

Day Six of the SIT: we must never again permit the partisan "weaponizing" of impeachment, which has made the process common in the US as opposed to the archaic tool it became in the UK (former US Solicitor General Ken Starr).

Day Six of the SIT: Dream Team's Pam Bondi addresses the Biden Ukrainian corruption charges which the Dems called "debunked conspiracy theories" and shreds the House Managers position like a tire being recycled. That will leave a big impression. #PamBondi #Impeachment

Day Six of the SIT comes to a close: the Dream Team's Alan Dershowitz confirms that the material leaked from the upcoming Bolton book does not improve the House Democrats' impeachment case. There is still no impeachable conduct.

Who caused the Bolton "kiss & tell" book leak? He and the publisher say, "not us". Presumably, the FBI is all over it. If Bolton is even partially responsible, I will support a #BoycottBoltonBook effort. #Bolton

Day Seven of the SIT (as the Dems are "Kavanaughing" the Trial): grounds for impeachment and removal are not to be malleable (flexible). The offenses must be clear. This Senate is being asked to remove the duly elected POTUS based on "policy differences"!

Quite a few of us agree with Sen. Lindsey Graham: no witnesses in the Senate as House has not presented a prima facie case (no HC and M). But if witnesses will be permitted, call both Bidens, Schiff, Chalupa, and the Whistleblower. POTUS will prevail.

Day Eight of the SIT: questions from the Senators to the House Managers and the Dream Team. It does not appear that there has been any movement on either side. There is a desire to get this over with the least amount of "whining" on the Left, but they will not be happy with just witnesses.

Liz Warren never met a "hair-brained" idea she did not embrace. The latest is to create civil and criminal liability and penalties for disseminating "misinformation". Really? I suppose that would include the beginning of the "truth police"? #1984 And at one time she was the Democratic POTUS leader for the nomination with a 2-point lead over Joe Biden?! That is truly disturbing. Her mission for an immediate end to fracking was and is not very popular in North Dakota, and it is not very difficult to figure out why.

Day Nine of the SIT: the questions and answers finally conclude with the same amount of repetitiveness we have seen during all the proceedings. The thirst for witnesses has been back and forth so many times that some heads are spinning. This could all be done tomorrow. Praying for that.

Day Ten of the SIT: the "spin" by the House and Senate Dems (before the voting) is out of control. Why should there be witnesses and additional evidence when the House case cited no "HC and M"? They claim a massive cover-up by the Republicans who are simply burying the Leftist fecal matter. #Liberals

Day Ten of the SIT: The effort to add new witnesses and evidence (the House's work) in the Senate fails as predicted from Day

One—on a 51-49 vote. Closer to acquittal with only closing statements and another vote to go. What a waste for America. We deserve better as the best country in the world.

Bring on the Waste Management Open, North Dakota hockey, and the Super Bowl! @FoxSports

Day Eleven of the SIT: closing arguments. The viewing numbers will probably show close to a zero. Were you expecting more?

"The Disaster in Des Moines"—not a soon-to-be-released thriller, but instead a real-time electoral catastrophe for the #Democrats and their primary in the heartland. The organizers passed on a DHS offer to test their new voting software (which failed miserably). Ouch! It is time for the Iowa caucuses to disappear.

Day Twelve of the SIT: the partisan preaching is grinding the #Impeachment proceedings to a halt like a 50-year old Ford Falcon. Thank you, Lord, that this attempted coup is almost over.

Bring on POTUS for the State of the Union speech tonight. The "State" is powerfully strong following three years of rebuilding America without much help from the "resisting" (or "blocking") #Democrats. Getting great again.

Congratulations to @RushLimbaughEIB on his being presented with the Presidential Medal of Freedom. He has earned it many times over in the Conservative trenches. #Conservatives

The #PelosiMeltdown continues in full view as the SOTU address ends—a tantrum tearing up her copy of the speech. Her actions of hate and division speak much louder than her occasional words of love and unity. Did the House Speaker violate 18 U.S.C. Sec. 2071(b) by destroying a public record (POTUS

SOTU address manuscript) duly placed into her custody? If so, she can be fined no more than $3000, jailed for up to 3 years, and lose her position. That could not be any more appropriate under the circumstances.

Differences of opinion on the SOTU address depending on the side of the aisle—"one of the best ever" versus "juvenile partisan cheerleading". And Rep. Debbie Dingell (D-MI) had hoped for more reconciliation? What planet is she from?

Day Thirteen (Final? And Lucky?) of the SIT: the Senators continue to express their positions (SOSO) and then a mid-afternoon vote to acquit or not. The best money is on the former.

Breaking News (and no surprise): Mitt Romney will break from the GOP Senators to vote for removal of President Trump. He cannot get over that @realDonaldTrump rightly dissed him for his loss to Obama (an election he should have won). Every party has a pooper and it might as well be Mitt—the newest poster child for the Leftist media. #romney

POTUS is forever acquitted of the House #Impeachment! #romney voted to remove President Trump for an Article 1 violation (Abuse of Power) based on his religious beliefs as a Mormon. We will eventually see if the Mormons in Utah agree with him. The rumors are that they will not.

The words of #PelosiMeltdown this AM: "I have tried to be gracious [toward President Trump]." How stupid do she and the rest of the #Liberals elite believe Americans to be? "Trump Affective Disorder" (TAD) has truly driven them to insanity.

An appropriate time for one of my favorite quotes, this one from Albert Einstein: "Weak people revenge; strong people forgive; intelligent people ignore." What are you telling me, as I was not paying attention? There has been an impeachment process going on during the past several months. Where have I been? Wink. Wink.

The "New Way Forward" proposal is a major step backwards. The lazy #Liberals in the #Swamp are trying to substitute this joke for the necessary comprehensive immigration reform — and the Right is not buying it. #LiberalLunacy

More journalistic "incest" and a significant error in judgment in our local paper on February 7, 2020. In the frontpage lead article, they featured the "Arts" writer for the newspaper and her husband about their journey to sobriety. This was an excellent article for the "Life" section of the paper, but hardly qualifies as "news". And with the difficult nature of arts promotion these days, we need to be very careful not to offend the strong supporters. In a photograph for the article, it showed her computer with a "RESIST" sticker adorning the exposed panel of the laptop. Such a display violates a general rule that for those who are arts spokespersons, they need to stay away from politics lest they alienate supporters on one side of the fence or the other. I hope that I was in the vast minority in even noticing that word which many of us have come to despise in these times of unprecedented incivility and division. And congratulations to the couple for their success in the battle against alcohol addiction.

Democrat 2020 POTUS candidate, Tulsi Gabbard, is fighting the Democratic elites in DC who are pulling the strings behind the competition for the nomination. Good luck with that?! Those "gators" from the #Swamp have really strong jaws and teeth!

Has the #Biden2020 campaign for POTUS run out of gas? He looks very tired, got clobbered in Iowa, is trailing by a mile in NH, and financial contributors are not doing so. It would be sad to see that entertainment disappear.

You can stick a fork in the Biden (did I ever get this wrong) and Warren campaigns…they are done (as of February 12, 2020)! And make sure the rest of you have your campaign obits ready as Socialist Bernie and "stop & frisk" Bloomberg are rising to the top.

The lemmings on the Left are calling for AG Bill Barr to resign following a DOJ reduction of the Roger Stone sentencing recommendation, without knowing the facts and ignoring the power of the Judge to decide the punishment. Fools. Follow up: The #Democrites come out of the woodwork senselessly calling for the resignation of AG Barr. What did the GOP do when AG Holder referred to himself as Obama's "wingman"? Nothing/ crickets. #GetALife.

You have undoubtedly noticed that most of the critics of President Trump are amphibious residents of "the swamp". They are also "green" and are alarmed about the reduction in the water level of their habitat. #DrainTheSwamp

Democratic 2020 Presidential candidate Bernie Sanders is the gift that keeps on giving to his party, now doubling down in his support of policies of former Cuban dictator Fidel Castro., and calling for free daycare. #Democrites should be afraid, very afraid.

Line of the Day: Question — "What was your impression of the Democratic debate last night [2-25-20]?" Answer: "It was either a train wreck or a clown car." Way to go CBS.

Shame on Pelosi and Schumer for weaponizing/politicizing the Coronovirus, sending some Americans into near-panic mode. Be glad you are not from North Dakota, as I would work here to have you removed from your position.

#Democrite disconnect: #PelosiMeltdown claims party unity while the POTUS hopefuls say that only they can defeat @realDonaldTrump. This is the real-time birth of our 5-6 party system in the US.

We know that China is serious about stopping the spread of the #coronavirus they started when they ban the consumption of dogs and cats in the country.

Television schedule for today (2-28-20) on HBO lists "Hellboy" followed by "Bill Maher" (or is it really two episodes of "Hellboy" in a row?). #billmaher

#FakeNews NBC with Lester Holt and a commentator saying as February ends that Americans are being urged to "stay home" and "don't go out to restaurants"?! Wha? Their next statement will be "don't breathe the air". #coronavirus

Political losers on the Left accuse POTUS of declaring COVID-19 a "hoax". No! Listen! He correctly said that your criticism of the administration response to the virus is your next #FakeNews "hoax effort"! Now that makes sense. DUH?

It appears that Democratic leader Donna Brazile is drowning in the mire of the "swamp". On #FoxNews today (3-3-20), she told RNC Chair Ronna McDaniel to "Go to Hell" (repeatedly) for weighing in on the Dem primary strategies, and then stated a strange pledge to be more civil during Lent? Too late, as the respect for you (at least from this observer) is gone. And that is too bad because some on the Right used to listen to her statements. Many of us who are Christians were taught that only God makes the call about Heaven and Hell, but maybe evidenced by these passionate proclamations Donna must know more than we do about such a decision. And please do not go there, Ronna.

Democratic Senate leader #Schumer threatens #SCOTUS Justices Gorsuch, Kavanaugh & Roberts three times in a matter of hours yesterday (3-4-20). Shocking, but not surprising for a person who is insane. Something has happened to the swamp dwellers after the calendar hit March. Schumer should pay with a minimum of censure.

The #Democtites 2020 POTUS platform is "Anything/Anyone to Beat Trump!" So much for a concise presentation of policy positions. Prepare for an incredible waste of money.

Liz Warren is OUT. Good call. She lasted about 3 months longer than many of us predicted she would. I will miss her Socialistic rants, but not her raised clenched fists, screaming, "twitchy movements", and "selfie" bragging. Back to some beer swigging for she and her husband to get over her dismal primary showing at home in Massachusetts.

Disgraced Sen. Crazy Chuck #Schumer continues to spread inflaming #FakeNews about the administration response to COVID-19 and the effect on the markets—without mentioning a 30-point single-day drop in world oil prices? He is "nuttier than a fruitcake".

The Liberal mainstream media and social media are responsible for most of the panic and hysteria we have today surrounding COVID-19. Is it time to shut them down (with the Wall Street markets)—just as we did following 911? #CoronavirusPandemic

In 24 hours (as of 3-16-20), NY Governor #AndrewCuomo has made a precipitous 180-degree flip on the issue of local/ state control of the COVID-19 response as being his best solution, to one that the federal government needs to handle this all and the same for every jurisdiction? Someone no doubt reminded him that he is a #Democrat first and a leader second (or third?). #Liberals

Two days later, #Schumer continues to criticize the @realDonaldTrump administration for its' response to the #CoronavirusPandemic and guarantees a "recession" while most of us are trying to stay positive. Apparently for some politicians it is impossible to avoid the whoring whenever there is an opportunity. Then, following another two-day break, the #Democrite becomes the contemporary "Chicken Little" on the Senate floor: "The sky is falling, the sky is falling!" Is it any wonder why those who listen to him are panicking? #CoronavirusPandemic

#Democrite #Bloomberg is giving $18 million to the DNC (3-21-20). How about instead giving those funds to our fight of the #CoronavirusPandemic rather than again trying to "buy elections"? #Liberals

Good News: Senators reach a #CoronavirusPandemic relief agreement (3-25-20). Bad news (for #Democrats): Their partisan antics at this critical time in our nation's history have sealed their dismal fate for the '20 elections.

The US Senate approved the $2 trillion CARES Act (COVID-19 stimulus bill) on March 25, 2020, followed by the US House two days later—one of the few acts of bipartisanship we have seen during the Trump administration. Congress has finally taken the American people into account in an effort to diminish their pain.

I will not write about what I am thinking on this Sunday in Lent (3-29-20), so I will wait until tomorrow to address the most recent pathetic and dangerous comments of Nancy Pelosi. Next day: Someday alleged-Christian #PelosiMeltdown will be given the "thumbs up" (Heaven) or "thumbs down" (Hell) by

God at the Pearly Gates. With her recent profane claims that the POTUS is "fiddling while people are dying", my money is being bet on the considerably warmer venue.

I finally hear discussion about what I have been saying for months—CoronaVirus Reparations (CVR) must be pursued against China. Thank you, #TomCotton!

I honor and salute all of you today, March 29, 2020 (and every day), who served in Vietnam during the war, as well as those 58,220 American heroes who never made it back alive to our shores. We can never thank you enough as a grateful nation. May God be with you and bless you. It is National Vietnam War Veterans Day. #HonorOurVeterans

The #MLM (mainstream Liberal media) calls for networks to not televise (sensor/boycott) the POTUS daily COVID-19 briefings. Such a plan would result in more virus deaths, but they don't care. So much hatred! #Liberals

CNN poll shows Biden leading Trump by 11 points as other polls show a "dead-heat"? Another problem for Dems is a 56% "enthusiasm" rate for the fall elections with Republicans at 80%. Just wait until Joe gets the trapdoor because of his condition. #Liberals #2020Elections

#Democrites blocking an additional $250 billion for the PPP which will run out of funds on 4-17-20. They want to add their "pork" that will be addressed in COVID Tranche 4. Remember this small business owners—enemies on the Left, friends on the Right!

The Leftist political hacks are now calling for a Commission to study the US COVID response, in the middle of the battle? The "resistance" becomes the dangerous micro-managers. There is a time and place for this when the dust settles! #Liberals

What is the love affair with NY Governor Cuomo all about? He is one of the "Chicken Littles" ("the sky is falling") (with NY Senator Schumer) of the COVID fight, making every effort to hoard for NY. We do not need a national leader like that. #COVIDHoarders It is laughable that he supports #StatesRights and claims that the #CoronavirusPandemic is a political "no fight zone" while stating that @realDonaldTrump is not a king and his COVID briefings are comedic. He is obviously ignoring himself and the #Liberal partisan clowns in DC! This happens in mid-April of 2020.

#ObamaGate (worst President in US history) takes cheap shots at @realDonaldTrump while endorsing #SleepyJoeBiden for 2020, followed by Liz Warren who joins the lemmings. Pile over the cliff into the #Democrites funeral procession.

#PelosiHatesAmericans blames @realDonaldTrump for the COVID economic shutdown and resulting financial devastation while blocking the immediate critical need for more PPP funds. She will hereafter wear a red "W" on her forehead. #Liberals Two days later (4-17-20), #Democrites are destroying thousands of small businesses every day with their continued blocking of additional PPP funding for #CoronavirusPandemic victims. They will pay the piper at the ballot box in November!

Louisiana Sen John Kennedy today (4-21-20) on Fox: he has been trying to understand why the Dems have been delaying the additional PPP funding vote "but I can't get my head that far up my backside". Never dull nor uncertain is the Senator.

Thank God for the #Liberals/#Democrats/#LeftistMedia! Without their material, there would not be nearly as much of the humor and laughter we currently enjoy on the Right! Keep it up!

#AOC has re-emerged from hiding under a rock (following the demise of #Bernie). She has a brilliant plan for low-income workers who have lost their job during the #CoronavirusPandemic: don't go back to work when the economy reopens? WTH?

Every time I hear what a poor job @reaDonaldTrump is doing in response to the #CoronavirusPandemic, I wonder where that drivel is coming from. Then I watch 5 minutes of CNN, MSNBC, CBS or ABC and the answer is clear. And the American people are apparently buying it?! Those of us on the Right believe he is doing an amazing job in a situation that has never presented itself in the history of our country! #LameStreamMedia

On April 28, 2020, #PelosiMustGo touts assistance for states and cities (okay with major limits) and guaranteed minimum income (no way) as part of a #CoronavirusPandemic Relief Part 4 package. The GOP will demand vital infrastructure projects. #Socialists

That same day #Schumer criticizes @realDonaldTrump and federal #CoronavirusPandemic testing assistance. What does he not understand about "state's responsibility"? #Liberals

Memo to Dems in Congress: your #CoronavirusPandemic investigation of @realDonaldTrump and failure to support sanctions against #ChinaMustPay for their negligence and malfeasance will destroy you in November. Your conduct is un-American and will be costly.

#TrumpDerangementSyndrome (TDS) hatred by the #Democrites rears its ugly head daily: today (May 12, 2020)

those #Leftists blindly criticize the @realDonaldTrump administration response to the #CoronavirasPandemic during #Fauci Senate testimony. #Liberals would spew their vile garbage at a kindergarten graduation.

Pork is in short supply on that same day, except in the #PelosiMustGo $3T #COVID19 relief package introduced in the House when the members are out of the Swamp! Her bill releases prisoners from ICE custody, makes payments to illegals, mentions cannabis 68 times, etc. Sen. Kennedy called it "as dead as fried chicken". Truth.

#Biden admits (changing his position) being a part of the #ObaMAGAte planning to surveil the @realDonaldTrump campaign in '16. More of these treasonous Swamp Rats will be unveiled soon. The proverbial cattle feces are about to hit the fan. #Liberal #HidinBiden: #COVID19 opening is now "public health versus the economy". No. We can have both when we base it on science and facts. Leftist dummy.

#Biden, Comey, Brennan & Clapper are among the names on the declassified list of those requesting the name of the unmasked @realDonaldTrump campaign official (Gen. Flynn) alleged to be colluding with Russia. That would be a big fat "OUCH"! #ObaMAGAte

Memo to #Obama on May 20, 2020: what "legacy" of your #WorstPresidentEver remained in early-2017 has been virtually obliterated by @realDonaldTrump. Assist #HidinBiden for 2020 at your peril or disappear and preserve some dignity. Your tough choice.

The #SusanRice self-serving "by-the-book" email to herself on 1-20-17 (Inauguration Day), 15 days after her WH meeting with #Obama, #HidinBiden, and #LyingComey. The full email was declassified on May 20, 2020. Sorry lying Sue, but we are not buying it.

#Schumer (Resister-in-Chief) accusing the Senate Republicans of foot dragging with COVID relief? That is more "Novel" than the virus. Let the dollars allocated settle in as we get #backtowork. And protect most US businesses from lawsuits (and that is from a lawyer who sees the potential for hundreds of thousands of them).

Message to the #Liberals in late-May of 2020: buck up buttercups and get #backtowork safely. That is the only way we can reduce the horrific domestic violence, child abuse, suicides, ODs, alcoholism, deaths of people not going to the hospital for diagnostics due to COVID fears, and mental illness we are experiencing everywhere.

#HidinBiden criticizes @POTUSTrump on May 19, 2020 for taking #HydroxychloroquineWorks for COVID prevention purposes, just as many would question Joe's decision to have a frontal lobe lobotomy...or maybe not? Choose your battles wisely, Oh Sleepy One. #noneofyourbusiness

About a week later as I am completing the manuscript for this book, candidate Biden during a CNBC interview says: "I can beat Joe Biden!" Wha? Yes, indeed you can, Joe, and probably will!

On 6-2-20, #PelosiMustGo warns that the "world will end" with four more years of @realDonaldTrump. That is more than we have seen as far a Democratic-Socialist platform in the past 3.5 years of "resist"! I believe that POTUS has the Left a little riled up. #Liberals

#Zoom (used by everyone during the pandemic for meetings) servers are in #Communist China. Is that a concern for you? It joins #TikTok as a danger to the safety and security of America.

US Rep Jim Clyburn (D-SC) denies @realDonaldTrump any credit for helping African Americans through the First Step Act, Opportunity Zones, and the police reform Executive Order on 6-16-20—more than any POTUS in 50 years+. Sickening partisanship causing blindness.

Sometimes in life it is important to laugh to keep from crying. Example: National Review columnist Andy McCarthy stated on 6-18-20, "when will we see a wave of adulthood in DC?" He went on to warn against expecting anything soon.

On 6-23-20, House Judiciary Chair Jerry Nadler reports that he will subpoena Attorney General Bill Barr to testify regarding the "legal" firing of a US Attorney by @realDonaldTrump, threatening if necessary to de-fund the Department of Justice to extort for an appearance? Nadler is a "poster child" for incivility these days in the swamp.

The #Liberals and their leaders on the Left are supporting "mob rule" in the US with efforts to de-fund the police. Fewer dollars for security equate to more inner-city deaths and armed camps elsewhere to assure protection which the police would not be able to provide. More insanity in the swamp.

Where is the indignation of the #Democrites toward those who are destroying historic American artifacts? Answer: they do not want to criticize a vital part of their voter base (the anarchy wing).

Dems will block Congressional police reform on 6-24-20 with a vote in the US Senate to not allow debate and consideration of the Senator Tim Scott bill—a win for #Democrites and a loss for America.

Have you ever noticed that being a minority carries with it a right to declare "racism"? Is that a racist standard? Oops! As a white person, I cannot say that.

Trump's biggest challenges for the 2020 elections are the burned bridges he has created which need to be crossed. One poll today (CNN on 6-24-20) had him down by 14%.

Welcome to "*1984*" (at the beginning of summer, 2020) as #Twitter attempts to block a valid @realDonaldTrump tweet warning unlawful vandals in DC. Say "no" to political censorship—break up Twitter to slow down the #Liberal "madness". Meanwhile, the #Liberal #CancelCultureCancer is bringing down Facebook by withdrawing ads. These "*1984*" #Leftists will not quit until they succeed at eliminating Conservative thought.

#DemocratsAreDestroyingAmerica believe the group "Black Lives Matter" is an asset for the party. Isn't that very Marxist of them? And what exactly have the #Liberals in America done for African Americans during the past 50 years? Approximately. The correct answer is "zilch".

CHAPTER 24

THE "WAR" ON MEN

A recent statement from a former First Lady (and now author), the much-respected Michelle Obama—"America now is like living with a divorced dad." Really? How incredibly shallow, elitist, and sexist was that thought, not to mention trashy and hurtful to compare America to such a situation, which could be amazing or possibly awful—and from a former First Lady? That is unquestionably a pathetic first from a former FLOTUS (except probably from "stand-by-her-man" Hillary).

"News" from Fargo: Our local paper in its' "Life" section feature touts a female makeup artist who has turned to painting? And that would interest the local readers in what way? Good for her, but it just does not pass the news "smell" test. We are interested in serious issues that we are facing in our lives, and that was not one of them (at least at that time).

Another battle in the war from my local newspaper—a front-page feature, "THOSE FEMINISTS" (really all in CAPS) by an area "cub" reporter, about the federally-funded 1977 National Women's Conference. That was two years after President Ford started an initiative to recognize more equality between the sexes (the same year that North Dakota approved the Equal Rights Amendment which eventually failed by three states). The story featured a law school classmate of mine and supported the proposition that today's children should be educated about the Conference. Really? How about the idea of civics training instead? The article was a "yawner", probably intended as a common "in your face" offering from the paper.

In my original book I discussed the collateral damage from the "war" on young men and boys. This is playing out in suicide statistics which are showing that the rates for this age group of males is growing by as much as twenty-five percent (25%) for some short periods of time. As a country we cannot afford to be losing so many individuals in any demographic categories, whether as a result of selective and exclusionary behavior or otherwise. We need to treat all segments of our population with appropriate support and respect.

The Liberals in America are living dangerously these days with their support of males who identify as females to participate in female sports, as a part of a team or in an individual capacity. This could result in the destruction (at least in part) of women's sports as we have come to know them. Watch for records to fall and be careful in the locker rooms.

A new phrase has been sweeping the country as a new "tool" in this war. Women are heard complaining about "toxic masculinity"—what I call the "Boys-Will-Be-Boys Syndrome" (or BW2B Syndrome). According to Wikipedia, the problem refers to "certain cultural norms that are associated with harm to society and to men themselves, as well as traits such as misogyny or homophobia used in promoting bullying, aggression, and sexual/domestic violence" [maybe a slight paraphrase]. There are also claims that the typical male tendencies toward competitive sports fuels the toxicity. I view such terminology as simply another "dog whistle" in the female trove used to demean the opposite sex toward a position of sexual inferiority. This is all supported by some on the Left who have shown a propensity toward the "kick-them-while-they're-down" mentality espoused as a viable alternative to the "high road" by former US Attorney General Eric Holder.

Query: why are the contestants on *"Wheel of Fortune"* always two women and one guy (except when it is all women or couples, or after I wrote this (on September 10, 2019) when there were actually two men and one woman?)? This is similar to a local television commercial advertising a new autism clinic in the area which features a care provider and an adolescent boy—no, a young girl?! My jaw nearly hit the floor. Minutia? Maybe. I have apparently just led a sheltered life, not knowing or having heard about too many girls suffering from autism.

The "war for women" is perpetuated and invigorated with stories around the US such as the one we read about locally on June 3, 2019, celebrating the 100 years of women's suffrage in America. Now that is a worthy cause for commemoration, as well as questioning why it took so long for women to be able to vote in our republic. We obviously made many mistakes as we were growing this country, and we are presently continuing to learn from our erroneous and imperfect pathways traveled to arrive here today.

On June 5, 2019, we are greeted in the morning by our local newspaper with the lead frontpage article entitled "THE DOCTOR IS ALWAYS IN", from the area director of a women's healthcare service unveiling a new virtual appointment system. Maybe one day they will develop such an important program that is available to men as well—or maybe not. After all, I suppose that men are always available to go into the clinic for face-to-face examinations? Don't hope for this to be applicable to men any time soon. Update: it took COVID-19 to bring men into the mainstream of video or e-conferencing between doctors and their male patients.

Our local newspaper advertises their daily online edition in the printed version, but always with a woman. At least I have never seen the ad with a man. I apologize if I have just missed it.

Is one of the reasons for the war that girls are smarter than boys from an early age? Sometimes it appears this must be the case. Our local "Dollars for Scholars" scholarship winners listed this past June consisted of 34 girls and 16 boys. Based on that, maybe girls are even twice as smart?

Gender movie producing has become very big today. This entails a balance of genders in the production of a film. New producers include Hillary Clinton and Michelle Obama. Has this resulted in an abundance of "chick flicks" during the past year or so? Maybe.

All political parties or groups need to be recruiting quality women <u>and</u> men for candidacies and leadership roles. I know that the Republicans are doing this and assume the same is true with the Democrats. Each should be wary of gravitating toward those of either sex or any sexual orientation who are too far away from the center, as we appear already to have those in politics who cover the distant corners of political thought and philosophy.

One of the latest by-lines in the war is "weaponized feminism"! It just sounds bad—evil! At the same time, I need to get in line to purchase the "Girls Like Us" book. Or maybe not. And how about the group "Code Pink: Women for Peace"? Their declared purposes are anti-militarism and supporting social justice, but their policies in the US have seemed to morph into an anti-Trump/anti-Republican diatribe including pro-Palestine and Iran, anti-Israel and Saudi Arabia, anti-drone, and supporting the close of the prison for terrorists at Guantanamo Bay. Their disruptions of Congressional hearings and occupation of embassies have seemed more fascism-orientated than their mission statement belies. My inclination is to pass on joining this effort even though I agree with some of their "neutral" and "apolitical" positions. "Real men" may wear pink, but not so much for this guy.

According to *"The Guardian"* (May 25, 2019) and writer Sian Cain, Paul Dolan, a professor of behavioural science at the London School of Economics, says that data and facts have determined that the happiest segment in the population is unmarried and childless women. The research apparently came from the American Time Use Survey (ATUS). Maybe I should have put this point in Chapter 1, as that group of individuals would also be considered as the most selfish category of humans. The baby boomers were brought up to prepare for and expect to be married and to raise a family (and to not be like Ebenezer Scrooge who married money instead of a woman). I am not sure about you, but personally cannot imagine life without my spouse and daughters, sons-in-law, and grandchildren. My non-scientific observations would be that some of the unhappiest and most unfulfilled people I know are what we used to call "old maids" or "spinsters". Maybe these women do live longer, but that cannot possibly make up for the reality of reaching retirement age and having no one to call immediate family. What a pathetic and loveless result for living alone with your "success" and "happiness". This is the epitome of being a self-centered person. Good thing to know what the facts indicate, but we will leave that information as "unconvincing" or "unfathomable". Whomever said, "successful women do not marry" was unquestionably "a few cards short of a full deck" (as we used to say).

Most Americans were probably supportive as fans of the FIFA US Women's Soccer Team during the World Cup in 2019. For some of us (including yours truly), that would change if the team became too political and turned down a post-championship invitation to visit President Trump at the White House. Sure enough (as expected), the team rejects such an invitation and accepts one to visit Congress instead. This decision was articulated by the team star and "mouth" Megan Rapinoe who ripped into the President for his alleged conduct of "excluding people". Such claims are not unusual coming from gay Americans who wrongly believe that Trump is "homophobic". Nothing is much further from the truth. In her explanatory diatribe, Rapinoe (that "one bad apple" we talk about) turns into a "troll" when she drops the "F" bomb in stating that she would not go to the White House but would instead accept an invitation from the Liberal mob to speak with those who agree with her positions. Now there is REAL exclusionary conduct! In her parade speech she said that everyone needs to "love more, hate less, listen more, and speak less", but she isn't one to heed much of her own advice. Even though I had now soured on my support for the team, I was still on their side that they should be getting paid the same amount as the US Men's Team, at least until I learned from *The Los Angeles Times* in late-July 2019 that the women have been paid MORE than the men since 2010. Ouch! This is yet another gross example of making sure you have your story right before you share it with the world. #EggOnFacesOfUSWomen'sSoccerTeam.

It seems as if every other day I learn of a new (to me) organization of women in my area or region, somewhere else in the US, or around the world. I will share some of those here for a little free publicity. I apologize in advance if I fail to list your group, either here or in other of my writings. And as I have pointed out, even though almost all of these associations would be required by US law to admit men as nonprofit public-sector entities, the chances of that happening based on the name of the group is probably slim to none. How about: "The Power of 100 Women Who Care — Red River Valley"? This sounds like an excellent bunch of people, but why couldn't it be "People" instead of "Women"? I actually know a couple of men who care — about something. "Momsstrong.org" — where are the Dads? Or how about adding them with "Parentsstrong.org"? And there is also "23 and Me", an organization of mothers and daughters. This will not be the end, even for this paragraph. Where are the sons in that organization? And how about the Facebook posts which are often shared, and which are created by "WOMEN WORKING". What is that group and what are they all about. I am sure it is all legitimate. Learned another new one recently—@soccergrl-probs. It seems that there is a need in America to use the female soccer community as another group to unite in their hostility toward and loathing of anything male. Wha? This is probably very deserving and far overdue. Call me very old fashioned, but I even get nervous when I see missions which include concepts such as "empower[ing]" or "sisterhood"—except for college Sororities of course. Our local United Way (I have been a leader over the years), in its' infinite wisdom, has set up a group named "35 Under-35 Women's Leadership Program" and announces their 2019 graduates. Great! Then in a couple of months they are soliciting members for a new class of participants. Simple question: Where is the men's program? Maybe it is the cynic in me, but I am not holding my breath. Along comes "Ford Warriors in Pink". I would join, except that I do not look good in pink. Our own Fidelity Investments announces the creation of the "Women's Leadership Fund (FWOMX)"—"Investing in Businesses Which are Investing in Women". I had not even realized that there was a corresponding "Men's Fund"—because of course there is not. I have invested in the Fund to avoid being labeled a misogynist. There is a group of women in North Dakota who are supporting efforts to assure ethical conduct by our state leaders. They call themselves the "Badass Grandmas". Apparently the "Badass Grandpas" are a "no-show".

On July 21, 2019, there is a political cartoon from local Liberal Steve Stark. "Women: what is the biggest MENACE to society? Those first three letters!" HardyHarHarHar. Not LOL. Stark is apparently a comedian as well as an artist!

Report out of neighboring South Dakota: women from around the country are visiting farms in the state. What do these women "have up their sleeves?" This is just one of those "mysteries of the mind" deals.

Many people around us today, especially politicians, need to be more careful with our words, as they can and sometimes do come back later to haunt us. During an interview for everyone's favorite news source, *Al Jazeera*, US Representative Ilhan Omar (D-MN) was quoted as saying: "Our country should be more fearful of white men in our country, as they are killing most of the people." Now just what that means, I am not certain. But if she was talking about the race of male murderers in America, US Department of Justice statistics from 2013 showed 52.2% of arrests were of African Americans and 45.3% were of Caucasians. Furthermore, most of the murders committed here have the perpetrator and victim of the same race. Please do not think of me as racist for pointing out the truth. I believe that my proposals of an education for all will reduce the numbers of murders across the board.

The "Mom's Demand Action" group (excluding the "Dads") marched on the White House during the summer of 2019 following the mass shooting in El Paso, TX, and the visual images were not very positive. What I witnessed was a bunch of women in common apparel smiling and chuckling for "selfies" to document their attendance at the event. How sickening. Who do you think you are disrespecting the shooting victims like that? Maybe this anger is due to my being an "old-timer" who was taught that there are appropriate times for various conduct, and that frivolity should not be associated with protesting the senseless deaths of 22 innocent people and the wounding of another 24! Sometimes being "old school" just does not match up with the decorum we see all around us today.

Now the MMIW (Missing and Murdered Indigenous Women) group has added a "G" for "Girls". Our local newspaper today lists four deceased Native men, ages 47, 48, 44, and 26. Where is the organization to investigate the early deaths of Indigenous men? And there is the story of a 36-year old man in Minnesota who is sentenced to twenty-five years in prison for the beating death of his three-year old son who became a "Murdered Indigenous Boy" (MIB). In a simultaneous development, the MMIWG Indigenous-led research group Sovereign Bodies Institute announces that they expect there will be an increase in the violence against Indigenous females because of the Keystone XL Pipeline construction? Now there is a stretch I did not see coming. It looks like the Bureau of Indian Affairs (BIA) officers will need to get busy to prevent anything like that from happening #MMIWG #EliminateReservations An update from late-January of 2020: I notice in a local newspaper article that they reference the MMIP group, now substituting "People" for "Women & Girls", just what I had suggested from the very beginning. We do not need to make this a sexist situation, as all of the residents of the Reservations at least in the Northern Plains are "at risk" of violence and death. And the movement takes a "big hit" as the mother of three missing from the Standing Rock Reservation in ND/SD has now been found safe in the Dallas-Ft. Worth area after having been missing for two months. The negative publicity comes from the facts that she was missing for an entire month before it was reported to authorities, that she may have become an MMIW as a result of human trafficking, and that foul play was expected. None of this turned out to be true when it was reported that the woman had apparently fled on her own when she learned there were multiple warrants out for her arrest in counties north of the Reservation. Indeed no one had taken her anywhere as she had in reality fled to avoid incarceration. It is stories like this in which parties are "crying wolf" to bring MMIP to the forefront, that diminish and demean valid attempts to raise awareness about the horrific conditions for Native Americans on and off the Reservations. There are very few people who do not want to help the Natives fight for safety and protection throughout the country, but such instances which falsify the truth leave a deep wound for those who come forward to assist in a perceived time of need and are subsequently discarded into the ditch. Let's get serious and factual in this MMIP mission.

There is a local announcement for our area by the metropolitan Chamber of Commerce that the participants (with their names and employers) have been selected for the 2020 "Women's 35-Under-35 Leadership Group". All of this is more reverse discrimination that is rampant these days and apparently ignored by the men. There would have been an "equal time" rule in my era. It is hard to buy the "oppression of the professional women" argument these days, especially in our neighborhood. It is possible they have taken a path following the State of North Dakota that has a "North Dakota Women's Business Center" without a corresponding "Men's Business Center". This may all sound very trivial to you, but to this writer it is simply as issue of basic fairness. We men will not be ignored.

There are basically two types of homeless shelters in the US — for men only, or for women with their children. There are a small number (far too few) of "family" centers. Hmm. Something appears to be missing here. This is not only more evidence of the war, it is also an effort to break up the nuclear family in America.

A local hospital in my area of the world sponsors a "Go Far Woman Health Expo". That is wonderful. Unfortunately for the men there is not a similar Expo for them, and it is certainly not because we are so healthy or that we are already living the perfect lifestyle. And there is also the excellent group "Beautiful Inside & Out Girls" which was formed in 2013, focusing on faith and athletics. It probably could have just as easily been

"People" instead of "Girls", but what fun would that have been? Besides, men and women have the University of Notre Dame and Liberty U on which to fall back for faith-based activities on an inclusive basis.

Our local newspaper features ads for "freedom of speech" exclusively with women. There must be some evidence that men are simply not interested in protecting this First Amendment right. And some of their articles attempt to lure the reader in with a "bait" headline. One recently was lead by: "THE REAL WONDER WOMEN" (actually in CAPS). I figured that the story and half page of photos would be about women who raise our children in the US. Negative with that expectation. Instead, it featured the nearly-forgotten US Cadet Nurse Corps that stepped in during WWII as the US experienced a nurse shortage during that conflict. The article was a great reminder of the sacrifice many men and women made during the War, at home and abroad. But I still believe that we do not praise our mothers and fathers enough for their critical work in bringing up the next generation to be good people and better citizens.

In a feature which followed in a few weeks (August 18, 2019) with huge photos, the headline in "pink" and "CAPS" read: "The PINK TAX". The definite "must not read" article was apparently about the assuredly unfair sales taxes on feminine products. Is there a man out there who would not agree with the need to change such rules for, among other reasons, eliminating the opportunity to continue to write about the problem on a semi-annual basis? Then the tabloid goes sharply off the cliff into the deep water two days later with a front page featuring MMIW talk from the 2020 Democratic Presidential candidates, Part 2 of a Savanna LaFontaine-Greywind revisit, and the current Liz Warren apology tour (fondly reminiscent of the Obama tours during his Presidency (and a necessary skill for any Liberal candidate who wants to be successful)). Is all of this swill coming from the "nothing burger" grill? For me such a front page screams out "no need to read me today". So I don't.

The "Life" section of our local paper four days later: "The Jeremiah Project and a 12-week empowerment program for women". I could shave, dress appropriately and attend, or just be patient and wait for the men's program which will unquestionably be announced soon. Hmm. I do want to be empowered! Decisions, decisions.

The North Dakota Women's Business Summit. Unquestionably an excellent event! So then why isn't there one for men? Same inquiry for the area Chamber "Women Connect" event without an opportunity for the men to connect. Or how about a "Fresh Grounded Faith" women's event in Fargo?

In mid-September of 2019, 2020 Dem Presidential candidate Elizabeth Warren is heard saying: "we're [women are] not here because of men at all!" Interesting thought from a female who is definitely not a biology professor. The last thing I saw in this direction was that it was still necessary to combine an egg with sperm to fertilize the egg to produce a baby. It does take two to tango. Maybe I am missing something here.

Female teens Iron Eyes and Thunberg make the frontpage lead article in our top area newspaper on October 9, 2019, based on their having met at the Standing Rock Rez to discuss the imminent threat of climate change. The story is filled with biased political trash rather than dialogue-provoking "news". It is these type of offerings which cause me to consider cancelling my personal subscription of 34 years—something I would do in a heartbeat if the paper wasn't providing the most incredible materials for my writing on a daily basis (what I refer to fondly as "mysteries of the mind"). A great example that same day in the "Life" section is a food feature of breaded pork cutlets for

"National Pork Month". The problem was with the calendar. That day was Yom Kippur (also known as the "Day of Atonement"), the holiest day of the Jewish year and the end of Rosh Hashanah (Jewish New Year). Most Jewish people do not eat pork and find the meat to be disgusting. It is one thing to severely dislike the current "PC culture" (as many of us do), but there is the option of being sensitive to special days of the year. Do newspapers no longer have editors and staff to make sure that these types of embarrassments do not happen?

There is positive publicity in the local media for an area business with a "Cleaning for Cancer" service. The company provides free home cleaning for women undergoing cancer treatment. That is all very nice, but not so much for men receiving cancer care. Do males somehow deserve this kind of exclusion based on their past conduct?

All of a sudden, we are learning of a group dedicated to addressing female brain injuries called PINK Concussions, Inc. Is there a group dedicated to uni-sex brain injuries named something like GREY Concussions? Is it that women's injuries have been pretty much ignored in the past? I am thinking "not". Do we need all this division when it comes to brain disorders from excessive head contact, male or female or otherwise?

There is certainly a lot of ingenuity in the marketplace. Out of Bismarck, ND (capital city) comes "BisMan Stiletto" (with the "BisMan" standing for the twin cities of Bismarck and Mandan) which defines itself on Facebook as "a group of professional businesswomen with a common commitment to serving our community. Stilettos are always seeking service opportunities. We welcome information on other local nonprofits to partner with and serve." Great mission, but what has happened to all the amazing service organizations of women and men in our communities which have done this and more for over a century?

I find myself somewhat bewildered that in our present world it is women who need to separate themselves from men in order to serve their fellow citizens. The men on the other hand seem to be very content to work with women to improve our communities. On an unfortunate note, I only learned of BisMan Stiletto from a news report that accused a former treasurer of the organization of embezzling funds from their accounts over three years. Better luck to them in the future on their quest to help neighbors in need.

A "hot" new development in female products—the "DIY Rape Kit"? How absurd is this? First of all, there is the problem of "chain of custody" which would make the results inadmissible in the courtroom. And how about the #MeToo product possibly leading to the abuse of changing a consensual sexual encounter into a "buyer's remorse" situation alleging a sexual assault? There have been challenges around the country with a backload in processing legitimate rape cases. Those delays need to be addressed and the results used to punish the offenders.

Bloomberg claims in November of 2019 that the male-dominated financial services industry is ignoring the prospect of listening to and tailoring products to women at a cost of $700 billion per year in lost revenues? This is according to management consultant, Oliver Wyman. The article sites the failure to target women for life insurance policies for instance. Another problem is the inability of investment brokers to convert billions of dollars in cash held by women to securities such as stocks and bonds, and therefore the lost commissions on those investments. When the dust settles, however, this all boils down to the claim of discrimination in the hiring of women to management roles in the lucrative financial services industry. Of course it does. I do not buy the magnitude of this claim.

Who was the "rocket scientist" that came up with the idea of a new version of "Monopoly" called "Ms. Monopoly"? Women and girls receive $240 when passing "GO", while males receive $200 each time they reach that point. Is that meant to represent reparations for being born as a female in the US? Whatever it is intended to accomplish, it is not difficult to question the logic. Pretty sickening.

As I have been writing over the past couple of years, I have seen advertisements for and read about more than sixty opportunities exclusively for women dealing with leadership development and basic skills training, and not a single one targeting men. Zero, nada. It is a pathetic time to be a man these days. A local college campus is sponsoring yet another program for women, called the 2020 NEW Leadership Development Institute. This is an "intensive" 5-day course to provide leadership training, inspiration, and support for women who do not have leader experience. It features particular emphasis on women from "groups typically under-represented in the political process"(?). Pardon me for being a little cynical, but I am guessing that the intention of this Institute is not to mass produce Conservative participants for the Republican Party. On the contrary, it is probably anticipated that the course could result in adding participants on the rolls of Liberal and Democratic causes, as any time most higher education is involved with anything it tends to err in favor of the Left side of the aisle.

What is the Women's Global Development and Prosperity Initiative (WGDP). It sounds pretty impressive, doesn't it? It was established by President Trump in February of 2019, as the first comprehensive effort to advance global women's economic empowerment. A major element of the Initiative is that such women who are successful re-invest in their families and communities, apparently different and somehow better from what empowered men do. Memo to self: get over it and let the facts lead to wherever they may.

According to a Kauffman Fellows Research Center study, start-ups in 2018 with at least one female founder raised 21% more in venture capital funding than similar ventures with all male teams (an average of $23 million versus $18 million), and yet only 22% of venture-funded firms during that year had a woman on the team. That is fairly straightforward advice to anyone's startup efforts.

A Minnesota sports summit will address the inequities in girls' sports in comparison to boys' sports. Suggestion: make sure you have the parents involved to explain how they are so much more supportive of one as opposed to the other. That is probably the single greatest factor in trying to justify the disparity.

Random factoid: there has been a 68% increase in female truck drivers in the US since 2010. Cool!

What planet have I been on since UltraViolet Action was formed in the United Kingdom (2011)? Am I the only person who did not know about this organization (for me until late-2019)? My first wind of this women's advocacy group was when I heard about them demanding the cancellation of a 2020 Democratic Presidential debate unless and until NBC "cleans up its' act". I am certainly glad to not be a part of that network. The purposes of UVA are to "raise equality between the sexes at a higher frequency", reduce sexism, and increase women's rights. Welcome to the battle. There are now unofficially two such worthy entities for every female in the world. This one will assuredly be one of the best and most successful.

Our largest local newspaper announces it has purchased and intends to continue building a magazine named "On the Minds of Moms". Never heard of it (or simply ignored it as a dedicated "Dad"). This follows and amplifies one of the serious obsessions of the publication and its' staff, and is unquestionably a very impressive move to those few men who are still reading the editions of the "all things female" paper. Update: the first post-purchase edition of the magazine is released on January 7, 2020, with a great deal of what I refer to as journalistic incest and self-promoting.

The much-maligned "glass ceiling" for women is being adjusted with the entry of a new term—the "broken rung". This refers to the difficulty which limits the ability of some women from achieving their first management position. No matter what terminology is used, we must be extremely diligent to erase the methods used by those who would limit the upward mobility of a person based on their sex or any other protected classification.

As we enter 2020, an article I read predicts that this will be "the year of women in movies", probably cinema with women, by them, and for them. It should be interesting at the end of the year to look back to see if this is the case. For those people like me who go to very few movies, there will probably not be much to this that will be memorable. A week later, there is a statement that 2019 was an historic year for "women working on films", yet with only "modest gains". It sounds like some sort of contest to me. One of the unfortunate victims of such efforts occurs when a classic novel and story is so distorted as to not even resemble the original. This is what happened with the 2018 bastardization of Louisa May Alcott's "Little Women" which was an Oscar contender for the awards in early-2020. The total changes were perpetrated under the cloak of redesigning the story to indicate the manner in which Alcott would have wanted it to flow and end, challenging reality with a feminist agenda. Really? Give me an adaptation of the real product any day rather than the new political twists on an old masterpiece.

There is a new effort in Minneapolis-St. Paul called "Matriarch Digital Media", created by women to "understand, encourage, and uplift women" through podcasts. This is coming at a time when some of the traditional annual events for females like the "Women's March" are seeking more relevance amid claims of stagnancy.

A local event is planned by the North Dakota Women's Business Center entitled "Strong Women, Strong Coffee". Oh boy! No. That would be "Oh girl"!

For an outspoken critic of our premier local newspaper, it becomes necessary for me to admit when they are totally on the mark with their heaping of praise and admiration on the frontpage for a deserving recipient, in this particular case one who had passed on too early. The woman in question was a trail-blazing police officer in Fargo who justifiably became Fargo's first female sergeant. She was a tough but compassionate and loving person who was destined to be the best in her field of first responders and dedicated civil servants. Many of her students whom she nurtured as a superior and mentor now make up the leadership hierarchy of the Department, including the Chief of Police. I and probably thousands of others were proud to call her "friend" and were saddened when cancer took her from us several years after she had retired from the force. She left a significant mark on the Fargo Police and in the hearts of all those she had touched during her time with us. You are now out of our sight, Val, but you will never be out of our hearts and minds. You were an inspiration to us all.

I do like to read an occasional book review, but have found that if I read the book it usually does not come off like it was portrayed in the review—and that is disappointing, making it less likely I will put much importance in perusing future reviews. Sometimes the "set-up" of a review will turn me away immediately, and that is appreciated. There was an opportunity for me in my local newspaper on 3-1-20 to read about "Speak: Love Your Story. Your Audience is Waiting." It continued "meet the woman who helped you connect with your 'Top Oprah Pick'!" That was enough. They had dropped the "O" bomb! Simply more weaponized and demeaning feminist sexism which the paper is noted for. Not interested. Turn the page.

The Fargo Roman Catholic Diocese was planning to host the annual "Trusted Sisters" Women's Conference, which used to be a "coed" (women and men) event. Unfortunately, it was cancelled this year due to the COVID-19 pandemic. Does the sponsoring of an event by a Christian body make the blatant sexism any more acceptable? Not sure about that one.

"Well-Read Moms" group works on a reading revival for women. Great. But why leave the men out? #WarOnMen

On April 29, 2020, the #MeToo Movement is permanently collapsing as some of their feminist proponents dismiss corroborated #TaraKeane claims against #JoeBiden2020 based on a #FakeNews #NewYorkTimes "investigation"? This is not quite the response of the #FakeNews media and the #Liberals when Dr. Ford came forward to attack SCOTUS Justice-designate Brett Kavanaugh. Okay, the uproar was not even on the same planet! The vast majority of female leaders and the #LameStreamMedia are shockingly quiet with their common input — chirping crickets. #DoubleStandard #Democrites #RememberKavanaugh

Ladybosses of Fargo-Moorhead will have a virtual seminar for its members and prospects in July, 2020. The mission of the group is to help women in business connect and to empower them. Of course it is.

On Thursday, April 9, 2020, I am writing the final two major additions to the *"AMERICA…Still Going"* manuscript, this one to complete the chapter relating to "The War on Men" and the other to close out the book with an update on where we have arrived to date in our battle against the Novel Corona Virus pandemic. These entries regarding the "War" are the most difficult, as this chapter is probably the most controversial subject matter for me with many of my female friends no doubt disputing that such a situation even exists as opposed to the continued domination of men over women in American business. I remain alarmed that I appear to be somewhat of an island in my evaluation of the gravity of this situation, especially the impact on the boys and young men in our country. There was a saying decades ago as the baby boomers were being raised: "Viva La Difference!" Roughly translated, that meant "celebrate and enjoy the uniqueness of traditional male versus female traits and variations". The intentions were never to my knowledge intended to condone and perpetuate negative stereotypes about women nor to create and support open discrimination against women and in favor of their male counterparts. Unfortunately, the boomers inherited a system which in ways treated females unfairly and as inferior to men. We have long since learned that these were unjustifiable and illegal conditions against women which were accordingly then accompanied by significant efforts to bring about total equality between the sexes. Our efforts to bring about change and the level playing field have in ways fallen short, probably as a result of less than full support by a minority of the men involved. It seems to me that these efforts for slow but sure improvement were met head on with the serious feminist movement of the 70s and 80s during which the female activists demanded deserved immediate action which was met by a masculine brick wall. This has resulted in the climate of reverse discrimination and female elitism which surrounds us today. The primary victims on the male side have been the young boys and teens who have been treated as second-class citizens for most of their lives. The dominance of "she" over "he" is everywhere, except to a major extent in the arenas of those sports in which men have shown a physical advantage. We now appear to be in the world of "Viva La Similarite". And here is where I break away from the pack. I am sensing that it has reached: "Pour égalité, nous dois se ressemble"—for equality we must look alike. We are creating a world of "Pats" (from SNL—the character who is virtually impossible to determine the sexual orientation without asking embarrassing questions). This includes clothing, hairstyles, tattoos, piercings, eyeglasses, lack of makeup, motorcycles, vulgar language and signals, reckless/highspeed driving, aggressive behavior and assaults, and other criminal conduct. Again, just call me old-fashioned, I guess. Do I have any suggestions to turn this around? Not a chance. I am way out of my element with these matters. I just hope and pray that the "War" does not get out of hand. I will leave the solutions (if there are any) to my children and grandchildren.

CHAPTER 25

THE OVERCROWDING OF AMERICAN PRISONS AND NEED FOR PRISON AND SOCIETAL REFORMS

In May of 2019, the "American Taliban" (Californian John Walker Lindh), a convert to Sunni Islam who was also known as Sulayman al-Faris, is released from prison after 16 years of a 20-year federal sentence for supplying services to the Taliban and carrying an explosive during the commission of a felony (after facing charges which carried a maximum of three life terms plus 90 years were dismissed in a plea bargain because the feds were deemed to have forced his confession to those crimes). These offences used to be considered treason, carrying a mandatory life sentence or death. But once again an ugly plea bargain thwarts justice for the country and for those brave soldiers with whom he had once served. This also serves as a huge stain on the federal employees whose over-zealous behavior led to the reduced charges and plea agreement.

Why has there been a recent explosion in car chases between the police and mostly young people? And almost without exception the driver arrested is charged (among other things) with Driving Under Suspension (DUS)—no driver's license. Does anyone have a driver's license anymore? At least some of us still have such identification based on my most recent visit to the local License Bureau Office and the long wait in line. Maybe these offenders simply do not like to wait in lines, as much as they like to drive very fast. They will not spend time in jail for the license offense, but often do for the other law violations (such as fleeing, drug possession, reckless endangerment, driving under the influence, or having stolen property in the vehicle).

The ACLU supports allowing US felons on parole to vote? I did not realize that all these former criminals are Democrats. How stupid have I been? The "L" in ACLU seems to always stand for "Liberals". I guess that I am simply naïve to believe that an organization operating to protect American civil liberties would be politically neutral, helping people on both sides of the aisle. #TheRightWithoutRights

A Duluth (MN) homeless man with mental challenges gets 4 years of probation, up to 90 days in jail, some hours for community service, and must pay $66K in restitution for "torching" an historic 118-year old synagogue there. Wha? And good luck for him paying back the damages (which is the amount the fire costs exceeded the insurance funds available). How about treatment in a suitable mental facility followed by a couple of years in a halfway house? This is Minnesota, however, so he should probably also be required to learn how to sing "Kumbaya". #JusticeForAll

There is a regional story in the press that twenty people have been arrested and eighteen charged with aggravated assault in black on white attacks over the weekend in Minneapolis. Liberal prosecutors say that they will not pursue obvious "hate crime" charges as they deem that the victims of the ambushes were beaten because of their level of inebriation rather than because of their race? Another example of cattle feces with that one. Prosecutorial discretion is very important in our American system of criminal jurisprudence, as long as it is dispensed fairly, evenly, and without discrimination. We must never permit it to be used as a weapon or otherwise to diminish the rights of one segment of the population in favor of another. I am not saying that this decision in Minneapolis was not justified, because I am not on the ground there and aware of all the facts. Who knows, maybe the attackers were part of a men's church group on an outing to preach temperance and the injured were belligerent and in the wrong place at the wrong time. In this case, it sure can suck to be intoxicated Caucasians coming out of a bar.

A 63-year old SD man has been executed on November 4, 2019 by injection for a 1992 murder during a burglary. This does not appear that uncommon as we have a local kidnapping, rape, and murder case that has been dragging on for over a decade since the death penalty was imposed and still no finality for the family, friends, and community. We had been used to an appeal period of five years or so, but now we are seeing appeals raised more than 20 years following a conviction. If we are going to continue with capital punishment in serious cases, it appears to be time to close the gap between capital convictions and the subsequent ultimate punishment. #CapitalPunishment

Speaking about timely executions, we have a story to tell in the Heartland that is more evidence of the delays we see today. In November of 2003, a member of the Gamma Phi Beta Sorority at the University of North Dakota was kidnapped from a mall parking lot, sexually assaulted and brutally murdered by Alfonso Rodriquez, Jr. At the time of the abduction, one of my daughters was attending the University, belonged to a different sorority, and knew Dru Sjodin through her best friend in high school who was also a Gamma Phi. This was a shocking development for the University and the City of Grand Forks. Rodriquez was convicted and sentenced to death in the late-summer of 2006. In 2019 (thirteen years after the guilty verdict), Rodriquez failed in another attempt to have his conviction and sentence set aside. At that time death penalty experts expressed their concerns that further appeals in the case could drag on for another ten years.

It doesn't seem like it was that long ago when a single appeal (possibly to the SCOTUS), once rejected at a high level, would be followed by a prompt execution. Obviously, that is no longer the case. This new system of "justice" is absurd and extremely expensive. If we are going to continue to provide for the death sentence in extreme cases, we need to make sure that we have convicted the right person, let an appeal run its course, and carry forward with the termination of life. Then we let God decide the ultimate punishment for the perpetrator. Imagine being a family member in these cases and having to constantly relive the horrible death of your loved one for decades. Unconscionable.

There are stories out that the recently promulgated "First-Step" Act has resulted in dangerous and violent criminals being released from jail? We will need more proof that this is happening, as it is the opposite outcome from what the legislative drafters contemplated.

In November of 2019, a former Warroad (MN) police officer who takes an "Alford" plea (not a guilty plea but acknowledging there is enough evidence for a conviction) is sentenced to three years in jail for kidnapping and sexually assaulting a teenager (ten times). Fair? That is for you to decide.

It is time that equal protection under the laws of the US should be extended to equal treatment of all persons under our criminal laws. Just as in education, there is no place for the outdated doctrine of "separate but equal"—because it is not. What a catalyst that would be for improving our places of incarceration if there were the same percentages of persons of all colors and socio-economic statuses being jailed for the same or similar criminal conduct.

Many of us in the US believe that there is a multi-tiered justice system that serves to protect certain people while ignoring those who are differently situated. Some of the recent names that come up during these discussions are Hillary Clinton, Andrew McCabe, James Comey, and Peter Strzok. What if you entered your apartment house, walked into a unit in the same location on a different floor as your apartment, and shot and killed the unarmed resident who happened to be an African-American accountant? Do you think there would be some potentially serious repercussions? Sure there would, like possible "life in prison". This is what happened to an off-duty Dallas (TX) police officer who was sentenced to ten years in prison. I was thinking about twenty years as being a fair penalty. That is from someone who loves our police, but also considers unjustifiable homicide as "murder".

There are many calls and numerous efforts today to reform our outdated bail system. It has become far too common for wealthy law-abiding citizens and criminals to be able to secure release from jail no matter how high the bail is set. I have held the position for many years that the need for bail (or none) should be based on the seriousness of the offense, the flight risk, and the ability of the accused to pay (such as a sliding scale). I do not agree with those who claim that the system simply discriminates against poor people and favors those persons of means. There are some jurisdictions that have decided to base bail on whether the offense was one involving violence, or not. A great example was recently from New York City where a non-violent ("gentleman") bank robber was released from jail without any bail only to shortly thereafter rob another bank and return to the pokey. Apparently bank robbing was much more serious in the 60s than it is today. Our bail system needs to be fair for all so that our jails are not filled with poor people awaiting trial when society would be better served with those harmless defendants at home until their "day in court".

The matter of prison reform and prisoner safety once again presents itself during the Corona Virus pandemic. Some jurisdictions are releasing serious criminals from jail because those in charge are determining that it is too dangerous for health purposes to leave the convicts in the confined spaces of jail with increased chances of catching the virus. It might sound good on the surface, but several places are finding that these "safe" prisoners are re-offending rather quickly and being sent back to their cells in short order. Certainly the good health of a law-abiding public needs to take priority within reason over the well-being of convicted criminals.

CHAPTER 26

THE NEED FOR NEW LEADERSHIP:
THE CASES FOR EMPLOYMENT
AND TERM LIMITS

Let's add something very important to then "*AGG*" term lim-its suggestions for members of the US House and Senate. Many of us believe that one of the major problems in our nation's capital is caused by retiring or defeated Congressmen and Congresswomen remaining in DC to work as lobbyists for special interest groups. These individuals come from positions of power and sometimes wield an undo amount of influence with their former colleagues. Conservatives invariably view these people as part of the "swamp" of Washington in need of "draining". Lobbyists clearly can be reduced in numbers without too much complaining, and we should also look at restrictions about how soon members of Congress are able to become lobbyists once they leave their elective or appointed positions.

A lot of people were saddened to learn in early-November of 2019 that Rep. Peter King (R-NY) will retire from Congress after 28 years of service. The New York-DC commute had finally gotten to him. Then the day following the impeachment vote, Rep. Mark Meadows (R-NC), a GOP leader for six years in the House, announces that he will not run for reelection. Thank you for your service to America, Peter and Mark! (Meadows actually resigns his position to become the Chief of Staff for President

Trump.) This is more evidence of the GOP "self-imposed" term limits. It is becoming a regular pattern to hear of Republican members of Congress who are "calling it quits" and returning to the real world of their district or elsewhere—not so much for Democrats who seem content to live out their years in the DC "swamp".

I rarely complain about lifetime federal judicial appointments… until a Judge #EmmetSullivan emerges lawless and unprecedented. #FreeGenFlynn The experts to whom I speak say that this NEVER HAPPENS—that a federal judge would question prosecutors who choose to discontinue a criminal case. Logically, there is no procedure in the rules for a court to continue a case in which the government lawyers decide to drop the charges. Sullivan even decided on May 22, 2020, to hire a lawyer to represent him when the circuit court (his bosses) request that he explain himself in a week or so. It appears that no one is immune from the insanity on the Left. This is updated later.

My political science professors would call me crazy on this one, but I strongly believe we are on the verge of a 5 or 6 party system in America—Republican, Democrat, Independent, Libertarian, Socialist, with a possibility of Green if they cannot uniformly find a home elsewhere. This is a clear sign that huge and irreconcilable gaps are forming on both sides of the moderates in some of our current parties. It is not uncommon around the world that members of multiple political groups are being forced to form a government through a coalition of parties with similar but not identical ideological platforms in order to represent a majority or at least plurality of the electorate. America appears presently to be on track for such a possibility.

There is a train of thought that the COVID-19 pandemic will change many of the institutions and building blocks which have been a part of the US landscape for many years. One of the victims of these changes may be "non-essential" employment. The health crisis has revealed that there are many businesses, departments of government, and vocations which have developed unnecessary layers of management that are wasting huge amounts of money, and could be operated much more efficiently and at considerably lower cost in the future. This could have a transformative and streamlining effect on what businesses and governments look like and how they perform moving forward. "Waste" may become a five-lettered word that represents a focal point in determining the way we operate and how we are employed in America in and after 2020.

Statehood for DC is expected to be passed (and is passed) by the US House as we reach the ides of June, 2020. This is a non-starter in the US Senate. I am opposed and would prefer leaving things the way they are or making the District a part of Maryland.

There is considerable consternation as the US continues to reopen amidst the COVID-19 pandemic. Most of the states with Democrats as Governors are much more cautious with those plans to #getbacktowork. These delays are having a devastating effect on the lives, livelihoods, and businesses of millions of Americans who are watching all that they have built over the years disappear in the matter of a couple of months, not to mention the domestic violence, child abuse, suicides, and deaths from curable causes with treatment being delayed all around us. This raises questions about the power of government to trample on the rights of its citizens. A sign during a recent protest of state delays in re-opening the economy: "My freedom does not end where your fear begins." Sad but true. The equal protection and due process clauses of the US Constitution do not permit Governors to act arbitrarily in continuing the closedown of America. #backtowork The words of our Founding Fathers cannot be denied from the very beginning of our Republic: "We hold these truths to be self-evident; that all men are created equal; that they are endowed with certain unalienable [inalienable] rights; that among these are life, liberty, and the pursuit of happiness; that to secure these rights, governments are instituted among men, deriving their just powers from the consent of the governed; that whenever any form of government becomes destructive of these ends, it is the right of the people to alter or to abolish it, and to institute new government..." from Thomas Jefferson in the Declaration of Independence (July 4, 1776). This passage is not only true but is probably the source of a quote or interpretation often attributed to Jefferson: "When tyranny becomes law, rebellion becomes duty." I leave you with those thoughts and with a passage from a Letter by Jefferson to William Stevens Smith on November 13, 1787, in which he stated: "What country before ever existed a century and a half without a rebellion?...The tree of liberty must be refreshed from time to time with the blood of patriots and tyrants. It is its natural manure." Food for your thoughts until we meet again.

CHAPTER 27

CONTINUING EFFORTS TO IMPROVE THE INNER CITIES AND LIVING CONDITIONS FOR ALL

We seem to be almost continually bombarded with proof that the political machine on the Left is destroying once-great cities from the core and out. More absurdity arises in Seattle as we come to the end of October 2019 — the largest tax/penalty on fuel oil in the US, which hurts the citizens who can afford it the least. Those "rocket-scientist" community leaders need to be thrown to the curb for this "stunt" which purports to be "eco-friendly" but instead will make it very expensive to heat lower to middle-class homes and apartments in the city. The Democratic leaders argue that these of their constituents should move forward for the planet to convert to a different and greener fuel for their source of warmth. And how many housing units do you expect to do that at a cost of up to $60,000 for each project? #HeatlessInSeattle Update on July 2, 2020: During the Pandemic and the rioting following the death of George Floyd, the City of Seattle leaders again blow lunch by allowing Marxists to occupy a portion of the inner city (Capitol Hill District) in a six square block area (the CHOP/CHAZ Zone that included a vacated police precinct building). This chaotic "occupation" continued for 20 days (which the Seattle Mayor had referred to as a possible long-term "Summer of Love") before the police moved in on July 1 (following the murders of two black teens and numerous lawsuits against the city) to disperse what was left of the protesters. This type of activity is not uncommon these days as the Liberal leaders of many US cities are not willing to use law and order in the streets against their constituents. Most of the demands of the occupiers can best be described as ranging from interesting to comedic to absurd. As the Trump administration attempts to build up the inner cities, the Left seems to do all they can to tear those efforts down. Truly sad and sickening.

Democrats responsible for inaction and deplorable conditions for over 70 years in our inner cities are now criticizing innovative and effective Opportunity Zones unleashed by the Trump administration as benefiting the rich. How blind and naïve is the "opposition" these days? #OpportunityZones What is wrong with attempting to attract capital to our major cities through public-private partnerships to expand business possibilities, employment, education, crime reduction, and everything else positive about productive urban development? Nothing, of course. The argument is that Liberal politicians have controlled the destiny of our inner cities for decades with promises of improving conditions to the mostly minority populations. And that those words of hope have gone unfulfilled. Along comes President Donald Trump with action replacing rhetoric. We can no longer allow these center-city areas to be forgotten and abandoned. So why is there opposition on the Left claiming that these efforts are merely another opportunity for wealthy developers to become even more successful? It is obvious that Socialists are always trying to convince Americans that capitalism and wealth creation is bad. And then there is an overwhelming desire that this POTUS cannot and must not be successful in anything he does, even though the country benefits enormously from the programs. This is how the unmitigated hatred by Liberals of anything and everything "Trump" has turned into insanity, plain and simple. In my corner of the universe (Fargo), we do not have a traditional "inner city". But that is not stopping focused entrepreneurs from using the Opportunity Zone programs to the advantage of the city and our inhabitants. This is similar to a time about fifteen years ago when Fargo became the "poster child" in America for "Renaissance Zone" project financing, turning a struggling downtown into a vibrant one. For these decades, we have been "Mach 2 with our hair on fire". Great Americans dream about a time when we can be talking about Detroit, Baltimore, Indianapolis, Kansas City (MO), East St. Louis (IL), Anniston (AL), Rockford (IL), or Monroe (LA), as proud for the successful efforts which brought these dangerous places back from the brink of total devastation. And many of us will be thankful for these amazing developments no matter who was leading our country at the time. My advice to the Republican Party for 2020 and beyond is to chant "OZ, OZ, OZ" to advertise their successful development programs in our urban centers. The decades of neglect are coming to an abrupt end.

While Rep. Elijah Cummings (D-MD) was alive and leading a US House Committee, Trump was criticized for verbally demeaning the home District of the Representative in Baltimore. The comments were basically that the city was a rat-infested and crime-riddled sewer. The President was defended by some, that he was speaking the truth. And the Trump administration was coming off the heels of expending $16 billion on the Baltimore area in 2018. Shortly after that it was revealed that Bernie Sanders had criticized Baltimore on camera in 2015 as having a "third-world" downtown. Two points here: "truth is always a good defense", and it is undeniable that the continued and precipitous decline of our inner-cities has come at the hands of and failures by the Democratic leadership in these areas (virtually without exception). Whenever those on the Right bring these facts to the forefront, they are always met on the Left with the constant chant of "racist"—of course.

A suspect in multiple NYC bank robberies was released without bail (under a new local law passed by the #BleedingHeartLiberals) and is caught on tape robbing another bank. The proper bail reform is not to eliminate it, but to use a sliding income scale and to keep likely recidivists in jail pending trial. In the past we called this type of extreme lawmaking "legislative overkill" and "throwing the baby out with the bathwater".

Sometimes it is enjoyable to read about the housing and living trends of people in the US. This applies to those of us residing in the Northern Plains. Elsewhere in the book, I relate that one of the fastest growing states in the country during the 2010-19 decade was North Dakota. We have an abundance of available high-paying jobs here (mostly in the energy, software technology, agricultural manufacturing, biotechnology, and healthcare industries), as well as the training necessary for an interested person to easily fit into a position. Our "cost of living" here in the heartland is on the low end of the spectrum. Often, we learn that our particular area in the east central part of the state is the number one relocation destination for the Minneapolis-St. Paul metropolitan area. We are family friendly with some of the best public and private K-12 schools in the country, a top environment to raise children, one of the best places to start and operate a business, the best air quality in the US, and a leading place for women to work and succeed in their vocation. We are a top choice for immigrant and refugee resettlement despite our winter weather "challenges". We are also aware that these same conditions to attract new neighbors are not prevalent in some other parts of the country. As an example, we hear on a regular basis that residents are leaving big cities and coastal communities on both of the east and west ends of the US due to high taxes, limited services, exorbitant housing costs, homelessness, crumbling infrastructure, pollution, crime, natural disasters, and poor education opportunities. Who in their right mind would not want to leave such a difficult living situation, especially when a much better life can be literally hundreds of miles away? The blame for such deplorable living conditions in many cases rests on the towns, cities, counties, and states that have driven good people away by losing sight of the basics in life that are a prerequisite to creating and maintaining decent neighborhoods and law-abiding residents. It is heartbreaking to see how some of the best and most beautiful parts of America have been driven into the ground, in more cases than not by the lack of leadership and vision of Liberal Democrats who seem more focused on protecting the rights of a few to the detriment of the many.

Then there are events/protests that detract from the efforts to improve the inner cities and bring more racial and income equality to those portions of our large metropolitan areas. Such were the protests starting in Harlem of NYC sponsored by a consortium of anti-police groups calling themselves "FTP [F___ the Police] Emergency Action". They were rightly complaining about a plan to enhance the monitoring of the city's subway system for fare jumpers with the addition of 500 police officers and a cost of $250 million to save $200 million over the next four years. The crowd went out of control in blocking subway traffic, resulting in 58 arrests. The plan for policing seemed somewhat excessive to this writer. Subway passes could have been purchased and distributed for a lot less money. Everyone needs to work together with intelligence and conviction for this all to move forward.

On May 22, 2020, Joe Biden was interviewed by a black radio show host who was asking the candidate for some ideas about what a Biden administration would do to help the minorities. Appearing to be taken aback by such a probing question, Biden responded: if you don't know who to support, Trump or me, "you ain't black"? How very elitist, condescending, and presumptuous of the former Vice-President. Have the decades of neglect by Democratic leaders of African-American issues and concerns throughout the country left the constituents with considerable cynicism about whether their problems will ever be addressed? We finally have a #Conservative President who is vigorously working to improve conditions for our minorities in America.

Just as great progress is being made with Opportunity Zones for inner cities in America, someone throws a large wrench into the machine causing it to be destroyed. On Memorial Day (5-25-20), a Minneapolis police officer named Derek Chauvin restrains an unarmed black man named George Floyd with a knee to his neck and resulting in the death of Floyd. The detention was based on the suspicion that Floyd had passed a counterfeit $20 bill at a neighborhood market. The killing was vividly filmed with cellphone cameras. It took prosecutors four days to charge Chauvin, and that was for third-degree (negligent) murder. I would have been more supportive of second-degree murder charges [which was eventually done]. The three police officers who were present and who apparently did nothing (or too little) to stop the assault have been fired but not yet been charged (as of June 1, 2020). (Update: later in the week they were charged with aiding and abetting second-degree murder.) Protests following the death spread around the US and some overseas during which peaceful gatherings turned violent leading to significant property damage, arson, looting, shooting injuries, and riots blamed on shipped-in agitators on the Left and allegedly on the Right. At the same time locally, a young white police officer is shot to death by a black man (who also killed his mother) being served with an eviction notice in nearby Grand Forks, ND. Where was the indignation and rioting following those deadly criminal acts? Nothing. Instead there were candlelight prayer vigils and huge funeral services. Peaceful towns and cities turned chaotic amid the continued efforts to reopen businesses during the COVID-19 pandemic. This was one of the worst things that could have possibly happened as a struggling country tried to claw its way back to some semblance of normalcy. The actions of four policemen from Minneapolis turned the entire US into an urban combat zone. Wouldn't you think that 155 years after the end of the Civil War our country would have moved on from racial prejudice and discrimination, especially with the lessons taught the baby boomers by the likes of MLK, Jr. and Bobby Kennedy about racial equality and tolerance? BOOM as the streets explode with more hatred and hostility, much of which is directed at mostly decent and fair law enforcement personnel. All good Americans want #JusticeforGeorgeFloyd, and we will not settle for less. May God save us from additional strife. Update: Calls for #DefundPolice during the first week of June, 2020, are more #Liberals insanity. Those who would suffer from the resulting mayhem would be our vulnerable minorities, and the major winners as the firearms retailers throughout the country from America continuing to arm itself for self-protection! Ninety-five percent (or more?) of our US police are great officers. The better plan would be for police forces to be enlarged to continue serving and protecting during these difficult times. Those proponents of "less is better" need to rethink those efforts to slash law enforcement numbers before it is too late.

CHAPTER 28

RANDOM TOPICS & THOUGHTS

There were no obvious places in the book to put these topics and thoughts, so I created a new chapter. Please bear with me as these matters are probably not of a cataclysmic nature but are rather random and sometimes inconsequential.

September 19, 2019 was the tenth and final day of date palendromes (91019 to 91919). When was the last time this happened for such a long period? That may be an easy question, but I decided to leave it for someone else to figure out.

How often do you see meteorologists becoming political? Not very often to this observer. We do have a lead meteorologist for the newspaper here who mixes weather and politics periodically. Sometimes it is very subtle, while at other times it is "in your face". And I do not ever remember this happening with the weather personality being a Conservative. The latest example of this was when he cited the climate change "controversy" as evidence of the current political divide. Unusual but probably true. A couple of days later he stirs the pot again with his supposition that the recent frequency of catastrophic flooding is likely a result of that same climate change.

Whenever a person leaves this earth as a living being (many times too early in life from the eyes of their loved ones) and upon hearing the story of the life they led and the challenges in the world left unsolved, I wait for those words which often follow. The family (or friends) of this wonderful human being are setting up a non-profit organization or foundation to carry on the legacy and passion of the dearly departed. Having been an attorney involved with the creation and administration of hundreds of non-profit/tax-exempt entities over the years, I learned firsthand that there are already too many of these benevolent vehicles on the road. With each of these new unincorporated associations, corporations, or trusts out there, we add another set of administrative costs and expenses, and other duplications of time and energy which are in many cases unnecessary and wasteful. I have throughout my life tried to follow the wisdom and advice of my dear father who encouraged me and others to do our due diligence in an effort to find an existing entity with the same or similar mission, and attempt to participate jointly in that worthy cause to provide more of the assets to be directly applied for the intended benefits. This was the same concept which he, I, and our families followed in support of the United Way over the years, realizing that the mission is to make a real difference for those in need rather than having personal ownership of an organization which cannot provide as much of an impact on the selected cause. Now, with all of that having been said, if you have $100 million to apply for one or more charitable endeavor(s), hire that attorney and accountant to get you properly set up and proceed to do those philanthropic works.

What is with this recent trend toward HUGE and COLORED glasses frames. I am not talking about those unique glasses worn by children with physical challenges. I am referring to those frames worn by members of the media and the Liberal elite. If the wearers are attempting to look like clowns, they appear to be succeeding. I am suggesting that many times the "shock" factor in fashion is not a good look. An excellent example of this trend is Al Roker of the *Today Show* and NBC News (as he prepares to leave that gig). His spectacles in "red" and "blue" (and then "orange") have become for this viewer more of a distracting factor that make it impossible for me to take what he is saying seriously. Another chronic offender is comedian Howie Mandel. It is probably me who needs psychological help because of this "phobia", and I can probably accept that. I do find such examples of eyewear to be amusing, which is probably an excellent contributing factor these days toward my regular disposition.

Currently there is an abundance of stories about animal abuse on the Indian Reservations in the US? I frequently hear from friends and family about rescue animals (primarily dogs) which have been adopted after having been rounded up on a Reservation. Do we need to assist the Native American populations with education about proper and humane animal care? I am suspecting that "where there is smoke there is fire" (another old adage the baby boomers were taught about one problem aligned with or related to another).

Other clichés which guided us in life during the 50's through the 70's: "it is better to be safe than sorry" (tread carefully); "life is there for the taking", "snooze and you lose", "where there's a will, there's a way" (go for it without needless delay); "gravy days" (the best of times which flow from past experience); "hand caught in the cookie jar" (busted); "between a rock and a hard place" (tough predicament); "mind your own business"; "is the Pope Catholic?" (DUH?); "NSS?" ("No S _ _ _, Sherlock?") (everyone knows that); "part and parcel" (an essential element); "put your money where your mouth is" and "put up or shut up" (care to wager on that thought?); "don't put all of your eggs in one basket" (a disaster could follow if the basket falls or breaks); in a much gentler era (50s and early 60s): "there is a time and place for everything" or "whatever goes"; "beauty is in the eye of the beholder" (the presence of beauty is personal); "the jig [gig] is up" (you have been caught); "you are preaching to the choir" (the listeners are already believing what you say); "stress quality over quantity"; "good riddance to bad rubbish" (we are better off without that person or thought around us); "they're a dime a dozen" (there are already a lot around); "hold your horses" (wait a minute before you act); "tougher than nails"; "cat got your tongue?" (nothing to say about that?); "read it and weep" (gotcha); "mark my words" (you heard it here first); "get out while the getting is good" (leave when you can); "you get what you deserve"; "what doesn't kill you makes you stronger"; "grasping at straws" (try it); "growing by leaps and bounds" (quickly); "you make your own breaks"; "any friend of yours is a friend of mine"; "lock, stock and barrel" (entirely); "calm, cool, and collected" (not easily rattled); "who's to quibble [argue]?" (tough to argue with that); "if you can't stand the heat, get out of the kitchen"; "what is good for the goose is good for the gander" (works out well for all involved); "nothing good comes easily"; "live and learn"; "you reap based on what you sow"; "often imitated, never duplicated" (a tough act to follow); "finders keepers, losers weepers" (which may or may not be true); "do not take things [good or bad] for granted" (do not assume anything); "by in large" (all things considered); "this is not my first rodeo" (I am experienced in such matters, but have never participated in a rodeo); "[conduct] adding insult to injury" (piling on); being "a glutton for punishment" (one who is drawn to difficult tasks); "eating crow" (personal punishment for something said or predicted erroneously); "Katie bar the door" (prepare for what is about to happen); "only time will tell" (wait and see what happens); "knowing what's what" (personal knowledge about the matter); "potted" (drunk and/or too high); "you can't have it both ways" (your arguments must be clear and consistent); "practice makes perfect"; "you can lead a horse to water, but you can't make it drink" (people, like some animals, will only do what they decide on their own to do); "even Steven" (the "score" is tied); "my foot" (I don't believe it); "a penny saved is a penny earned" (Ben Franklin—fiscal responsibility can begin small); "if it ain't broken, don't fix it" (don't try to change something that is fine already); "let sleeping dogs lie" (leave it alone); "going ballistic [or bonkers]" (over-the-top behavior); "stupid is as stupid does" (a person's lack of applied intelligence is clearly revealed in their behavior); "before you buy the 'sizzle', look at the steak!" (something may sound like a good deal before you do a thorough evaluation); "hang in there" (stay the course); "don't cry over spilled milk" (keep your emotions in check for the critical events in life); "don't bite off more than you can chew" (don't take on more of something than you can handle); "the horse has left the barn" (it is too late to do anything about that); something has reached a "fever pitch" (a high level of excitement or concern); "you only live once" (make the most of your time here); "keep your hands to yourself" (do not invade the space of a person near you); "worry wart" (one who chronically expects the worst outcomes); "the apple of my eye" (the cause of my affections); "keep your eyes on the prize" (focus on your goals); "good gravy", "oh my gosh", "goodness gracious", "fooey", or "egad man" (expressing shock or anger without profanity); "enough is enough" (don't you know when to stop?); "double entendre" (a statement with two possible interpretations, one of which may be "for mature audiences only"); "Rome wasn't built in a day!" (it can take time for good things to happen); "whole kit and caboodle" (all of it); "four eyes" (you wear glasses); "local yokel" (you are from a backward part of our area and have some challenges); "cute as a bug's ear" (very cute—even cuter than the ear of a bug); "hob nob" (to associate on very friendly terms); "nothing ventured, nothing gained" (you must take chances for success); "good things come to those who wait" (be patient to experience your success); "fiddlesticks" (not the "League of Legends" champion)(No Way/I don't believe you!); "I get your drift" (understood); "quaff" (eagerly and excitedly consume an adult beverage); "this too shall pass" (the present dilemma will end eventually); "hoisted on your own petard" (inadvertently damaged by your own devious actions/poetic justice); "many happy returns" (Happy Birthday); "lollygagging" (being lazy about something/loafing/standing idly by); "splurge" (spending more money than anticipated); "low and behold" (much to my surprise); "hold your tongue!" (don't say anything); "salt mine" (where one works); "by and large" (all things considered); "beef" (complaint); "give 'em an inch and they'll take a mile" (don't let a bad thing get started as it can become tough to stop).

The "crack cancer" challenge is the latest ill-conceived waste of edible food to raise funds for a rare type of the disease. Don't get me wrong, I am totally supportive of most efforts to increase the funding for cancer research. I just do not ascribe to wasting food to show one's commitment to finding a cure or preventive tool.

In my first book, I referred to the importance of us being decisive in life. It is difficult for those who suffer from "analysis paralysis" to be successful in just about anything important. While it is critical to get all of the important information about an issue or process, it is seriously necessary to be able to "pull the trigger" when the sights align with the target, squeezing rather than abruptly pulling. That is when the next steps are put into motion—monitoring, evaluating, adjusting, and measuring to assure the desired goal is reached. This may sound boring or tedious to some, while many of us find this entire process to be truly invigorating. As Benjamin Franklin once said about life's roadmaps and paths: "If you fail to plan, you are planning to fail." Truer words have seldom been spoken.

Do you ever notice in your local newspaper that big advertisers tend to get special treatment in articles related to them, or in the "opinions" section of the paper? It is no different anywhere I have been a witness. This is common in Fargo, especially when they highlight businesses which advertise as contributors on a particular topic. When it doesn't make sense to me (as if I know anything), I refer to it as "journalistic incest" and "lazy journalism"—what we used to refer to as "tooting one's own horn" or tooting the horn of a good customer. This is great for many of us as it reduces the amount of reading we need to do from that edition. It is even worse (and very common) for the paper itself to publicize one of their own television or radio stations, other related businesses, or some of their news staff. We saw this in full force as August, 2019 ended, and the paper had an article by the publisher's spouse. Then there was a half-page ad inviting the readers to meet one of their female writers (haven't seen these ads for the male writers?). Or how about the area boomer reporter who argued that the country does not need a "Space Force", now apparently an expert in the matters of intergalactic security and protection. This seems to be lacking somewhat in futuristic vision that is not really that far off. For this guy, all of these "I-am-from-the-sticks" stories create "thanks-but-no-thanks" moments.

What a difference a couple of years can make. Joe Biden's son, Hunter, is expelled from the Naval Reserve in 2014 for cocaine use based on a failed drug test. Later that year he is earning at least $50,000 (some reports were of $83,333) per month as a Director for Ukrainian oil company Burisma, while he was also a Director in a Chinese private equity firm (BHR) which received $1.5 billion from the Chinese government. The young Biden had traveled to both countries with his father, Vice President Joe Biden, on Air Force 2. Only in America can you find such an amazing success story!

"*Collusion*" by Newt Gingrich is a "must read" if you have not done so already. He is the same guy who came up with one of my favorite labels in 2019 when he coined "the looney Left" (9-10-19), similar to my "#LiberalLunacy".

A survey is showing that 40% of the people responding are getting physically sick over politics. This sounds like the same result as we see from Seasonal Affective Disorder (SAD).

The baby peregrine falcon on a bank tower in Fargo is given the name "Savanna" after a Native-American woman kidnapped and murdered (August, 2017) in the city with her daughter cut from the womb. Really? Is this done to disturb us, to remind us of the heinous murder, or to honor a woman who became famous because of a dastardly deed? Or all of the above? The local paper brings back the story for no apparent reason about once a month. One such article proclaimed "Loss of Savanna still very fresh"—to whom? I hadn't thought about the crime during the past month, since the last article about the horrible event. The frequency of stories must be at least partly as a result of the MMIWG (now MMIP (as I had always suggested to be inclusive)) Movement and the impact it has had at least on the staff of the newspaper. Later, they feature the story of a local artist with her painting of the deceased woman (Savanna) being escorted to Heaven following her death? To publicize the MMIWG or MMIP crisis? The cynic in me believes this to be somewhat opportunistic, and a little creepy.

I will take another opportunity to share thoughts I was taught at a very young age by my parents about worthy recipients of charitable gifting. The two "givens" were our local, state-wide, and national church and the traditional arts groups in the area (symphony orchestra, community theater, opera company, and dance/ballet troupe). For most of the other support, we were steered toward United Way, as they were built with a system of determining the needs of the community with fiscal responsibility and vetting. All of this was rounded out with the schools we attended for K-12 and college. Above all, it was emphasized to maximize the "bang for the buck" by giving where as much as possible of a gift goes for program rather than administration. Give until it hurts.

NATO ally and Turkish President Erdogan is in Russia with Putin as the cease-fire in the invasion of Syria by Turkey is about to end. Not what NATO friends do. Time for the American "no-fly zone" over Syria and a blockade of Turkey?

We learn that the trial for the 911 conspirators will begin at Guantanamo Bay on January 21, 2020, 19.5 years after the attacks. What took so long—Khalid Sheikh Mohammed? I may update this entry depending on the timing in completing this manuscript. Update: the trial date is again delayed, this time to January 11, 2021? We are used to delays in our US judicial system, but this is getting pretty crazy.

Congratulations to Tiger Woods for tying Sam Snead with a record 82 PGA tournament wins (happening October 28, 2019 at the ZoZo tourney in Japan)! And I suspect Woods is not done yet.

It was wonderful during the 50s and 60s to enjoy "variety" shows on the television, first in black & white, and later in technicolor. This was a major source of family entertainment at home. Some of these productions were "The Ed Sullivan Show", "The Dean Martin Show", "The Carol Burnett Show", "The Smother's Brothers Comedy Hour", "Rowan and Martin's Laugh-In", and "The Red Skelton Show". The common theme was comedy, but it went beyond that as well. For those of us who watched these shows, it still brings a smile to our face just thinking about them.

In 2019, we need to be cautious about the apps we download, as the software owners may not have the best interests of the users in mind. One such product is Russian-owned FaceApp which takes a facial image and applies AI and probabilities to "age" the face for a period of years. At last count over 100 million people had downloaded the app. Not too shabby. While there is no evidence at the present time that FaceApp is using those images for any nefarious reasons, the potential for abuse remains as the company servers contain names and images which might be an attractive prize for a bad person with a lot of money. And with facial recognition as a popular recent means of identifying people and protecting others, who knows what the possibilities could be. As the boomers were trained: "caveat emptor" or "buyer beware" and "better to be safe than sorry".

There are many people who complain about Daylight Saving (or "Savings") Time (DST)—"Spring Forward" and "Fall Back". They have even abolished it/opted out in Arizona and Hawaii. At the time of this writing, seven states have made DST a permanent fixture for their locale. It has made a lot of sense in the agricultural heartland of the Northern Plains (especially prior to GPS-controlled farm equipment), as it allows farmers to be outside in the fields during the summer with natural light until as late as 10:30 PM. I especially enjoy those people who are so opposed to DST and then celebrate how long they can be outside during those beautiful and elongated summer evenings, particularly in the Northern Lakes Country of the US.

Lesson 15 in "Hollywood Greed": Cher is returning to Fargo in 2020 [then postponed due to COVID-19]. She last performed here during her 2004 "Farewell Tour" (one of her MANY farewell tours" ever since). "Like a bad penny, she just won't go away". #TimeForCherToRetire

SCOTUS Justice Ruth Bader Ginsberg is in the news again, another day with a different sickness or healthcare problem. She refuses to let any of them slow her down or stop her. She is obviously one tough character. This time it is pancreatic cancer (which is commonly terminal). She claims to be "on her way to being very well". While there are many of us who do not agree with her partisan preaching when not on the bench, we cannot argue about her being a role model and an iconic jurist.

It is not a shock in late-2109 that the Mayo Clinic has again been named as the top hospital in the US. For many decades, it has had an amazing reputation for successfully treating people from all over the world. I hear from friends and colleagues on a regular basis about the positive care they or a loved one received there. But no hospital can do it all and all the time. In 1992 my father was treated for prostate cancer at the Mayo/St. Mary's campus in Rochester, MN. He had the cancer surgically removed. When he returned to Fargo, one of my first serious questions for him was: "when do you start the chemo?" His answer was swift and certain: "there is no need for chemo, they got it all [the cancer]." With no family history of cancer, I did not think too much about the situation. Three years later he was dying before our eyes as he had cancer throughout his body. He passed on to Heaven in January of 1995 at the age of 71. As the years went by following his death, I heard from two of his good friends who had virtually the identical condition, surgery, and results at that facility. I never blamed the Clinic for his condition nor his passing. I am certain that this was the program they followed with nearly all the patients with the same circumstances. Personally, I suffered severe pain senselessly for about 6 months of my later years while being treated for a misdiagnosed pinched nerve in my back when instead the problem was my two hips that were "shot". This stuff happens constantly. I did not write in *AGG* nor here about our healthcare challenges in the US. We need to find the best way for us to insure and treat as many of our citizens as possible and in the best ways with as little expense as practical. Even though I practiced law for decades representing medical facilities, healthcare plans, and insurers, the future planning for these complex issues needs to be left to those who are currently in the trenches. Update as we battle COVID-19 in May, 2020: there is much division about how to treat the condition as we attempt to re-open the country. It appears that we will not know until hindsight as to how we should be doing this as it is new ground for us all. That is scary at this time of miracles in medicine and we cannot battle a "Novel" virus with much certainty.

There is speculation in the science world that a meteor strike on Mars caused a Mega-tsunami and killed the planet (or at least led to it). Concepts and stories like this have always fascinated me and many others who are interested in the history of our universe.

As we approach Thanksgiving of 2019, Mayor de Blasio bans foie gras in NYC. Good use of your time, Bill, as your city continues to crumble into the dilapidated sewers. Looks like I will need to be content to continue getting the foie gras back in Fargo. #AllAmericanCity

Greta Thunberg is named as *Time Magazine* 2019 "Person on the Year". She is the Swedish teen who came to America to "quack" about climate change. Some believe she is an example of child abuse, a pawn of her father and the global Left. What a slap in the face to the brave and heroic advocates for democracy in Hong Kong. Shame on you *Time Magazine*. I will never touch another product of yours. #ClimateChange I was over in Hong Kong as the city was preparing for the transition to rule by Communist China and easily predicted this same outcome. The riots for freedom and self-rule were inevitable. #HongKongers Update on the topic of Hong Kong from March 25, 2020, as we pray to God on an earliest-possible Memorial Day for the souls of all our Veterans who gave their full measure on the battlefield: Communist China now proposes to impose a National Security Law for #HongKong in violation of its "hands-off" agreement for 50 years. This could end very poorly for the Hong Kong patriots (as many of us suggested would happen when "The Handover" was signed on July 1, 1997).

You know that you are doing something right on Twitter when you "Tweet" one day and the subjects of your Tweets are all over the news the next day. Obviously just coincidence. Or not? This does happen quite often. I guess that it is simply a sign that my tweets are "timely". #Conservative

UN climate change talks in Madrid end in mid-December of 2019 with few agreements and new doubts. Duh? The US is one of the few countries doing something about the problem of polluting the planet. This is America again taking the lead by walking the walk of helping save the earth. #ClimateChange #CleanCoal

Another example of "strange bedfellows" from the recent (end of 2019) Russia/China/Iran joint naval maneuvers in the Middle East. One of the countries is predominantly Muslim while another puts their Muslims in "retraining" camps. Am I missing something here? That does not seem to be a natural affinity for one another. Then again, who is Iran to complain about the human and religious rights violations by another country?

North Dakota is named by Loudwire and Vivid Seats as the "Most Rockin'" state in the US with the most rock and heavy metal concerts and attendance per capita in the country. "North Dakota loves 'rock', and 'metal' the most."

PTSD is being treated in an expansive way these days with everything from the '16 Trump election results (TAD—Trump Affective Disorder) to receiving excessive "boo's" to someone is "looking at you" claimed as the PTSD cause. Too bad for those who really need such attention: our military and first responders (and then our Doctors and Nurses battling COVID-19 on the frontlines). #Liberals

Forty-seven percent (47%) of America's homeless population is in California. That appears to be one of the main reasons why that state has lost one million of its' residents since 2010.

"Stay away from negative people, as they have a problem for every solution." Albert Einstein. This will be expanded upon later in this chapter.

Affirmative action (AA) was started by the JFK administration in 1961 and then developed by President Lyndon Johnson when the boomers were in various segments of K-12. It was intended to reverse years of education discrimination in favor of or to the detriment of one group of people at the expense of another, especially based on sex, race, and country of origin. In essence, it was "reverse discrimination". So how is it that the numbers of black and Hispanic college students are less now than back in those early days in the 60's? AA has now been dumped after numerous legal challenges. Good call.

"White privilege" has been receiving a lot of publicity lately [even before the death of George Floyd]. Some persons in a position of authority, especially men, have been apologizing for it in their past history. According to *Wikipedia*, it is: "the societal [advantage] that benefits white people over non-white people in some societies, particularly if they are otherwise under the same social, political, or economic circumstances". I have substituted "advantage" for "privilege" in their definition based on how I was taught while growing up to never use a word in the verbiage explaining it. I guess that it does not apply to me personally as well as to many of my peers, as we were not raised alongside persons of color. The existence and benefits of white privilege probably exist to a greater extent to those born and raised in some other parts of the country, including large cities, coastal areas, and throughout the South.

Report: 53% of Americans support military action against Iran in order to stop their nuclear weapon development. That majority might very well get their wish.

Late in 2019, the United Kingdom announces that it is on the verge of approving a 5G Internet network for the countries from Chinese giant and government puppet, Huawei. Now that is one of the dumbest (bonehead) plans I have ever heard—in my entire life. Is the UK not concerned in the slightest degree with its' national security? Update: As I am completing this book, there is information out of the UK that they have possibly come back to their senses and will reject this partnership with China. Ya think?

This was a tweet by this author on February 18, 2020, the day following the running of the rain-delayed Daytona 500 ("The Great Race"). Near the end of the final lap, driver Ryan Newman was leading until he was clipped by a driver behind him and spun out into the wall and oncoming traffic. It was a horrific fiery accident, especially when the Newman car was spinning on its roof and was struck by another car in the driver's side window area where Newman was strapped in the car. "We are praying for a full recovery for you, Ryan [Newman], and a return to the track. You are a great driver and a tough trooper. #NASCAR #NASCARJoinHandsForNewman" We learned on the night of the accident that Newman was in serious condition from the injuries which were miraculously non-life-threatening. Update: A full recovery is expected for the driver from what easily could have been a career or life-ending accident. Amazing!

Interesting sentence commutation by POTUS for Blago (former Illinois Governor Rod Blagojavich). I never thought that there was a serious attempt by him to "sell" the Obama US Senate seat and felt that the sentence was too long when he was convicted. He became the third of the last five Governors of that state to go to prison. The move by Trump will definitely spice things up for a while. #blagojavich

2FA ("two-factor authentication") as we attempt to access our financial data online is becoming a time consuming and wasteful "pain in the ass". Apparently, hackers have a lot of financial information about all of us, but the chances of them having certain multiple random factoids about us is more limited. It all adds up to much more minutia we need to have at our disposal to reach our important accounts and their contents.

The COVID-19 #lemmings have been activated and are quickly headed to the cliffs and certain death. How naive we were to think that so many people in America have a brain, let alone the ability to use it. Panic Reins Supreme!

Who would have thought that in this day and age China could take down the US with a good, old-fashioned medical virus as opposed to a computer virus? The impossible has become the probable. #coronavirus

Breaking News: Ilhan Omar has just gotten married (for the umpteenth time), and it is allegedly not to a brother!

"Ethical Wills" are popping up in America, and this is of interest to me as an estate planning lawyer over the years. These documents focus more on who the person was rather than what property they had to give away upon death. I can see the usefulness in such devices, just as I have also recommended videos of the person during life to express their feelings following death about those family members and friends they left behind. Creativity in this field can be enlightening and invigorating when done the right way. Make it happen.

All is fair in love, war, and sandwiches. Popeye's restaurants brought back a popular chicken sandwich for sale on Sundays (when competitor Chick-fil-A locations are closed). This initial offering was cut short when the chain ran out of the chicken for the sandwiches. Best "layed" plans, as in chicken eggs.

Virtually every gathering of any size in America is being shut down as of and after March 11 & 12, 2020, from an unprecedented overreaction to the power and potential spread of COVID-19. Some of the most important cancellations are the NCAA post-season tournaments and games in basketball ("March Madness") and hockey, the NBA and NHL seasons, the MLB pre-season, SXSW, and "yes", even the 20th Annual Fargo Film Festival. Will "The Masters" golf tournament and the 2020 Tokyo Summer Olympics be next? (Update: "Yes", The Masters has been delayed by a few months, and the Tokyo Olympics by a year to 2021!) Colleges around the country are following up Spring Break exclusively with online courses ("for a couple of weeks?"). No. You can stick a fork in the 2019-20 collegiate school year. This insanity/madness is CRAZY!

Should the world seek and expect to receive #CoronavirusPandemic reparations (#CVR) from China? Their initial mishandling of the virus without transparency has resulted in one of the greatest health threats in world history. It appears that the answer is a resounding "yes"!

#FakeNews at the former news power NBC on 3-16-20 as businesses are ordered closed because of the #CoronavirusPandemic: "Are mandatory business closures the new norm?" What the? How irresponsible to use that following a unique and singular situation. #Liberals

The next day, #China threatens to throw the US "into the mighty sea of coronavirus" by limiting the sale of vital products and pharmaceutical drugs to us? They will rue the day they made this statement. We and the rest of the free world will bury them (the Communist Party of China as opposed to the wonderful people of that country). As I described in *AGG*, my father became a China scholar following my parents' travels there as one of the first groups of foreigners to visit the Communist country after President Nixon opened up that travel in 1972. Initially my father believed (as an accountant/bean counter) that there was nothing to stop them if their people started moving in the same direction. Over time, however, he learned that there was so much disharmony among the various ethnic and religious factions within the country that it would be impossible for them to do much of anything in unison. I have believed for years that China will face a civil upheaval during the next decade or so, and it may become COVID reparations that leads to that level of discontent within the country. China as we know it today will disappear in a fiery demise. I encourage your reading of "*The Coming Collapse of China*" by Gordon Chang.

Still in March of 2020, some of us are already tired of the #CoronavirusPandemic verbal repetition and lack of creativity. How about "increase" rather than "ramping up", "Social Separation" as opposed to "Distancing", and "isolate" rather than "hunker down"? Where is the "good ol' fashioned" American journalistic ingenuity?

In North Dakota, the love-hate feelings for President Trump can generally be compared to those for lutefisk, grilled liver, sushi, raw oysters, local caviar, Rocky Mountain oysters, and cilantro. There is very little middle ground involved.

Generally not a big fan of new words, but this one (on 3-14-20) from the Urban Dictionary is a good one: "#COVIDIOTS" refers to those who ignore the "facts" of COVID-19 and/or are the product hoarders. You all know who you are. Shame on you! Let's get back to work.

The question I keep asking myself as COVID-19 is waning in China is: "would we be doing all of this (basically shutting down the country) anyway based on the much more serious, widespread, and deadly seasonal flu outbreak in the US which will kill tens of thousands of people each year?" And the answer I give myself is consistently "No". We have not and we will not. This "scare" may (and hopefully will) go down in history as one of the greatest "busts" of all time. With COVID-19 we simply sit back while the financial lives of millions of people are being destroyed. We will look back and judge the decisions of our leaders at a time in the future, considering the entirety of the damages inflicted by the pandemic—including those precious lives lost to suicide, other unmet serious health conditions, and drug overdoses, among others. As much as I believe that China should be held financially responsible for this worldwide mess, I will not hold my breath until that happens.

Young people in their teens and earlier in life have died from various diseases at those tender ages over the past 70 years. We all certainly remember when it happened to someone we knew. There was seldom much publicity about these tragic passing's in deference to the privacy of the grieving family. Today it seems that many such deaths are over-publicized and even glamourized well beyond the extent necessary. It would be nice if some sort of middle ground could be reached to memorialize these young-sters who left us too soon and then honor and celebrate those who must move on with life. We certainly want to avoid giving young minds the wrong and potentially deadly impression that they would receive greater recognition and appreciation in early death than they would in future successes throughout life.

It would be unfortunate for me to have a fear of "Friday the 13th", as my wife was born on the 13th day of March. Such a fear is also known as "paraskevidekatriaphobia" or "friggatriskaidekaphobia". Why not just "fridaythe13thphobia"? It is fun to celebrate on the 13th day of the month whether it falls on a Friday or not! And I am glad to not have the disorder.

FB Post on 3-31-20 amid COVID-19: What a day to miss (and I do not post about many of them). Yesterday was National Doctor's Day! And why did I not see nor read anything about it? A belated "thank you" to all our physician heroes out there, during these tough times and all the other days, weeks and months when we simply take your skills and expertise for granted. You are a key to the great living in America!

That same day we are closing out the most catastrophic month in world history since the "passion" of Jesus Christ. As the month began, the US economy was exploding with success and today it is virtually shut down. China will pay for the $20 trillion in damages (so far). #CoronaVirusReparations Is there any question that the #CoronavirusPandemic will increase the number of people throughout the world who believe in #God?

Two Days Later: A typical "spring" day today in Fargo…the Red River is flooding (cresting today), a winter storm arrives with rain, sleet, graupel, and snow, and we are having to deal with a pandemic. Wimps need not apply! #NorthDakota

China is now warning about a "second wave" of the COVID virus. It is about time for America to get back to work and save what we can of our economy and people. Protect the elderly and vulnerable and start living again. #CoronavirusPandemic

Today (April 7, 2020) is "National Beer Day"! At or about 5:00 PM CDT in the Heartland, I will be quaffing down one (or possibly two) tall cool ones. And congratulations to 22 Northmen Brewing Company on its first NBD! Enough said. Skol! #BeerDay @beerventurous

Dr. Fauci (of the Trump COVID Response "Dream Team"): We need to end handshaking—permanently? That will not happen during our lifetimes. Was he ever taught about looking into someone's eyes and delivering a firm handshake? How about instead working on better personal hygiene? #babyoutwithbath-water #getagrip

Much of what we receive from the federal government in mone-tary assistance and how we are represented in the US Congress is determined by a Census every ten years (at the beginning of each new decade). That makes 2020 the year to conduct this "canvas" of who and how many of us live around the country. As we were gearing up for the 2020 Census, COVID-19 descended upon us. As of today (4-8-20), not too much is being said about the logistics for the Census which is dependent in part on door-to-door visitations to fill in gaps. This will be clarified as *"ASG"* is being published and I may be able to place that update here as almost everything else is being postponed or cancelled. Update: on 4-15-20 there is finally some mention of the Census (and probable need to delay it for a while until things are back to some semblance of normal).

British Study: Action by China three weeks earlier would have eliminated 95% of the problems today. Sounds like the Communist regime and the WHO may have more blood on their hands. #CoronavirusPandemic

I have never liked the term "going viral", having viewed enough of the garbage that did just that. We can only hope that our current #CoronavirusPandemic will necessitate a change in that description in the future. #Viral

Question: Is there a possibility that having received a pneumonia vaccine like Prevnar 13 could lessen the effects of COVID-19? I have been properly inoculated against such a condition and wonder if this aspect of the virus which often results in a similar symptom could be reduced by this vaccine which most elderly and vulnerable people should have received. #SpecialReportQuestions

Two years ago, the US government questioned the safety of the Wuhan biolab where COVID and bats were being studied. And some still believe the #CoronavirusPandemic started in a wet market there? #ChinaVirus The COVID-19 damages worldwide could be a catalyst for the implosion of Communist China and fall as a world economic power. Huge mistake and costs for their constant lack of transparency. Must read book: *"Coming Collapse of China"* by Gordon Chang.

Have you identified gaps in the #CoronavirusPandemic unemployment benefits? I have one at home: commission salespeople who are still employed but their ability to earn income is gone! #NoPersonsLand Also at risk are those self-employed individuals who did not receive much income in 2019, at least not enough that would have entitled them to state unemployment coverage and benefits in 2020.

China increases the Wuhan #CoronavirusPandemic death toll as of today (4-17-20) by 50%! This is what the OK #Boomers call getting caught with your hand(s) in the cookie jar. Can you say #CoronaVirusReparations #CVR? #ChinaMustPay

Fauci to #Democrite Governors: enough of the "testing is everything" crutch on the Left. Normality can return without "testing for all" (will not happen) or a vaccine! #OpenUp

The China commie propaganda machine spreading misinformation like manure will not save them from bankruptcy with claims mounting in the many trillions for their #CoronavirusPandemic malfeasance. #ChinaMustPay

#ChinaMustPay started the #CoronavirusPandemic (in a Wuhan biolab?), hid it from the world with the help of #WHO, hoarded PPE from around the world, and is now gouging in selling the equipment. Those decisions must bring down Goliath with a rock to the temple. #CoronaVirusReparations

With the arrival of spring comes "noise pollution". Since when is it okay and legal for motorcycles and pickup trucks to sound like jets landing, only louder? The laws are on the books, but like just about all traffic offenses the enforcement by our "finest" is probably not one of their top priorities. #TooLoudCycles

As I am on the final lap of proofreading and adjusting the manuscript for this book on April 29, 2020, the most critical crisis in America today is not the #CoronavirusPandemic (with more than one million infected and almost 60K deaths), a US economy which has been nearly destroyed by the virus closing it down, nor threats from our enemies China, Russia, Iran and NoKo, but rather it is the censorship of the Right by the Leftist authoritarian "Big Tech" (FB, YouTube, Twitter, Google) — cracking down on what they consider and deem to be "political misinformation" (what the Right believes to be lawful and protected "dissent"). This is the very essence of *1984*, except that the enemy of the people today is those companies who control the content of the Internet rather than a government trying to control the masses by destroying individualism and personal freedoms. This serves as a factor which intensifies the need for leadership of our country following the 2020 elections which will be responsive to this threat to the Republic by breaking apart Big Tech and assuring that those who control the "Tech Swamp" are playing with fairness to all Americans rather than only to the Leftist elite. You are not hearing as much about this threat as you should be as it appears that the Liberals in America are content (and even anxious) to move our country as far Left as possible with the only results being Socialism followed by Communism. The children and grandchildren (and eventually great-grandchildren) of the boomers will be on the frontlines of these battles for our future and cannot fail us in our mission to preserve the country envisioned by our "Founding Fathers". A Conservative in America (yours truly) on #Twitter for a year now with among the best, factual, and most consistent posts, and yet only 28 "followers"? (Update: down to 25 on July 3, 2020.) That is literally impossible. Big Tech Blocks! #DivideBigTech #Liberals Second Update: Thank you, Sen Josh Hawley (R-MO) on 6-17-20 for your bill attacking #BigTech for their political censorship aimed at #Conservatives. These dangerous companies need to be reeled in and broken up in order to save our democracy.

The next day, a headline article in the once Conservative local "dying *Forum*" (Fargo): "[Gov] Burgum rolls dice in restarting ND economy" and "Governor bets on testing, tracing, health care capacity"—all of the standard Liberal "dog whistles"? #Burgum is so right! #BackToWorkNOW

A Twitter post by me on May 6, 2020 (National Nurses' Day) (Thank You, Nurses!): I come across this quote (one of my favorites) today during the final proofread of my follow-up book to *AGG*: "Stay away from negative people, as they have a problem for every solution." Albert Einstein. Very appropriate as many people are now suffering from "COVID Obsession" (CO). That seems to be all they think and talk about! And CO can bring on similar problems as does carbon monoxide (the other CO) poisoning. Notwithstanding CO in the country, our nurses in America "rock"!

As the Summer of 2020 approaches, previously laid-off workers because of COVID who refuse re-employment need to be identified and lose their unemployment benefits, including the federal funds. There should never be a lucrative incentive (like the government dole) for persons to not work than for them to be re-employed and receive a reasonable wage. That is the "American Way".

As June of 2020 ends, #NativeAmericans want to destroy the Mount Rushmore monument (how about the Crazy Horse monument at the same time?). Try it if you feel lucky. This is simply another example of #Leftist insanity and anarchy. These are the "destroyers" in America versus the visionary "builders". Update: Trump decides to visit the monument on July 3, 2020, met by a chorus of "BOOs" from the #SwampRats. #NativeAmerican (Lakota Sioux) leaders claim that Mount Rushmore is located on sacred tribal grounds?! Stupid me. I thought the monument was located in South Dakota and <u>NOT</u> WISCONSIN (where their and my sacred tribal grounds are located)! One of those #NativeAmerican leaders says that every time he looks at #MtRushmore he is reminded about how the white man stole tribal lands. Suggestion: maybe it is time to ignore things over which you will never have control.

"Brainiac Idea of the Day" on 7-3-20: The "Black National Anthem" will be played at NFL games. How very patriotic of them! I did not even know there was such an anthem. And where exactly is this "Nation of Black" located? Teddy is rolling over in his grave.

Fact: there were an all-time record number of gun purchase ID checks in June of 2020. Forty percent were for first-time buyers. Get ready for more of these records in the future as the "Arming of America" continues!

A poignant moment following the July 4th (2020) weekend shootings and deaths in Chicago: an African-American family spokesman says "if we [the black community] do not believe that 'Black Lives Matter', how can we expect others to believe that 'Black Lives Matter'?" Violence by blacks against blacks needs to be a part of the dialogue to restore faith and trust in America.

CONCLUSIONS AND A PROPOSED PARTIAL SOLUTION

I have an "add on" to my *AGG* proposal for a mostly government funded P-14 system in the United States—reinstatement of the "draft" (this time for young men <u>and</u> women), just in case the country is thrust into a predicament in which we need to mobilize and train a large number of capable citizens to protect our mutual interests. The last program of "conscription" in America was abolished in 1973, as the Vietnam War had ended, in favor of an all-volunteer military. The program would only be used as deemed by the government to be necessary to augment our voluntary warriors. We cannot afford to be caught in the future with a critical need to amass a fighting or protecting force and no means of immediately effectuating the creation of such.

I have a strong suggestion to the US electorate for the 2020 elections. As we were preparing for the 2018 midterm elections, I warned that a resulting Congress with a divided control (one party with a majority in the Senate and the other with a majority in the House) would result in "gridlock"—and that is exactly what happened. The last three years have been virtually wasted with little or no efforts toward bipartisanship for the betterment of the country. There is nothing worse in my opinion than mindless bickering in Washington between the Right and the Left, as the ultimate losers are those of us in the middle who make up the majority. The solution: elect a moderate President from one party and enough similar Senators and Representatives from that party so that the Democrats or Republicans (my preference) can get work done for the country. Then you have the opportunity two years and four years later to "throw the bums out" if they do not live up to your standards or if you feel that they are steering America in the wrong direction. I expect that one day our government in Washington will be able to work together in some semblance of harmony, hopefully during my lifetime. Written prior to the Corona Virus pandemic: Are you concerned about the rising US deficit? Blame those who voted in 2018 to give the #Democrites control of the US House, and vote for the Republicans in 2020! And the COVID-19 pandemic did not help our bottom line! Bad news for all the Liberal "Trump-haters" out there. They have been diagnosed with MHS ("Mass Hysteria Syndrome"). The good news for the Conservatives is that the only known cure takes "four more years" to be effective. And the POTUS recently made a remark that echoes my personal thoughts about 2020: "Whether you like me or not, you have to elect me!" There are quite a few people whom I believe will realize that to be true. At this point there is simply no viable alternative to a Trump re-election in this first year of the new decade.

Where does this item go in "*ASG*"? It should probably be here as we consider proposals for the future. Is it time for students from mainland/Communist China to be excluded from attending college and/or working in the US? This has been a question of mine for the past ten years. Some of us who are routinely attracted to "conspiracy theories" believe that we have thousands of Chinese students spying on Americans for their government (especially on college campuses) and involved with espionage in the theft of our Intellectual Property. The Beijing-based Chinese have become an immensely powerful and successful nation over the past twenty years, much of which has come from what our country willingly and sometimes unwittingly surrenders to them. This proposal and plan would presumably come to an end when we can again trust that what is created and developed in America can stay here and be shared (where and when appropriate) at a cost to be paid to the asset owners. Update on March 18, 2020: In the past two days Communist China has threatened to throw the US deeper into the COVID-19 mess by reducing necessary prescription drug exports to us and has reported that they will be expelling American journalists from their country. There is no denying the evil of such a God-less country which persecutes and punishes its' own people. The Communist Chinese government in Beijing is unquestionably the "Great Satan" of our era. Update on May 18, 2020: Over the past three months, professors from American colleges (including Harvard and Case Western) have been arrested and charged with aiding China efforts to steal vital US trade secrets and have been paid millions of dollars to do so. At the beginning of the COVID-19 outbreak, China purchased much of the personal protective equipment (used to protect doctors, nurses, and other first responders) from around the world and is now gouging those same countries in selling the equipment back to them. These programs of plundering have got to be ended immediately! Update as of May 21, 2020: Pharmaceutical companies, vaccine scientists, and colleges around the world have been warned that China is actively hacking computers to steal information about efforts to treat patients of and create vaccines for the COVID-19 pandemic they are responsible for creating. And Confucius Institutes to control Communist propaganda are being closed at many US colleges, US professors are being arrested for China spying, and these Institutes have also crept into our American K-12 system. It is clear that "no good deed goes unpunished" applies to our country based on these recent and recurring efforts to be friends with a totalitarian regime.

As I was creating the finishing touches on this book (4-9-20), it was time to close it out with an update about the Novel Corona Virus pandemic which has the US in the midst of a 100-year event caused by China and for which that Communist regime must be held accountable. As of this AM we had 432,438 confirmed COVID-19 cases and 14,808 deaths in the country as the virus is peaking in some areas and just getting started in others. (Update on May 18, 2020: these numbers have increased to 1,487,447 US cases and 89,567 deaths!) We have been fortunate so far in North Dakota using one of the highest percentages of testing and experiencing among the lowest levels of per capita infections and deaths. This is one of the most serious situations that any of us have faced in all of our years, even though the numbers so far (in early April) represent about one-third of what we experience each year during the seasonal flu outbreak. This virus is more concerning as it is unpredictable, easily contracted, spread by unwitting victims who are experiencing no symptoms, and without a vaccine, known treatment, or cure. Hydroxychloroquine (a malaria drug) does show some promise as do plasma injections from those who have survived the virus. (Update as of July 3, 2020: a study of hydroxychloroquine has shown that it can be effective in reducing the severity of the virus in patients who are seriously ill.) The experts say we will have the vaccine, treatment, and cure about a year to fifteen months from now, while I predict all will be accomplished by the end of 2020. A "unified face" has reduced the amount of political turmoil we have been experiencing since the virus descended upon us, but those who are insane on the Left have still found it difficult to let the Trump administration help manage the pandemic without their micromanaging and grandstanding. With the 2020 elections just seven months away, those campaigns have been curtailed to a virtual trickle. It looks like Trump v. Biden now after Sanders pulls out, but I am not personally sure that Biden will be able to handle the challenge based on early signs of memory loss and confusion. We will see as it relates to the virus and to the elections. I continue with my position that we made a mistake in closing down virtually the entire US economy in response to COVID-19 and should have instead protected the vulnerable elderly, infirmed, and others with immune system/respiratory challenges while continuing on with business as usual. The economic shutdown has resulted in the destruction of financial conditions for tens of millions of Americans that I considered a too severe price for an illness that did not and will not adversely affect many who were sickened. We will never know except by speculation whether the cure will be worse than the illness itself. I will further update this if possible. Update on April 25, 2020: as some states are starting the process of "re-opening" while the pandemic continues to rage, there is considerable difference of opinion about whether this is prudent. It is readily apparent that the Left and the media that feeds it want the US economy to be destroyed and the Trump hopes for re-election with it. Liberals seem content with the idea of killing off American entrepreneurism and small business in favor of Socialism and the global giant Amazon thriving. They argue with their "dog whistles" that everyone in the country needs to be tested multiple times (for the virus and/or the presence of antibodies) which would probably require at the very minimum approximately 1.4 billion tests as the dust settles. The Right and red states want to get back to work before it is too late to salvage as much as possible from what was the most vibrant and successful economy in the history of the world just three months earlier. There will probably be more deaths from the virus under the Republican plan, while not nearly the number of deaths from suicide and other causes that the Left would prefer to see with more chaos from the crushing of financial lives by a continued close of the country. Whatever happens to the economy of the US, the results could be very ugly, and determined by the party in the driver's seat starting in early-2021. Update on May 18, 2020: what once appeared to be a time of greater unity in the US has now devolved back into partisan bickering and finger-pointing. I suppose this was inevitable as we are in an election year. Great news abounds as there are already several very promising COVID vaccines emerging. More signs of states re-opening their doors while summer approaches as the Right supports this move and the Left balks and seems content to not stop short of total economic destruction. What a catastrophe of epic proportions. Final update on July 3, 2020: amid the reopening of the country, the US has a record number of new COVID cases of over 55,000 in a single day. Some states are backtracking on the plans to expand open businesses, especially FL, TX, AZ and CA. There are some positive reasons for the increases in numbers (such as more testing), but the speed of getting "back to normal" will certainly be slowed considerably. This is all very tough to watch and experience. Meanwhile, India expects that the COVID vaccine it is working on will be ready for distribution by August 15, 2020.

Now to place an ending on this two-book series. I have always believed in the words of writer and philosopher Mark Twain: "Humor is mankind's greatest blessing." Nothing beats laughter with others and at ourselves. I cannot think of a better way than with some levity from one of the most important writers and humorists in our history, and who was also an actor and member of the Cherokee Nation. Will Rogers is one of the most cherished icons in American lore. Like many of our most respected commentators from the past 250 years, he was able to poke fun at himself as well as others. Much of what he said still holds true today, whether we want to believe it or not. From 1923: "If you ever injected truth into politics, you have no politics." And a couple of thoughts from 1932: "I am not a member of any organized political party. I am a Democrat!" and "Democrats never agree on anything, that's why they're Democrats. If they agreed with each other, they'd be Republicans!" Here is looking at you, Will—an American treasure and proud Democrat we can all still enjoy!

The final words of one of my American heroes, Teddy Roosevelt, as he left this world on January 6, 1919: "Put out the light." So be it, and may the God of us all be with us.

POSTSCRIPTS

May 26, 2020 FB post from a story about some good deeds once allegedly performed by Donald Trump in response to all of the Liberal angst displayed by many who responded: David Bailly I never cease to be amused when I read about bleeding-heart Liberals with so much hatred since having contracted what I labeled as Trump Affective Disorder (TAD) and what others call Trump Derangement Syndrome (TDS). Trump is not a perfect person — far from it. How would you feel if you had thousands of people in a press corps and tens of millions of others criticizing your every move, glance, word, decision, or gesture for each minute over a period of 4+ years. I would be a basket case after a couple of months. I was taught in a Christian upbringing that a person without sin should cast the first stone at the sinner, which is certainly not me. I wrote about all of this in *"America Going, Going..."* and am following up in *"America...Still Going"* which should be out on the shelves in a few months. What ever happened to the lessons the baby boomers were taught by the Greatest Generation as we went through the 50s, 60s, and 70s? Those principles have been discarded in favor of a mostly selfish society. May God help us as we try to return to some semblance of "we" instead of "me".

A letter to *The Forum* (Fargo, ND) Editor on May 27, 2020 following their announcement on May 26, 2020 that the current five-day per week printing and delivery of the newspaper will end on June 24, 2020 with printed and mailed papers only on Wednesdays and Saturdays, effectively ending the publication in print (which I had predicted for many years):

It is a very sad day for the F-M-WF area and for the Northern Plains of the US. We are losing one of the bastions of our lives in the Red River Valley. Although some of us have seen this coming for many years, it is still shocking when the day arrives. This coincides with a national pattern that mirrors the observations I have made and the predictions for the future set forth in my first book (*"America Going, Going..."*) and those which will be coming soon in a follow-up writing. And don't blame this on the pandemic which surrounds us, it has been inevitable based on strategic decisions made by the newspaper over the past ten years.

In the books, I write about "The Death of 'True' Journalism". We have experienced this firsthand in *The Forum* as it has been reduced from a first-class news publication to a biased tabloid with opinion and first-person narratives replacing the important issues and developments of the day. This is compounded by the clear obsessions of the publishers and staff which dominate the writings which remain. We used to be able to read through the lengthy newspaper while experiencing very few typos, grammatical errors, duplicate articles, and senseless bias from the lunatic fringes on both ends of the spectrum, all of which we now experience on a daily basis—in a much smaller package. During the past year, I considered cancelling my subscription to the printed paper and the daily delivery, but I remained committed to our carrier and to the rich materials being provided for my writings.

The first clear sign in this decline of an institution occurred with the modification of a section of the paper becoming "SheSays". I questioned periodically as to where was the section entitled "HeSays" while I skipped by the demeaning and patronizing focus on women. Much to my shock, "HeSays" did eventually show up for a single day, which happened to be an April Fool's Day. I got it. Then, adding insult to injury, our Pulitzer Prize winning publication decided to "farm out" its national news coverage, initially to *USA Today*. That was palatable until the paper, in its infinite wisdom, veered sharply to the Left with this service moving to *The New York Times* and *Washington Post*. Now that was a horse of a different color. One of the special moments experienced recently was when *The Forum* featured special recipes for National Pork Month — on Yom Kippur. Not sure about that timing.

During this time, *The Forum* had developed a much-praised online presence with *inForum*. I am assuming this appeals to GenXers, millennials, and GenZers, an occasional OK Boomer like me, and all of the expats out there who want to keep up on the area happenings. Getting news from a computer or cellphone has not been my deal, but then again this is not about me — it is about us and the bird we had in hand over the past century plus. The intense pushes toward the digital version have been obvious over the past six months, lending an ominous signal of what was about to transpire. Many of my peers have said "no" to the *inForum*, but I will continue to subscribe as the written paper fades into the sunset. Something is probably better than nothing.

I remember going downtown to *The Forum* building hundreds of times over the years to see a friend, an editor, a writer, a staff member in advertising or personal ads or notice publications, and lingering in the building or entrance to view and read front-page articles from historic times for our region or country. I have always loved the history. Those days are probably now numbered. I can see portions of the beautiful headquarters being repurposed for office space or condos.

The Forum as we have known it is almost gone, but we will never forget the important life-changing information you brought to us. And I will miss leaving gifts outside for our carrier in recognition of a job well done. They say that «all good things must come to an end», although it certainly isn›t «all». Some of us will miss you and what you brought to us every day for all these years. Thank you and bon voyage from a proud Fargoan and subscriber!

One of the new uniform programmed talking points on the Left is that the street violence around the US following the death of George Floyd is caused in part by elements of the Far Right (in addition to the Antifa fascists). Where is the proof of this? Two weeks later (6-9-20), what a disgrace at the funeral for #JusticeForGeorgeFloyd. "Will anything positive come from his death?" Participants in the service claim that first the White House needs to be cleaned out [in November of 2020 elections] (ending the Presidency that has done more to improve inner cities with Opportunity Zones than all of the #Democrats running them for 50 years). America must not do anything more than the Floyd riots to destroy the possibilities and indeed probabilities the Zones have created for the mostly minority centers of our major cities.

The #Leftists media and social media call on America to block and ban "unsafe" opinion and rhetoric. Really? How very objective of them. Like this tweet, I suppose. Now that is scary! Welcome to the #USASR. We are creeping closer to "*1984*" with every day that passes.

More agreement with Alan #Dershowitz on 6-10-20: the #Liberals in America are continuing in their efforts to "#erasehistory" in our country with the removal of everything from the past that symbolizes the mores (of many) from a painful different time. And how exactly do we learn from these errors when the evidence of them is all being removed?

Congressional #Democrites wearing kente cloth stoles in their US Capitol Building photo op (on 6-9-20)—seems to me to be "cultural misappropriation"? How disgraceful. Their approval rating will deservedly plummet even further. Americans need these elitist Liberal Senators and Representatives to be gone with the swamp water.

Good-bye to dear friend, Dr. Michael Weiner, who passes on 7-1-20 in AZ. Cancer. We will one day see you on the other side, God willing. +

ABOUT THE AUTHOR

DAVID BAILLY is an entrepreneur, and business and estate planning attorney from Fargo, North Dakota. His undergraduate college studies prior to law school were focused on accounting and political science, all in his beloved North Dakota. He has been a writer for his entire life, mainly in his career, with daily journaling, and for opinion editorials. He has been active in numerous local, regional, national, and international businesses and charitable causes/organizations. Bailly has traveled extensively throughout the US and the world. His life commitments have always been centered on faith, family, profession, and friends. He has held leadership roles in many groups with a spirit and drive to be proactive in those positions rather than reactive. Bailly has excelled in his passion for helping to build skills in others through mentoring and motivational coaching. With all of this, he has continually tried and mostly succeeded in keeping humor as a part of any equation and solution. "Life is already too serious to not have some fun as we journey along its pathways." He dedicates this writing to his wife (of 41 years) and family, and always to his God. His first book, "*AMERICA Going, Going...*" (published in June, 2019) was written to recognize how his parents (part of the "Greatest Generation") taught him how to live and love in the 1950s and 1960s.